BIBLE STORIES

David Kossoff's *Bible Stories* were published in 1968. The book became, and still is, a runaway bestseller.

This unusual and remarkable success story began quietly. Late in 1963, Kossoff, an award-winning actor and an occasional writer and teller of his own stories, was invited by the BBC to contribute and perform 'A Story from the Bible' on television. He took great care with this, his first story from the scriptures, and chose Jonah. It made a great impact and the letters poured in. BBC Radio, sensing a new voice, offered the old-established 'Five to Ten' morning programme for an experimental month.

It was an immediate success. He became a sort of institution. Soon he was given his own television series. His audience was huge; addictive. Soon, too, by demand, records. One of his favourite stories, Adam and Eve, was given a musical setting by Wilfred Josephs, 'for Narrator and Orchestra', with a Festival Hall premiere! He began to do 'public tellings' of his stories. 'Everywhere. From Welsh Baptist chapels with a miner's choir, to hippodromes with a jazz quartet! – And once, in a summer dusk, in Coventry Cathedral.'

BIBLE STORIES

RETOLD BY

David Kossoff

Fount
An Imprint of HarperCollins*Publishers*

Fount Paperbacks is an Imprint of HarperCollins*Religious*
Part of HarperCollins*Publishers*
77–85 Fulham Palace Road, London W6 8JB

First published in Great Britain in 1968
by William Collins & Co. Ltd

This edition published in 1999 by Fount

1 3 5 7 9 10 8 6 4 2

Bible Stories by David Kossoff
is published in Great Britain by arrangement
with the British Broadcasting Corporation

A catalogue record for this book
is available from the British Library

ISBN 0 00 628102 8

Printed and bound in Great Britain by
Caledonian International Book Manufacturing Ltd

CONTENTS

Foreword by William Barclay viii

IN THE BEGINNING 1

Adam and Eve 3
Cain and Abel 6
More Trouble 8

THE FAVOURED FAMILY 9

Abraham, Isaac and Israel 9
Whither Bound? 11
Fair Shares 13
The Promise 15
Don't Laugh! 16
Friend of God 17
Fire and Brimstone 19
Son and Heir 20
'God Will Provide' 22
Isaac and Rebekah 24
Isaac's Sons 25
Esau's Birthright 27
The Blessing 28
Jacob in Exile 31
Wrestling with God 33
The Sons of Israel 36
Brotherly Love 38
Potiphar's Wife 40
Dreams Come True 41
More Dreams 43
Corn in Egypt 44
Separate Tables 46
A Different Judah 48
Israel in Egypt 49

BIRTHPANGS OF A NATION 51

A Prince of Egypt 53
Midian and Marriage 55
The Burning Bush 56
'Let my People Go' 58
Bread from Heaven 61
The Law 63
Forty Years On 65
The New Man 66
Making an Impression 68
The Walls of Jericho 69
The Hard Way 71
Gibeon 72
What's in a Name? 73
Gideon Receives Orders 74
Resistance Leader 77
Samson Takes a Wife 81
Exit Samson 86
Ruth and Naomi 89
Back to Bethlehem 92
Boaz 93
Harvest Home 94
Birth of a Kingmaker 97
Samuel Takes Over 99
The Ark of God 100
Samuel in Command 102
The Lord's Anointed 103
Giant Killer 106
David and Saul 108
The Last of Samuel 111

THE KINGDOM OF DAVID 113

A Real Big Sin 114
Absalom, my Son 116
Choosing a Successor 118
The Wisdom of Solomon 120
The Building of the Temple 122
Solomon in his Glory 123
Idols at Court 125
The Kingdom Divided 126

PROPHETS, PRIESTS AND KINGS 128

Elijah versus Ahab 130
The Still Small Voice 133
Naboth's Vineyard 134
Elijah's Mantle 136
Elisha in Shunem 138
An Unprofitable Servant 139
Man of War 141
Elisha the Kingmaker 143
Another Kingmaker 145
Never Kill a Prophet 147
'The Rod of God's Anger' 149
Enter Isaiah 150
Jeremiah and the Fall of Jersualem 151
Ezekiel Foretells the Return 153
Home Again 155
The Second Temple 157
Ezra and Nehemiah 159

IN FOREIGN LANDS 162

Jonah the Prophet 162
A Second Chance 164
In Nineveh 166
Poor Blind Tobit 168
Tobias Falls in Love 171
Happy Ever After 175
The Beauty Queen – Esther 176
The King's Vizier 178
The Tables Turned 181
Daniel and his Friends 183
Nebuchadnezzar Humbled 186
Belshazzar's Feast 188
The Lion's Den 190

THE NEW JERUSALEM 192

'Abomination of Desolation' 192
A New Resistance Movement 194
The Temple Lives Again 197

FOREWORD BY WILLIAM BARCLAY

There is no more difficult task than to make the old new and the familiar interesting. This is specially true of the Bible stories which many of us have been hearing from childhood. The Bible presents another problem. We often have the feeling, perhaps unconsciously, that the world of the Bible is an unreal world removed from the kind of ordinary world and ordinary people we know. The biblical characters tend to move in a world where the people are like characters in a fairy tale, remote from the 20th century. They never become real people and the narrative of events never seems to move in the live actual world.

This is the reason why I have read with such pleasure and delight David Kossoff's *Bible Stories*. To my mind there is no doubt at all that he makes these stories come alive. He has the gift of making old stories new for he is a born story teller.

But there is something in his book even more interesting than that. Gilbert Murray has said that if we are to interpret anyone's writing we must at least to some extent repeat and share the experience of that person. This is to say that we must enter into their minds, see with their eyes, speak in their words, and above all think with their thoughts. This is precisely what Mr Kossoff succeeds in doing. He has an astonishing insight into the mind of the characters involved and the way in which he makes them speak and think is both vivid and authentic. He not only tells what one might call an external story but he enters into the internal being of the characters he is describing.

I can think of no better way to make the Bible stories real to children, and to adults, than to present them with this book.

IN THE BEGINNING

Try to imagine, if you can, what it is like to have no possessions at all, nothing, not even the language of the country you've just arrived in as a refugee. Mind you, very few people are able to imagine such a thing, though there are thousands of men and women and children alive now who could tell you from experience what it is like to have nothing at all.

To understand the first story in the Bible, we have to imagine something a hundred times harder. Not just to *have* nothing at all, but when there *was* nothing at all. The very beginning of time. The dawn of history. Page one. Nothing at all. The earth, as the Bible itself beautifully puts it, 'without form, and void. Only (even more beautifully) the Spirit of God moving over the face of the waters'. An emptiness; formless; a dark, endless waste of water. No living thing. No plant or tree. Nothing. Only God.

The Bible tells a million stories of what God did later. Miracles. Mighty happenings and small matters, judgments and punishments, second chances, endless forgivings, great grace, mercies beyond counting. All to do with people. But this is before all that. Before people. Before anything at all. A void – and God. God had done no miracles, made no judgments, and punished nobody. Nobody to punish, or judge, or forgive, or show mercy to. No seas to part, no bushes to burn, no tablets of law to hand down, no slaves to free, nobody for God to bless or arrange a miracle for or make a prophet of. Nothing. A void.

It must have been dull for God. I've thought so since a child. I was the sort of child who liked to know why and I once asked a learned uncle why God made the world.

My uncle thought hard. My aunt too. I waited. They were both clever.

Then my uncle said, 'Well, he had to do something. To occupy himself.' And my aunt said, 'You ask *why*? Tell me, why *not*?' ...

And the thought was planted. And grew into a picture in the mind. A picture I have to this day. A picture of God looking out over an endless dark sea. A God who'd been by himself for a long time. A quiet, thoughtful God, feeling sort of empty. A bit bored perhaps. Maybe even lonely. Sitting silent, still. And then suddenly thinking, 'I know, I'll make a world. I need to do something. To occupy myself. Why not?'

Mind you, before God started to make the world, he gave it a lot of thought. Big job. Not much to go on. No previous experience in such work. No really good materials either. Just a vast midnight, always dark, covering a great waste of nothing but water.

'Right,' said God. 'First things first! Some light to work by. Let there be light!' And there was.

'Pleasant effect,' thought God and turned it off and on a few times. He could see that permanent light might not be so good after all, so he said, 'Some of each. Turn and turn about. Sometimes more dark, sometimes more light. Light will be called Day and the dark time will be called Night. One of each together will be called *a* day. Good.'

Then God looked at the endless water. 'Too much,' he said and decided to halve it. But where to put the other half? Nowhere to *empty* it. So he pointed upwards and the water heaved and lifted and boiled upwards into a gorgeous roof over the water below. Every colour, every kind of cloud. God looked up. 'I will call that Heaven,' he said. 'Beautiful. It looks a nice place to live.' And he moved in.

From above God could see everything. No different from today really. Except that then there was less to look at. Unbroken water, you remember.

So God drew on the water with his finger and the land came up. It was interesting to draw the different shapes. 'All the pieces of land,' said God, 'will be called Earth and all the water will be called the Seas.'

All the shapes of Earth looked rather bare so God thought about it for a while and then covered all the bareness with trees and plants and vegetation of every kind. 'And every kind,' he said, 'will contain its own seed, and thus continue.'

Then God thought of a way to improve on his Day and Night invention, which was a bit hard on the eyes in its sudden change. He hung outside his home two globes of light. One large, to look after the Day and the other smaller, for the Night. No sudden changes; as one dimmed, the other came on. Nice effect. Also he named them. The larger he called Sun, and the smaller, Moon. Then he made a million smaller moons and called them stars.

God was enjoying himself. The greatest artist of them all was having fun and not feeling so lonely.

'Next,' said God, 'things that move. That fly, and crawl, and swim, and walk.' And he used every colour and shape and texture that came into his mind. Huge sea-monsters, tiny birds, exquisite insects, delicate dancing creatures, and slow, heavy ones. Nothing was forgotten. Not a feather, not a fin. Remembering his arrangement for the plants he gave to the living things their seeds too. 'Multiply,' he said. 'Fill the seas and the sky and the land. There's plenty of room.'

God was pleased with his work but had an odd feeling still of loneliness. Of something still to do. He sat looking down into a calm lake, down at his own reflection. Then he smiled. 'That's it,' he said. 'I'll make someone to talk to. A man. He can look like me.'

Adam and Eve

Now, when God decided to make a man to live in the brand-new world he'd just created, he hadn't thought much about it other than that he would use himself as model and do the work with his own hands. All the animals, plants, birds and fishes he'd sort of *imagined* and said, 'Let there be', and there they were; but the man, the most exciting, he wanted to *make*. Special job.

So he looked around for a suitable material and chose mud. Not because he knew what we were all going to turn out like but because mud is good for modelling. We don't know what colour the mud was. May have been black, of course. Or yellow.

Anyway, God worked quietly and happily until he'd made a fairly good likeness and then he let it dry. It. Not he; it. A statue, lying down, made of mud. Wet dust. Then God bent over and blew gently into the nostrils of the statue, and it changed and became skin and bone and hair; and then its chest moved and its eyes blinked and it got unsteadily to its feet and they looked at each other.

God was pleased with his work. 'Your name is Adam,' he said, 'and you will live in a garden where the trees and plants are not only beautiful but will give you everything you need for food. We'll go there now.'

God had chosen the site for his first man's home with great care. A place he called Eden, well watered and mild. And it *was* beautiful. He showed Adam round rather proudly.

'You will be in charge,' he told him, 'too look after everything and to grow things for yourself. Keep things tidy. I am very fond of this garden,' said God. 'I often walk here in the evenings. I hope you'll be very happy.' He turned and then turned back. 'Oh, one more thing. There are two trees in the garden that you must not touch in any way. Fruit trees. There, right in the middle.' Then God left and Adam settled in. A sort of gardener. He had no one to learn from.

But God forgot nothing. Such skills as Adam needed were given to him. His hands were shown how.

God visited often and one day told Adam he had a new job for him. 'Before I made you,' said God, 'I made all the animals and birds and so on. Well, none of them has any names, so I'm going to arrange that every animal and bird will visit the garden in turn and you can decide what to call them. Also – and this is important – look among them for a helper, a companion for yourself. Sometimes you seem a bit lonely and we don't want that, do we?'

Adam did all that God said, but although he admired many of the creatures there was not one he felt he could make a real friend of. He was drawn to animals that he'd called Dog and Cat and Horse, but only to a limited extent were they company for him. He told God.

So God put Adam into a deep sleep and, whilst he was under this anaesthetic, did a little surgery on him. He removed a rib and healed the wound and from the rib made a new sort of creature. Not an animal, not a bird; in fact rather like Adam, but with little differences. Softer, rounder. 'That should do it,' said God. Then he woke Adam and showed it to him.

Adam was astonished.

'It's called a Woman,' said God. 'I named it myself. A companion for you. You are a male, she is female. All I told you about your garden you can tell her.'

Adam was very pleased to have someone to talk to at last. 'I shall call you Eve,' he said, 'and the first thing about this garden that you must know is that you must not touch the fruit of the two trees in the middle. Anything else; not those.'

Well, the time passed quickly. Adam and Eve enjoyed each other's company and they had a simple primitive innocence that indeed was God-given. They lived in the sun. Quite naked, but they knew nothing of clothes anyway. Like babies on a beach. Neither touched the two trees.

Now, when God had made all the animals, he also gave them very different levels of intelligence, or cunning, or craftiness. Some more, some less. One of the creatures who seemed to get a double share of cunning and craftiness was the serpent. 'More subtle,' says the Bible, 'than any other creature.'

A serpent lived in the garden (many animals did) and it used to watch Eve as she, curious, would look up into the two forbidden trees. 'The fruit is delicious,' it said to her one day. 'Delicious. A rare experience. Try it.'

Eve looked at the serpent. 'If we eat, or even touch it,' she said, 'we shall die.'

'Nonsense,' said the serpent. 'The tree is magic and, if you eat some of the fruit, not only will you *not* die but you will be much wiser in every way.' He had a smooth tongue, the serpent, and eventually Eve picked some of the fruit and talked Adam into eating some too. Then they waited to be wiser.

Poor Adam and Eve! The wisdom in the tree was the knowledge of right and wrong. So right away they knew with their new wisdom that they'd done wrong – and were ashamed. With their new wisdom they looked at each other and were no longer innocent primitives. No longer babies on a beach. They saw themselves guilty – and naked. They hid their bodies from each other with garments made of leaves and they hid themselves from God, who walked often in the garden.

But God knew. 'Where are you, Adam?' he said. 'Why did you hide?'

Adam came out. 'Well,' he said, 'I heard you about and I wasn't dressed.'

'Why,' said God, 'are you wearing those leaves?'

'Well,' said Adam, 'you can't go around naked, it's not right.'

'How,' said God, 'do you know you were naked, or what naked means, or what is right, or wrong?'

Well, Adam blamed Eve and she blamed the serpent.

God listened. So soon disobedience, so soon the need to punish. 'You will leave the garden' he told them, 'and never come back. Because of your disobedience life will be harder for all who come after you. For women childbirth will have pain, and men will have to work, to toil and sweat. Paradise like this garden will have to be earned, it will not again be given free. And all will return to the material which I used to make you – dust. Dust to dust.'

God was not angry; he was sad. It had begun to go wrong. There was worse to come. A whole Bible full!

Cain and Abel

Now, when God threw Adam and Eve out of the garden of Eden, it was not only because they had disobeyed him and eaten the fruit of the tree of knowledge of Good and Evil. No, God was afraid they would also eat from the tree of Life, and live for ever. He didn't want that; in fact, after that business with the serpent, he wished he'd never made them at all. However, God is merciful and doesn't hold things against people. So he didn't as it were write them off. He found them somewhere else to live and showed them how to use skins instead of leaves for clothes.

Then God had the idea that maybe a new pair of people would be an improvement. So he remembered how he'd given to the plants and animals and birds and fishes their own seeds so that they could multiply. Even insects. 'Seems to work well with birds and bees,' thought God. 'I'll arrange something similar for Adam and Eve.'

It worked well for them too and soon they had two sons. Cain and Abel. Different types they were, as brothers often are. When they were old enough Cain worked the land with his father and Abel was the shepherd. Rather gentle, quiet person. Thoughtful. Cain was none of these things. Quick-tempered, violent, jealous, quarrelsome. He had an evil streak. Adam had often to act as peacemaker between his sons.

Adam remembered well his fall from grace and the beautiful garden. He had good reason to be grateful for God's mercy and he brought his sons up to fear God and to show respect. At certain times of the year sacrifices were offered. Abel loved these simple ceremonies; Cain less so.

God observed Cain's attitude on a number of these occasions and did nothing. But then one day he both rejected Cain's offering and told him off.

Cain burned. He watched his brother's sacrifice accepted and saw Abel's simple happiness. When Abel went back to his flock, Cain followed him. And in a lonely, hidden place he killed him. Then he went away from that place back to his own field. His anger died away and fear crept in. The wind died away too and the trees grew quiet. Everything grew quiet. No birds sang.

Then God spoke. 'Cain, where is Abel your brother?'

Cain was sweating. He blustered, 'I don't know,' he said. 'Am I my brother's keeper?'

God didn't waste too many words. Cain's punishment was terrible. He was made a wanderer, a fugitive. He had no place to go to and no God to turn to. He felt the face of God and the hand of every man to be against him.

But God made him live long and marked him so that men would know that though he had killed his brother they must not kill him in return. All life was to be sacred. Even Cain's.

More Trouble

So. We began with a picture of God, rather lonely, sitting in the dark dawn of time, and deciding to make a world. And working hard at it and being pleased with his work. And then making a man, and from a man a woman, and from them two sons. One family. A mother led into wickedness who took her husband with her; and a first-born who murdered his brother. One family. It's difficult to resist another picture. Of God watching Cain walk away from him and thinking, sadly, 'Maybe making a world wasn't such a good idea after all.'

And for the next hundred years or so he had no reason to change his mind. In fact, things got so bad that even God was discouraged. He picked Noah and his family and decided to go back to page one. The story of Noak and the ark and how he saved a pair of every living species from drowning has been told so often that I don't propose to tell it again now, only to remind you that, when the waters subsided and the ark finally rested on Ararat and Noah and all the animals came out, God promised Noah that he would never do it again, and then hoped for the best.

The years passed and then God had the Babylon business to look after. Up till then the whole world had one language, nice and simple. But purely to protect himself and to stop the people at Babylon from building that idiotic tower of theirs God fixed it so that everyone spoke differently. Confusion and suspicion ever since!

So. God had thought Noah worthwhile and had chosen him and his family for special work. But even after Noah God was still a bit wary of these 'people' he'd made and the Tower of Babel made him even more so. He watched and waited for someone really special to turn up. He waited about four hundred years, a fair time, even for God. But this had to be the right one, for this person was going to start a *new* kind of people, God hoped, so he chose carefully. As we shall see.

THE FAVOURED FAMILY

Abraham, Isaac and Israel

Now, you would think that God would pick someone young to start a new kind of people. Someone who hadn't seen much; who was perhaps mystic, deeply religious; who lived remote from worldly things. Well, God chose a middle-aged man who'd lived in large cities all his life. A mature man with a good-looking wife, no children, and well used to the good things. He had a good business, a fine home and many servants. His name was Abraham. Into whose mind God spoke of fantastic things, and who listened with perfect faith. Abraham, who did not question; and when God said up and go he upped and went.

But understand first the sort of life he went from. By 'large cities' I didn't mean a bigger than usual collection of tents and mud-huts. Not at all. Abraham was born in the City of Ur near the Persian Gulf where the River Euphrates empties. After he was married he moved with his wife, his father and his nephew, whom he was bringing up, to another city far north called Haran. Both Ur and Haran were civilized and sophisticated places. Fine houses, rich plantations, elegant cultured people who knew of music and poetry and mathematics. People who dressed in beautiful clothes and had jewellery made of gold and silver and every kind of precious stone. These cities had many temples. Well, the people had many gods. Gods of all shapes and sizes. Gods they could see and touch. Familiar gods. No home complete without three or four. Regularly dusted.

So you can imagine what Abraham's family said when he told them that the GOD that spoke to him was a voice only: No idol; no *thing*; just a voice. They thought he was mad.

'Tell me again, my son,' said old Terah, his father, 'you say a god spoke to you. Which god? Which one?'

'The only one,' said Abraham. 'Don't ask me how I know he is the only real one, I can't tell you, I just know. All the other gods *we* made. This one made *us* – and everything else too. He made the world. I'm sure of it.'

'Tell me again what he *said*,' said Terah.

Abraham spoke gently and patiently for he loved his old father and knew he was upset. 'He said I was to leave your house and go where he would lead me. He said he would make my name famous and my family into a great nation.'

The old man shook his head sadly. 'Your family?' he said. 'You have no children. And no sense either to remind poor Sarah of the fact. She has longed for a child as long as I have longed for a grandson..

Abraham crossed to his wife. She was near to tears. 'Forgive me,' he said, 'but I must go because I believe. I cannot explain but I believe the words. Will you come with me?'

Sarah took his hand. 'Without a child, you are my whole life. What will be will be. I'll come.' Then she smiled. She had a little humour, had Sarah. 'Your god says he'll show you where to go, and that he'll make you famous. He doesn't say anything about doing your cooking and washing.' She kissed Abraham. 'It may be that you *will* be famous,' she said, 'but it won't be for looking after yourself, you're hopeless!'

The young man, Lot, had listened to everything without speaking. He knew his uncle Abraham rather well. He looked on him almost as a father since his own had died. He was part of Abraham's family and he had a good job in Abraham's firm. Import–Export business. One of the biggest in the City. Beautiful house in town; another down by the river; lovely possessions; many servants. All this to be left? Walked away from? Maybe his old grandfather was right. Maybe his uncle Abraham *had* gone mad. Then Lot raised his head from all this thinking and his eyes met those of his uncle. Abraham's eyes were not mad. They were calm, affectionate, a little amused. Abraham was known and respected throughout the City as an honest, shrewd and far-sighted man. Not young, remember, well into middle age. But active and strong – and he knew about people. He knew about his nephew Lot too. Liked him.

'Well, son,' said Abraham, 'what about you? Grandfather won't be coming, I'm giving him the river house and four servants. Everything else we are taking with us. I need a second-in-command who knows my ways. What do you say?'

Lot grinned. 'I say, Yes please,' he said.

Whither Bound?

Well, it took weeks. There was a great deal to do. Abraham seemed never to sleep and often ran Lot to a standstill. The business and the big house were sold. Camels and mules were bought. Flocks of cattle, sheep and goats were made ready. Drovers and shepherds were hired. Also more servants and craftsmen of all kinds. All were encouraged to bring their families, for Abraham told no lies. In answer to the question 'Where?' he answered, 'I don't know yet.'

Two days before the great caravan left he said, 'South.' And south they went.

Now, there came a morning not all that different from any other morning when Sarah, Abraham's wife, decided to have a little nag. Mind you, she had fairly good reason. Listen.

'Abraham,' she said, 'I am not a complaining woman, I've not any cause to be. But frankly I'm a bit scared. When you came home one night and told me we were going to sell up and move because a voice had told you to, and I said whose voice, and you said the voice of God, and I said which one, and you said the only one, I didn't argue. You are not mad and not young and we are not poor and, if you want to pull up your roots, it's my place to help and I did. I won't say you haven't done it well, we are like a small village travelling from place to place, you've thought of everything. But when are we going to *arrive*? We've been weeks and weeks on the road. Hundreds of miles. Passed through some lovely places too. Damascus was a dream. But every time I thought we were there, you said no. In two places you built great monuments because the voice spoke to you there. But we didn't settle. We went on. And,' said Sarah, 'here were are in Canaan in the middle of a famine!'

Abraham looked at his handsome wife, still a beautiful woman, no longer young but full of vigour and character. He felt a bit tired.

'Yes,' he said, 'a famine and a great many mouths to feed. We will go down through the Negev desert to Egypt. It will be hard but we've no choice. There will be great heat and little water. We have, with rationing, sufficient food. There will be bandits but I have armed all the men. In Egypt there is no famine.' He stopped and Sarah waited. She knew he was not finished and was puzzled by what she sensed was a slight embarrassment in Abraham.

'One more thing,' he said. 'It is said that Pharaoh King of Egypt, not past his youth, looks only to the north for the women of his house. He is not attracted to young girls but to mature women. He has been known to kill a husband to get the wife, to destroy a family to steal the mother. We are from the north, and you are beautiful, my Sarah.'

'What can we do?' said Sarah.

'It may be,' said Abraham, 'that a spinster sister will attract the king less than another man's wife. We will say you are my sister and you will dress plainly and keep out of sight.'

It didn't work. Abraham and Sarah hadn't been in Egypt more than a week before Pharaoh had them over for dinner and told Abraham that his sister was to be given the honour of joining the harem right away. As second favourite. 'Your sister will live like a queen,' said Pharaoh, 'and you will be rich beyond your dreams. Cattle, servants, gold and silver, jewels. I pay well.'

He did too. And got nothing for it. God looked after the whole thing. Sarah moved into the palace and Abraham was paid off. Pharaoh gave a huge party to celebrate his latest wife and in the middle of a rather cocky speech was stricken by a sort of paralysis. So were all the other men of the court. And it went on. The women of the court nearly went mad with boredom. Pharaoh's soothsayers finally told him they thought the trouble had some magical connection with the latest wife. 'Maybe,' they said, 'the lady Sarah is protected by a god – or is betrothed to a god. Maybe her brother Abraham is a magician in league with some god.' They weren't far off. 'Get rid of her,' they said, '*and* her brother. Ask for nothing back. Tell them to go back up north where they came from!'

Poor Pharaoh. He gave the orders and began to feel a bit better. When Abraham and Sarah went to his sickroom to say goodbye, he looked from one to the other.

'You don't look like brother and sister,' he said. 'I think you're man and wife. Oh well,' he said, 'never mind, whatever you are your family god knows his business.' He was right. As we have seen.

Fair Shares

Well, Abraham and Sarah and Lot his nephew made their way back to Bethel – somewhere in the middle of what we now call Israel. The journey down to Egypt and back because of the famine seemed now like a bad dream. Although the great flocks and presents given them by Pharaoh were real enough. It wasn't long before these great flocks of cattle and sheep and asses and camels began to give Abraham a deal of worry. The country round Bethel did not really provide good enough pasture for all those animals, many of which Abraham had given to Lot as a wedding present. Finding good grazing was difficult, and there was much bad blood between the herdsmen and shepherds of the two men. Not between them personally; Abraham had brought Lot up and treated him almost like a son, having no children of his own. And Lot respected his uncle.

So one day Abraham said to Lot, 'Tomorrow we will ride out into the country and stand on the highest hill and look to every side. As long as your herds and flocks are with mine there will be trouble, therefore let us separate. If you choose the east I will move west, if you want the country to the north I will go south.'

Lot listened and knew his uncle was talking good sense. When they came back from their ride he took some men and journeyed east. He was gone some days and when he returned he'd made up his mind. 'The Jordan Valley,' he said to Abraham. 'Plenty of room and plenty of water. Also,' he said, 'I've decided I've done enough travelling, so I'm going to live in a town. There are two, and they seem quite lively places. Plenty going on.'

'Oh,' said Abraham, 'what are they called?'

'Sodom and Gomorrah,' said Lot.

Well, the dividing up and the sharing out and the farewells all duly took place and Lot went east. Abraham after a while went South to Hebron and settled there. He missed his nephew but knew that he'd done the right thing.

Time passed and Abraham leard little of Lot other than that he'd chosen the town of Sodom to live in. Which for quite a long while seemed a good choice. It was a wicked place with a bad reputation but Lot kept out of things and lived as Abraham had taught him. He was rich, had a nice wife and a couple of small daughters.

Then suddenly one day, a day of confusion and terror, Lot found himself a prisoner of war! His home and the whole town looted and he and all the other captives being marched north. It was a rebellion, a civil war. One of his servants escaped and made his way south to Abraham who, although a man of peace, didn't like the family interfered with. So he gathered together all the men who worked for him, over three hundred of them, and went off to war. He made up in cunning what he lacked in numbers and had fought off enough bandits in his time to know how best to use a small force. Nice thought; middle-aged Abraham a first-class commando-leader. But he was. He chased, and caught up, and harried, and attacked by night, and after about two hundred miles of this he turned the tables completely and Lot and his neighbours and their families took all their looted belongings back home to Sodom.

Abraham and his men helped also to take back the great treasures stolen from the King of Sodom. Who of course was very grateful, especially as his own troops had not done so well in the defence of his city. The King wanted to heap gifts on Abraham, gave a huge party for him, but Abraham wouldn't take a penny. 'Reward the men,' he said. 'They fought for you. I fought for myself and to save a kinsman. It would be dishonest for me to accept anything. You see,' said Abraham, 'I was never in any danger. God made me a sort of promise. Not very detailed, but it certainly didn't include getting killed fighting for you.'

God listened to all this and was pleased, and decided to be a little more detailed with Abraham about that promise.

The Promise

One day when Abraham was sitting quietly outside his tent in the cool of the evening he began to get the tense yet drowsy feeling that he knew from experience meant that God was going to speak to him. He wasn't frightened, and when he felt a sort of velvety black darkness close his eyes and surround him he reckoned that what was about to be said must be more important than usual. It was, although a lot of it he didn't fully understand. God again told him that his descendants would be a special people and live in a beautiful land. 'But first,' said God, 'they will be slaves in a foreign land for four hundred years or so and I will free them from their bondage with plagues and miracles. They will walk through a sea and eat food dropped from heaven.' God continued for some time in this rather serious prophetic way and then after a while Abraham woke up.

He woke as always with a tiny nagging thought in his mind about the word 'descendants'. He and Sarah his wife were childless – and Sarah was well past the age for having babies. It was a subject that Abraham had learnt to avoid with Sarah. She also believed in God, and was very pleased that her husband had been singled out by God, but she too couldn't make sense of that word 'descendant'.

One day she said to Abraham, 'Look, it's ten years since God told us to leave Haran and go wherever he said. We've been to a fair number of places but we seem pretty settled here in Hebron. Well,' she said, 'I've been thinking about this descendant thing. It can't mean *my* son, it must mean a son of your house. Now I know you've never wanted a concubine – it's a great compliment – but I want you to consider Hagar my maid. You know her well and she's a nice young woman who, I'm sure, will give you a fine son.' Then poor Sarah, a bit choked up, went to her room.

Well, it took a long time to convince Abraham, but no alternative arrangement was suggested by God and Hagar was duly delivered of a bouncing boy. She was told it would be a boy by an angel, who also told her that the boy would be a 'wild ass of a man' with many enemies and an enemy to many. The angel also told her that the wild ass would have twelve sons who would become a great multitude. And they did. They are called Arabs.

But Abraham thought that this fine baby, whom he called Ishmael, was the one, the son, the first descendant, the beginning of the coming true of God's promise. And God let him think so until Ishmael was twelve years old. Abraham and Sarah were quite elderly now and lived quietly and contentedly. Well perhaps not so much in Sarah's case. She'd never really got over having no children and sometimes when she looked at Ishmael and his mother she felt very sad indeed. God, who was preparing quite an important statement to give to Abraham, noticed this one day, and decided that something ought to be done for steadfast old Sarah. So when the statement was finished he went to see Abraham, in a dream.

'Now,' said God, 'nearly twenty-five years have gone by and I'm very pleased indeed with the way you've obeyed me and looked after things. I made you then a promise that you shall father a multitude of nations and you will. I said that a land shall be yours; it is *this* land of Canaan, for ever. The land I promised. The promised land. Your son and his sons and their sons shall have no other God but me.'

'Indeed,' said Abraham, 'I have brought Ishmael up to believe in only one God!'

'Ah yes,' said God, 'Ishmael. But he is not the one. Ishmael also shall be a great nation but the son I speak of will be *Sarah's* son. Who will be born this time next year.'

The dream faded and Abraham awoke and thought and, as morning came, he looked at Sarah sleeping. A beautiful woman; but a white-haired beautiful *old* woman. A marvellous wife Sarah had been to him. A son for Sarah! It would hurt her feelings even to suggest such a thing at her time of life. So he decided not to. Stupid of him really. God has his ways of telling people the things he wants them to know. As we shall see.

Don't Laugh!

Now, Abraham and Sarah lived rather quietly in their old age, so Abraham was rather surprised one day when three rather tired hungry-looking people suddenly came round the house. He just looked up and there they were. Surprised or not, Abraham knew the laws of hospitality. He made the men come in and rest in the garden. He had a servant bring water so they could wash and refresh themselves. He asked them whether they would like to eat in the garden and arranged that a good meal was prepared. While they waited for the food to arrive he and the three men talked together. They gave no details of where they were from but said that they were on their way to the two towns of Sodom and Gomorrah. Abraham was interested and told them about his nephew Lot, who lived in Sodom with his wife and two daughters.

One of the men, the tallest, then said, oddly, 'We know. You brought him up well. He remembers and lives decently. A rare thing in Sodom. Or Gommorah.'

Abraham was astonished for he'd said nothing about how he'd brought Lot up. And the men had said they were going *for the first time* to Sodom and Gomorrah. Indeed they'd said they didn't even know the way. Abraham began to have a strange feeling, but before he could say anything the tall man said, 'Where is Sarah your wife?'

Abraham blinked. He hadn't mentioned Sarah's name. At that moment Sarah was just bringing the food out. She heard her name and stopped. Just inside the house. Unseen. The tall man then said, 'We shall pass this way next spring and Sarah shall have a son.' Abraham was now sure that his visitors were from God and he sat silent. And so did they. And into that silence they heard old Sarah laugh. A sad sort of laugh, with tears in it.

The tall man got up and helped Sarah and the servant bring in the food. When the servant had gone, he said gently, 'Sarah, is anything too hard for God? Why did you laugh?' Sarah was about to laugh again, then she looked up into the tall man's face and didn't.

Friend of God

After the men had eaten, Abraham showed them the road to Sodom and gave them Lot's address and they left him. He stood awhile and pondered. He was an old man and next spring his old wife was going to give him a son. He had no more doubts about it. He felt God to be very near. He was right. But when God spoke it made him jump.

'I feel it only right to tell you, my old friend,' said God, 'that I am going to destroy the towns of Sodom and Gomorrah. The people are wicked and cruel and worthless. Your nephew Lot and his family will be all right; the three men will see to that. But everyone else – finish.'

Abraham was shocked. This seemed suddenly a new sort of God bent on a sort of wholesale revenge. There was a silence and then God asked Abraham what was up.

Abraham decided to risk it. 'Thank you for saving Lot,' he said, 'but what of the other good men? There must be *some* worth saving. Or is it too complicated to sort out?'

There was a silence and Abraham thought he had gone too far.

Then God said, 'If I find fifty good men I'll spare the lot. All right?'

Abraham said, 'I've heard it's a pretty wicked place there; what if you only find forty?'

Another silence. 'All right,' said God, 'forty.'

'Er, thirty?' said Abraham.

'I'll forget the whole thing if I find thirty,' said God, without anger.

Abraham took a deep breath. 'There *may* only be ten,' he said.

God chuckled. 'Abraham,' he said, 'I wasn't wrong about you. All right, ten.'

Well, by this time the three angels were well on their way. The two towns lay just below them. Further away, looking oily and still, the dark water of the Dead Sea. Around them the dead-looking hills with the strange shapes, rather bare jagged hills, made of lava, and limestone. Hills erupted, and sinister. It was evening and the air was oppressive and close.

'Well,' said the tallest of the three angels, 'there they are, Sodom and Gomorrah. God has just told Abraham that if we find even ten good men down there the wiping-out is off. The towns and the people will be spared.'

'Will we find ten?' said one of the others.

'No,' said the tall angel. 'Only one. Abraham's nephew Lot. He and his wife and daughters will be saved. No one else. The arrangement stands. Well,' he said, 'I'm off. You handle this one between you.' And he was gone.

Fire and Brimstone

The tall angel was gone and the other two angels, both disguised as rather dusty travellers, went on down into the valley and into Sodom and to the house of Lot. He was outside getting some air. Around him to every side the noise of the nightly wickedness and debauchery was beginning to increase. Lot got to his feet. Brought up well by Uncle Abraham he offered the two men food and rest. 'Come in,' he said, 'for safety's sake. Lately in Sodom no stranger is safe. The robbing and killing of travellers has become a sort of sport. In the night it's much worse, the gangs are out, they are mad with drink and drugs. Come in, please,' he said, 'I know your arrival has been noticed.'

The two men entered the house and Lot bolted the door. They washed and Lot's wife made them a meal.

Night fell and the noise in the streets grew louder. Lot was nervous for he could hear a great mob gathering outside his house. He shuttered the windows. The two men sat quietly. Lot's wife and daughters stood white and trembling. A stone hit the shutters and then another. A great banging on the door began and the mob roared for the two men to be brought out. Lot tried to speak to them but it just made things worse. The mob ringleader, a huge bearded man, crushed Lot against the door. 'We were only going to burn your visitors,' he shouted, 'now we'll burn you all!' Suddenly the door behind Lot opened and his two guests were on either side of him. There was a great animal shout from the mob and they surged forward. And stopped. And stumbled; and there was no shouting. One of the men took Lot's arm. 'Come inside,' he said. 'They are all blind. It was necessary.'

The man closed the door on the nightmare scene outside and said, 'Pack your things; not too much. God is about to destroy this town and Gomorrah completely. No one will survive. The sea will engulf what is left after the fire has come down. You will leave at dawn.'

And as day broke the two men and Lot and his family left the house. There was a terrible hush in the streets. Here and there groups of people, groping, sightless. They left the town and as they climbed the road out of the valley a great earth-shaking rumbling began. The hills on either side of the two towns erupted and the air was filled with falling rocks and clouds of ash. Then the hills overflowed and split and a sea of red-hot molten lava poured down into the valley. It was difficult to see or hear or breathe. Lot looked round and saw his wife standing still a little way below him. As he shouted to her a shower of stones and fire enveloped her. His own clothes began to smoulder. One of the men appeared out of the smoke. 'Come,' he said, 'she should not have stopped, or looked back.'

Long after, when Lot went to the spot where he'd last seen his wife, there was a rough stone standing on end where it had rolled, or dropped from the sky. Like most of the rock in the valley it was white and crystalline, and in the sun it glittered ... like salt.

Son and Heir

Well, Abraham and Sarah, who had moved so often in the past twenty-five years, moved again. And this time not because God had said so, but because Abraham was being extra-considerate to Sarah who was soon to present him with a son and heir.

Sarah had brooded rather after that awful business at Sodom and Gomorrah when his nephew Lot had lost his wife. Sarah had brought Lot up, and this trouble had worried her. So Abraham and Sarah moved south, down to Beersheba, with all they possessed. Flocks, servants, everything, a whole village of people. Abraham was a cattleman, and rich. Also he was old and wise and rather special and people liked him at sight. Not surprising really, for God had chosen him very carefully indeed.

They all settled into Beersheba quite quickly and Abraham improved the wells and planted trees and made friends and waited for his son to arrive. Sarah, who didn't like to be laughed at, had told no one of God's promise, but servants have sharp ears, and proud old Abraham had dropped a word or two, and by the time the baby was due the whole place was buzzing with excitement. This was no freakish thing, no devil's work, this was a miracle promised by God.

And the day came, a calm cool beautiful day, and Sarah was delivered of a boy. The promised son. The 'descendant' who was to continue the line of Abraham and make a new and special people. All promised by God. Sarah, old Sarah, looked at her son and wept with joy. She'd waited so long.

Abraham named his baby son Isaac, which sounds rather like the Hebrew word for laughter. Certainly there was much laughter. A fat, healthy baby, no halo, quite ordinary. Slept a lot and was made much of. The celebrations went on for days. People came from far and wide and Abraham would point out gently to his rather heathen visitors that to *this* God, the *only* God, *nothing* was impossible. God would listen to his old lieutenant and smile.

Now, you might ask, where did all this leave young Ishmael, Abraham's son by Hagar, the concubine chosen for him by Sarah? Well, Ishmael was now about fourteen years old and a fine lad. He loved his new brother and spent a lot of time amusing baby Isaac. Abraham was pleased to see it, but less pleased at the atmosphere of tension that began between Sarah and the much younger Hagar.

Abraham waited for Sarah to speak her thoughts and one day she came out with it. 'I know it was my idea,' she said, 'that you should have a son by Hagar my servant, but the way things have worked out I don't want my servant's son to be equal to mine. *My* son is your true heir; God said so.'

Abraham was troubled by all this but knew better than to argue with a woman's logic so he told it all to God, who listened and said, 'Sarah is right, and you are to do as she says. Send Hagar and Ishmael away, but don't you worry for either of them, I will look after everything. Ishmael will be the father of twelve princes and they also will become a great nation.' They did too. We call them Arabs.

Abraham was comforted by this and he arranged everything in his usual kind and considerate way. Then he and Sarah settled down to enjoy to the full every minute of the growing up of the son they'd waited so long for. The seasons came and went and baby Isaac grew into a fine boy. His old parents were careful not to spoil him and he was a credit to them. Abraham prayed his thanks to God every day but heard little *from* God for years. But one night God spoke to him again. And what God said was something that brought all his happiness to an abrupt and sudden end.

'God Will Provide'

God had spoken to Abraham quite clearly. 'Take your son Isaac,' he said, 'your only son, whom you love, take him to a mountain I will show you and offer him as a sacrifice. A burnt offering.'

It had been no dream. It was many years since God had spoken in the night to Abraham but the old man knew it was no dream. And now he sat, a large-framed, still active man and his chin was sunk in his beard.

Old Sarah looked at him and then looked again. She knew that he was under some strain. The old couple were very close and since the miraculous birth of young Isaac to them in their old age they had lived in a glow of happiness. Sarah didn't say anything for she knew that if she was to know what was troubling Abraham he would tell her without asking.

Poor Abraham. He was very troubled indeed but this trouble he could *not* share with Sarah. He raised his eyes and met hers. 'I have to go on a journey,' he said carefully. 'I have to go and make a special offering to God who gave us our son Isaac. I will take the boy with me and two of the young men of the house.'

'How long will you be away?' said Sarah.

Abraham got to his feet. 'I'm not sure,' he said. 'It is an order from God. A week perhaps. God spoke of a mountain. None near here.'

The next morning early the young men saddled the asses, packed the food and cut the wood for the sacrificial fire, and they set off. Isaac, on his first long journey, was excited and chattered away. He was about eleven, a good-looking intelligent boy who was determined to enjoy the whole thing. With the two young men for company he didn't notice how silent his father was. Old Abraham rode a little ahead and they stopped only to eat and sleep.

On the third day they came to the base of a high mountain and Abraham dismounted. 'Stay here with the asses,' he said to the two young men. I will take the pot of fire and Isaac can carry the firewood.'

It was midday. The old man and the boy climbed steadily till the young men could no longer see them. They came at last to a little level clearing and Abraham stopped. 'Here,' he said.

In the middle of the clearing was a great stone with a flattish top. 'Pile the wood on there,' he said.

The boy worked hard and then jumped down and came across to Abraham. 'Father,' he said, 'we forgot to bring a lamb for the sacrifice.'

Abraham looked into the face of his beloved son. 'God will provide the lamb,' he said. 'And now I want you to do as I say without question; as I obey God without question.'

Isaac stood still and Abraham tied up his hands and feet. Then Isaac looked into his father's eyes and saw they were wet with tears and the boy knew it wasn't a game. He kept silent as Abraham bound his eyes. Then he felt himself lifted gently and placed upon the pile of wood. He heard his father strop the knive on the great stone and he heard his father in a choked voice try to pray and give it up. He felt his father's left hand steady him and a movement as though the right hand, the knife hand, was raised high. Then the boy heard his father say, 'I am here, Lord.'

There was a little silence then, as though his father was listening. Then he felt a tear fall on his face and a kiss and he was lifted down. The cloth was taken from his eyes and he looked into his father's face.

Old Abraham pointed. 'Look, my son,' he said. And there, caught in a thicket by his horns, was a ram. 'You see,' said Abraham, rather unsteadily, 'just like I said. God himself provided the lamb. Come, you can help. It must be painless and perfect.'

And when it was done, the old man and the young boy, hand in hand, walked down the mountain.

Isaac and Rebekah

Well, Isaac was all the closer to his father after that. You can imagine. And to his mother. He grew to be a handsome young man, who adored and respected his old parents and gently took over the reins of Abraham's huge cattle business. When Sarah tentatively hinted at marriage, Isaac would chuckle and call her a marriage-broker. 'And where,' he would say, 'would I find a wife like you?'

When Isaac was twenty-seven years old, his beloved mother died and he and Abraham bought some land just north of Beersheba for a burying-place and there old Sarah's body was laid to rest. Abraham mourned a long time and came to lean more and more on Isaac.

The years passed and one day the old man called his oldest servant to him. 'Eliezer,' he said, 'I think I've been a bit selfish; this mourning for the past has gone on too long, and so has my keeping Isaac by my side. He doesn't complain, he's a marvellous man, but it's time he was married. Last night I dreamt his wife came from Haran where I come from. It is an omen, for I don't want him to marry a woman of Canaan. So, old friend,' said Abraham, 'will you take a caravan of ten camels and gifts of every kind and go north to Haran. Trust God. He will guide you to the wife for my son, for my son belongs to God.'

It was a long journey for old Eliezer and took many weeks, but all went well and God overlooked the whole thing. They arrived at Haran in the evening and rested by the well. Eliezer got off his camel, very stiff, and closed his tired old eyes. He began to doze when a voice woke him. A young woman's voice, who offered him a drink of water. 'And while you rest,' she said, 'I'll see that the camels are watered.' She was beautiful and pleasant and Eliezer's quest was over. Her name was Rebekah and her grandfather was Abraham's brother. She took the old man home with her, he distributed the rich gifts of his master and proposed on behalf of his master's son. He also told the long story of Abraham's work for God over the last fifty years. The family talked together and then left it up to Rebekah. 'Will you go?' they asked her. 'Yes,' she said, 'I will.' She took only an old nurse as companion and they left the next day.

It was Isaac's habit, in the cool of the evening, to walk and think in a pleasant small meadow near his house. There were trees and flowers and long shadows. And it was here that Rebekah first saw her gentle-voiced handsome husband. Isaac was in his late thirties and a mature and sensible man but he fell in love with the abandon of a boy and Rebekah returned his love.

Eliezer went to Abraham and related the whole journey. 'A fantastic coincidence,' he told him, 'that I should find this lovely amiable girl right off – and she turns out to be your own grand-niece! Amazing!'

Old Abraham lifted his head and smile. 'Old friend,' he said, 'you were an unbeliever when I took you into my service and you are an unbeliever still. What coincidence? Why amazing? I told you before you went that God would guide you. You were never alone – as I am never alone. And my son Isaac and his sons and their sons will never be alone. Because you see,' said Abraham, 'God is interested in this family.'

Isaac's Sons

The Bible tells us that Abraham died in a good old age, full of years. When he died Isaac's twin sons were fifteen years old. Their names were Jacob and Esau.

Rebekah had waited a long time to be a mother. Nearly twenty years. After his marriage Isaac had moved nearer the coast. A place called Gerar, where his old father too had lived for a time. Like his old father, Isaac was in the cattle business. And like his father he became rich. So rich that people started to get jealous. Some of the Gerar people, who were called Philistines – a nasty lot, we shall hear more of them – took to blocking up his wells and so on. So Isaac and Rebekah moved. No small job with thousands of head of cattle and sheep and a big staff. They tried a number of places but the Philistines kept turning up with their well-blocking tricks. Eventually they came back to Beersheba. The Philistines had filled in the wells there since Isaac's childhood, so it was all to dig again. But Isaac was fond of the place and that night he prayed extra hard. He told God that if he could see his way clear to give them all a bit of peace it would be very acceptable. 'Rebekah,' he sold God, 'is miserable enough about being childless, let alone this Philistine business with the wells.' God listened and then said to Isaac, 'All right! Beersheba. This place. Make your home here. There'll be no more trouble with the Philistines. Leave it to me.'

So there they settled. Isaac and his vast herds and flocks and huge household. And Rebekah. Still no children. And they'd been married nearly twenty years. But God had not forgotten and one happy day Rebekah was sure she was going to have a child. Well, she didn't have an easy time. Towards the end of her pregnancy she was feeling so rough that she said to God, 'If this is what I've waited for so long I must tell you I don't think I can live through it.' Then God explained, although it didn't mean a lot at the time. But one point he cleared up right away. 'It's twins,' he told poor Rebekah, 'and not just two babies. They will be two nations; two peoples. One will be stronger, and,' he said, 'the elder shall serve the younger.' Well, the prophecy part of what God said didn't disturb Rebekah much, although I'm sure she remembered it later on when the boys had their big quarrel. So Rebekah at last had her family and everyone was very happy for her.

An odd thing happened when they were born. It was said that the second twin was born gripping the heel of the first. In those days such things were taken notice of and people tried to work out what they meant. This omen had them all a bit puzzled. Could have meant that Jacob was tenacious – the kind that hangs on. Certainly that would have been proved right. He was the younger by about one minute and that minute caused a lot of trouble. Out of that minute came strange and wonderful happenings – great promises from God himself, double dealings, two clear cases of fraud, great anger, and great forgiveness. But it all started because Jacob was younger than his twin by one minute.

Very different they grew up to be, the two boys. Even in appearance. Esau was a powerful, muscular sort of boy; red-haired; not very clever, but an active, outdoor, rough and tough kind of lad. Not given to any deep thinking. Not like Jacob. Jacob was a very thoughtful quiet person. He stayed home – and Rebekah, who hardly saw Esau except at meal-times, found Jacob good company. They became very close indeed.

Esau's Birthright

Rebekah was the sort of woman who will treat all her children with fairness and equality but who will have a great possessive protective love for only one. We all know people like that. Not really happy people. And Rebekah wasn't happy either. It was that birthright business. In those days the eldest son was like the firstborn of a King, the inheritor by right of birth. By birthright. Think what that meant to Rebekah. Here was her favourite, Jacob, who was clever, good at figures, farsighted, and who was obviously the better one to take over the business when Isaac retired, but who couldn't because his brother Esau was one minute or so older and thus by right of birth the firstborn. She wouldn't have minded so much but Esau didn't really care one way or the other. As long as he could hunt and be in the open and mix with the cowmen and shepherds he was happy. Always a strong, reliable, obliging fellow. People liked him. People didn't like Jacob as much. He was a bit secretive was Jacob. Kept himself to himself. Very close to Rebekah; held everyone else away.

And so they grew up. And as Rebekah favoured Jacob, so Isaac rather favoured Esau. It goes like that in families. He liked this hairy, bearded ruffian, who had no clever talk but gave off a sort of loving warmth. Jacob used to watch his father and his brother together and became absolutely obsessed with the thought of how much better suited he was to succeed his father than his brother Esau.

One day Jacob was in the kitchen with his mother cooking up a long-time speciality of his. A sort of meat and lentil stew. As skilful as Esau was at hunting meat so equally skilful was Jacob at cooking it. Esau hadn't been home for days. Suddenly there were shouts outside and a very dirty, very tired, absolutely starving Esau lurched in. 'What's that marvellous smell?' he said. 'I haven't eaten for two days – I know what it is,' he said, 'it's that stew! It's like a dream come true – at this minute worth more than gold!'

Jacob, who hadn't spoken since his brother had burst in, straightened up. 'Never mind about gold,' he said, 'is it worth your birthright?'

Jacob's eyes were oddly bright; he looked a bit mad. Rebekah watched everything silently. Jacob said clearly, 'You can have as much stew as you can eat if you give me what you don't want anyway – your right to succeed Dad – your birthright.'

Esau looked from his brother to his Mother. 'If I don't eat soon,' he said, 'I'll die – and a fat lot of good my birthright'll be then.'

Jacob picked up a ladle and a large bowl. 'D'you swear?' he said.

Esau, who now was way out of his depth, said, 'Yes, I swear. Now for goodness' sake dish up!'

Jacob filled the bowl and Rebekah handed it to Esau. 'Eat,' she said, 'and remember, to swear a promise is serious and I was here and witnessed everything. Say nothing to your Father. I'll tell him.'

But she didn't tell Isaac. Which was wrong. As we shall see.

The Blessing

Now, we didn't give a lot of time to the selling of his birthright by Esau to Jacob for a bowl of meat-and-vegetable stew. Or mess of pottage, if that sounds more familiar. More familiar; less appetizing. Well, the reason was that the detail of the happening is not important. Jacob and Rebekah his mother played a sort of wishful-thinking trick on Esau. It meant little and did them no good at all. But it shows us how much Jacob wanted what Esau possessed just by being a minute or so older. The right to succeed his father in the business. He just *knew* he was best suited for the job. And Rebekah his mother thought so too. Hence the nonsense with the bowl of stew. Don't dwell on it too much; the later, far more serious business of the blessing is more worth your attention.

Now, this blessing affair took place long after; when Jacob and Esau were grown men. And their father Isaac was really rather old. He had been forty when he was married and was all of sixty when the twins were born. Now he was in his late eighties and rather frail, and blind too.

Now, like a good many old people, Isaac didn't do much with his day. He slept a lot and looked forward to his meals. With no sight, his sense of taste was important to his contentment. He had favourite dishes. One of them was a savoury sort of casserole made with baby goat and herbs. Although there were goats among his own flocks, he preferred, he said, 'the wild hill goats that Esau hunts'. One day old Isaac asked Esau to try to catch a goat or two so that this favourite dish of his could be prepared. Esau, who was off on a day's hunt, said he would do his best. He kissed his old Dad and Isaac breathed in the coarse warm smell of his favourite son. It was long since he'd seen Esau, but the feel and smell of him was loved and familiar. Esau turned to his mother and said, 'I'll be back tonight or early tomorrow. I'll have the baby goats with me. I know where to go for them.'

Rebekah stood still for a moment and then like a flash the idea came. The scheme that was to change all their lives. And it did; but not the way she meant it to. She ran from the tent and found Jacob. 'Listen,' she said, 'and do everything I say. Your father just sent Esau to hunt wild goat for his favourite meal. And I know that your father is giving a lot of thought lately to the giving of the blessing.' Jacob stared at his mother. The giving of the blessing was the handing on to the firstborn the authority of the head of the family and with it the land and the flocks and the herds and the whole tribal leadership.

'The giving of the blessing,' murmured Jacob, 'is it time?'

Rebekah came closer. 'Your father is old and weak and he knows he has not got much longer to live and he's blind. Blind,' she said. 'Go at once to the flock and bring two baby goats. Your father shall have his beloved dish from *your* hands, not your brother's. Your voices are similar and you shall dress in your brother's clothes so that when you are near to your father he will smell the wool and fur. Serve your father and ask for the blessing after the wine and prayers. Try not to say too much. The blessing cannot be twice given or taken back. It must be this way. Abraham the founder, Isaac your father, Jacob the son. I know I'm right, Jacob. Not Esau.'

She stopped. 'What are you afraid of?' she said. 'Would I tell you wrong? You are my life?'

Jacob said slowly, 'I've watched my father with Esau. They sit close together. Often my father puts his hand on my brother's head or on his arm. Esau's hair is long, to his shoulders, and his arms are hairy. Mine are smooth and my hair is short and my neck bare. My father is certain to feel the difference when he places his hands during the blessing.'

Rebekah thought for a moment. 'Animal skins,' she said, 'long-haired fur for the back of your head and short-haired fur for your arms. Go for the goats. Leave everything else to me.'

And the whole shameful business worked perfectly. Old blind Isaac was a bit surprised that his splendid meal turned up so soon. But Jacob, copying Esau's voice, said that God had blessed the hunt. While Jacob served his father, the old man's doubts were stilled. He could smell Esau's coarse robes and he could feel the hairy arms and when he placed his hand lovingly on his son's neck he could feel the long hair. One thing though, rather unusual, he could feel his son trembling. Esau was not the trembling kind, a noisy happy rough sort of man, Esau, afraid of nothing.

'Why do you tremble my son?' said old Isaac moving his hand up onto his son's head. Jacob, muffling his voice in his sleeve said, 'Leave your hand on my head father and give me the blessing.' And the old man did. And when it was done, this important unchangeable thing, he heard his son and Rebekah his wife say Amen and quietly leave him.

The old man, sleepy with food and wine and very content, dozed a little. Then he was awakened by Esau, this time the real one, and soon a confused nightmare that he couldn't see was going on round his old head. When Esau realized what had happened at first he cried like a wounded animal, for he loved his old father and set as much store by the love in the great blessing as the honour and authority it contained. The old man, whose blind eyes were now wet with tears would have given anything to take back his blessing, but they both knew he could not. So they sat together awhile and then Esau asked his father to bless him too. 'Have you only one blessing?' he said. Old Isaac steadied himself and explained that Esau must serve Jacob now, but one day, 'one day,' he said, 'you shall be free of this yoke.' Esau kissed his father and went to find Rebekah. She looked at him silently. 'While my father is alive,' he said, 'Jacob is safe. When father dies I will kill Jacob. And you,' he said to his mother, 'and you I will never forgive.'

Jacob in Exile

Now, you might say, if this Jacob was one of the great elders of the Bible, the father of the twelve tribes and all that, son and grandson of men close to God, where was God while Jacob was behaving so disgracefully? Didn't he care about Jacob? Well, believe me, God was there and he cared. Jacob, you see, had to learn humility and some of God's lessons were going to be a bit rough. Look at Jacob's scheming to rob his twin brother Esau of their father's blessing. It had succeeded. Isaac had blessed Jacob with the blessing of the firstborn instead of Esau. Very crafty of Jacob. A lot of good it did him. His poor blind old father heart-broken and hurt. His brother had sworn to kill him. And his mother, who had really planned and plotted the whole thing, was now urging him to flee for his life away from all he'd hoped by his trick to inherit. 'You must go at once,' she said. 'Go far away – to Padan-Aram to your uncle, he will give you a home until your brother Esau may forgive you.'

And so Jacob left Beersheba and the huge flocks and herds which were his father's, and he left alone in the clothes he stood up in. He left in a hurry and in fear. He was full of shame and deserved to be. As he walked through his father's lands he wept. He walked all day and as night fell he found himself in a sort of rocky hollow. It was chilly and he was very tired. He found a smooth stone to use as a pillow and lay down. He felt absolutely forsaken. His mind kept on going over the day and sleep just would not come.

It was pitch dark; dead quiet. Perfect conditions for a vision – or a special sort of dream. Till he died Jacob was not sure which it was. It began with a feeling through his closed eyes that there was a great glowing light above him. He half opened his eyes and at first he couldn't make anything out at all. Then he got used to the light, and the light seemed to be a pure gold sunbeam that reached from the black midnight sky down to the hollow where he lay. Not straight down but like a sloping, steep road from earth to heaven. On it there seemed to be people. Tall beautiful people in robes the colour of the light. They seemed to glide and float, some going up, some down. 'They are angels,' said Jacob to himself and felt his eyes drawn up to the top of the beam where it seemed as bright as the sun. He tried to close his eyes. Not because the light was hurting them, but because he knew suddenly that he was looking into the face of God and to stare didn't seem right. And God spoke. 'Jacob,' he said, 'you are not alone. I am with you and always will be. You shall own great lands and your descendants will be a multitude that will spread through the world. Wherever you go I will never forsake you.'

Slowly the great glow faded and was gone. Jacob was stiff and cold but he felt comforted and safe. When morning came, he took the stone he'd used for a pillow and set it in the ground as an altar, praying his thanks to God, and then continued his journey.

It took a long time, many days, but at last he came to what was in those days called the Land of the People of the East. Top corner of Syria; near Turkey. A long way. He came at last to a well and was pleased to see it for he was parched. There were some shepherds there and they told him his long journey was over. This was the well nearest Haran. The shepherds actually knew Jacob's uncle. One of them, a big friendly chap, said to Jacob, 'If you wait around here one of Laban's own shepherds will be along. Owns a lot of sheep Laban does. They're all watered here.' And sure enough soon there was the sound of sheep bells and a cloud of dust and a large flock arrived. Jacob made his way across to the shepherd and just as he was about to speak the shepherd turned and Jacob looked into the face of the most beautiful girl he'd ever seen. Wonderful moment. Love at first sight on both sides.

She was Rachel, Laban's younger daughter. Jacob's cousin in fact. She took him home with her and he met the family. Laban was the brother of Jacob's mother and was like her both in appearance *and* nature. Pleasant enough, but a rather hard calculating man. Very shrewd. Rachel's older sister was named Leah. Rather plain girl who didn't look as if she was going to find a husband very easily. Jacob settled into the household very quickly. He was soon very useful to Laban because he knew a great deal about sheep and cattle farming, he'd grown up in it.

After about a month Laban, who was delighted with this clever nephew who'd happened along right out of the blue, offered Jacob a more secure job. 'All very well,' he said, 'me being your uncle and all that, but you ought to have some wages.' No fool, Laban; this wasn't generosity, he knew he had a good man and wanted to keep him. Jacob thought about it. This was now his home and he wasn't complaining. He was in love and occupied and happy. So he told Laban that he would work for seven years just for his keep, if he could marry Rachel at the end of that time. Laban agreed right away. And why not indeed!

But when the seven years were up he played a nasty trick on Jacob. When the ceremony was over and the bride lifted her heavy veil, it wasn't beautiful Rachel – it was plain Leah. Jacob hit the roof and began to have a sneaking idea that, although God was on his side, his side weren't doing too well. 'Now look,' said Laban, 'don't get excited. Poor Leah is the elder and if her younger sister gets married first she'll *never* get a husband. It's like that round these parts. Next week you can marry Rachel and do another seven years.' Well, what else could Jacob do?

So Jacob served his two lots of seven years and some on top. Laban was now very rich indeed and owed a great deal to Jacob. And he knew it. So did Jacob; who really still only worked there. Hadn't been made a partner or anything. So Jacob with a little help from God started to work a little for himself and crafty old Laban watched himself being outsmarted time and time again.

The years passed and now *Jacob* was the biggest sheep and cattle man for miles around.

And one day Jacob decided to go back home. He was enormously rich, he had two wives, two concubines, eleven sons and a daughter, huge flocks and crowds of servants but also he was homesick. He gathered his family together and said, 'We go tomorrow.' And they did. Remarkable journey. In many ways. As we shall see.

Wrestling with God

Now, things may not always have been easy between Jacob and his uncle Laban. Both crafty characters. But now that Jacob had started the journey home, he began to worry about his brother Esau. The thought of Esau began to cost him a lot of sleep. He woke one morning very low, depressed, full of pessimistic thoughts. He'd hardly slept and was feeling very much alone. And when you're feeling very alone is a good time to talk to God. Which Jacob decided to do.

'God,' he said, 'I'm frightened. Twenty years ago I ran for my life from my brother's anger. My brother Esau swore to kill me and I deserved it. You know what I did to him and I've been ashamed ever since. I shall never forget that first night on the run all by myself and you sent that dream or vision or whatever it was and you gave me your personal promise to look after me. Wonderful the confidence it's given me all these years away from home. Frankly,' said Jacob, 'I was a bit surprised you bothered with me after that business with Esau – especially as I was in the wrong. When you spoke to me that night I had nothing – and nobody. Now I have a big family and many servants and more cattle and sheep and horses than most people have ever seen. I know it's all your doing and, believe me, I'm very grateful. And when you sent an angel to tell me to pack everything and go back home I did everything you said. I didn't argue; I never have. You've got your own ways of doing things and your own reasons. And I'm sure that telling me to go back home has good sense behind it. And believe me I want to. But my brother Esau is on my mind. A few days ago I sent some of my men on my fastest horses to take a message to Esau. My men got back today and I now have my brother Esau's reply. Look, God, I'm sorry to go on so long but the point is that he is coming to meet me with four hundred men. Four hundred. We are not half that number and we have many women and children and I'm afraid for them. God, you said you'd look after us on this journey home but I must tell you I'm scared stiff. I'd be grateful for any suggestions.'

First thing God did was to give Jacob a good night's sleep. When Jacob awoke God's suggestion was clear in his mind. He got up and got started on it right away. He called his herders together and told them to count out from their flocks two hundred and twenty goats, two hundred and twenty sheep, thirty camels and their young, forty cows and ten bulls and thirty asses. 'All animals in separate herds,' he said, 'and at least one hour between herds. The goats are to leave first. Next sheep. And so on. When the first one meets Esau my brother he is to be told the herd is a present from me and that I am following. Each herder will say the same and hand over the animals. Start now.'

All this took most of the day and with the rest of his servants and workers Jacob set to moving his huge caravan across the shallow stream where they'd been camped for two days. The last to leave was his wife Rachel. She loved her Jacob and knew him very well. They stood together quietly. He explained to her, although he didn't need to really (she was no fool), that he hoped to appease Esau with the great train of presents so that when they met there would be a chance of forgiveness. He kissed Rachel. 'Go to the children,' he said. 'I shall stay this side of the stream tonight. I've a feeling God wants me to.' When Rachel had gone Jacob lay down. It was soon pitch dark. Across the stream, far off, the lights of the camp went out one by one. Jacob waited. Wide awake. His mind churned and raced. Time passed. No vision occurred; no dream came. Jacob got to his feet and decided to cross the stream and join everything he possessed and loved.

But he couldn't. Something, or somebody, blocked every move he made. He could see nothing. The man, if it was a man, made no sound. Hands gripped his arms, and shoulders as strong as his own pushed against him. Jacob was a strong man and his terror made him twice as strong. To get across that stream to everything he loved – his family, his children – was now the most important thing in his life. He fought till the breath in him sang like the wind. It went on and on, this nightmare, and as the sky at last began to lighten the Being suddenly stooped and Jacob screamed as his thigh was dislocated. The pain was terrible and Jacob, exhausted, collapsed against the hands that had wrestled with him for so long. The hands now were firm and gentle and lowered him to the ground. Then a voice spoke. 'Jacob,' it said, 'you have striven with God and with man – and with yourself – and you have done well. From now on your name shall be Israel and your descendants shall be called Israelites.'

Jacob fainted with the pain of his thigh. When he came to, the pain had gone but his leg was twisted and stiff, so that he knew it had been no dream. And Jacob – or Israel – limped across the stream. There were things to do. Twisted thigh or not, new name or not, he still didn't know how Esau was going to be when they met. He ordered the camp to be tidied and that his children be dressed in their best. Food was to be prepared and plenty of wine. After all Esau had four hundred men with him. Jacob tried his best not to worry too much about those four hundred men.

Suddenly there was a shout. Esau and his men had been sighted. Jacob lined up his children and behind them the women of the camp. He waited tensely till Esau dismounted then he went forward, bowing low at every ten paces. This was not only extremely formal but very difficult with his new limp. But Jacob was taking no chances. He needn't have worried. Esau ran forward and took his twin brother Jacob in his great arms and laughed and cried with the joy of finding him again after all these years. There was so much to tell. Esau was marvellous with the children and they responded right away to the rich kind warmth that came from this new uncle.

When everyone had eaten the two brothers looked at each other. Jacob, who had had great trouble making Esau accept the presents, felt that God was very near. Maybe, he thought sleepily, Esau with his goodness and kind eyes and his warm tolerant forgiving nature was a sort of *lesson* from God. As was his twisted leg and his new name. And you know, somehow I don't think Jacob was very far wrong. Do you?

The Sons of Israel

Now, you'd think that, when Jacob had sons of his own, the one thing he'd certainly try to avoid was making the same mistake as his mother had done. You'd think he'd have said to himself, 'All right, I was Mother's boy. And a lot of good it did me. Exiled; worked for years without wages for an uncle I didn't like; lived in fear of my brother's revenge for a quarter of a century. No, there'll be no favourites among *my* lot!'

Well, he may have said it. But he didn't take much notice. He was worse than his mother. With her it was simple; she had twins, she preferred Jacob to Esau. Jacob had thirteen children; twelve sons and a daughter. And the apple of his eye was Joseph. Son number eleven. Mind you, we must be fair, Joseph was the child of Rachel, Jacob's first and true love. You remember he worked seven years for Rachel, and then her father switched sisters and Jacob was landed with her elder sister Leah – and eventually two concubines as well. And Leah and the two concubines between them had had ten sons and a daughter before poor Rachel had even started. Very sweet and gentle woman, Rachel. She longed to have a child and at last she did. And that baby, the eleventh son, was called Joseph. She later had another son, making twelve in all, from all the ladies.

However, to get back to his father's rather ill-judged favouritism of Joseph. Jacob's business was livestock. A huge concern. Cattle, sheep, goats, asses, camels, everything. Very rich man indeed. Not city people. They lived well, but far out in the country. The boys grew up rough and tough. Jacob was a cattle farmer, and his sons were herdsmen and shepherds, and everybody worked. The younger sons did a shorter day, and Joseph was the second youngest. Not that Jacob needed any excuse to keep his favourite near him. Jacob's word was law and his love blinded him to the jealous feelings of his other sons. Mind you, Joseph *was* different from his brothers. He was gentle and quiet, where they were coarse and loud-voiced. He was clever, and learned things quickly, and was a logical and pleasant person. He enjoyed his life, and respected his father, and grew into a handsome, well-built seventeen-year-old whom most people liked a lot. Most people. Not his elder brothers; they couldn't bear him. But Joseph could shut out their dislike by enclosing himself in dreams.

Yes, Joseph was a dreamer. A visionary. And his brothers would jeer and roar with laughter at what they called his dream-talk. Sometimes, though, when at the evening meal he told of his dreams, there was no laughter and no jeering. Just a ring of dark hard eyes. For his brothers construed some of his dreams as meaning that they would all one day be his servants. That he, Joseph, would reign and that they, older than he, would be subject. It may be that God was sending Joseph these prophetic dreams. It would have helped a bit if God had sent also a little tact. Even old Jacob was rather put out once or twice by what seemed to be the obvious meaning of Joseph's dreams. But in Jacob's eyes Joseph could do no wrong. Silly, really, for favouritism always causes trouble in families. At a time when nearly everyone wore a sort of overall of rough-weave or skins, Jacob had made for Joseph a beautiful *coat* of specially woven fine cloth using many different colours – and with *sleeves*.

The brothers were livid. Sleeves were for princes – an idiotic present for the young dream-talker!

Jacob was oblivious of the bad atmosphere and one day – one bad day – he sent for Joseph. 'I want you to go and see if all is well with your brothers,' he said. 'They are with the flock at Shechem.' Joseph went and found that the flock and his brothers had moved on to a place called Dothan, so he followed. Dothan was about fifty miles from home and in those days it took a fair time. His brothers spotted him before he saw them. They were hot and tired from the sun and the shearing, and the sight of Joseph was just about the last straw. One of those mad, hate-filled, wild-eyed conspiracies began. 'We'll kill him' they said, 'we'll say a wild animal did it. We'll toss his body down a pit. Him and his blasted dreams!'

Now the eldest of the brothers was called Reuben and he calmed down first. Also he was fond of his Dad and knew that Joseph's death would just about kill the old man. 'No,' he said, 'no killing. Toss him in a pit for a day or two to teach him respect, but no blood!' He was quite a decent fellow, Reuben, and his plan was to pull Joseph out of the pit when the others had moved on with the flocks. And the others listened. When Joseph arrived his brothers roughed him up a bit and got rid of a lot of stored-up irritation but did him no great harm. Then they took his beautiful coat away from him and put him into a dry well with steep smooth walls and took the rope away.

Brotherly Love

Joseph lay there, rather bruised. The well was pretty deep and he could not hear a sound from above. He'd no idea how long he'd lain there or what was going on.

Good thing too. For what was going on among his brothers was all bad. Reuben wasn't there, he'd gone to check how things were going with the shearing at the far-off points of the great flocks. He was the eldest and in charge. His brothers were together and were settling down to a meal. One of them was a powerful quick-thinking man called Judah. Just as he was dipping his hand into the big pot of food he looked up. Far off he could see a caravan of traders approaching.

He knew by the time of year that they would be from Gilead on their way down to Egypt.

'Now listen,' said Judah to his brothers, 'I've an idea that will get Joseph out of our hair for good. Reuben was right, killing him would have been wrong – so we'll not kill him. We'll obey Reuben – and we'll show a profit! We'll *sell* him.'

His brothers looked at him. They knew Judah to be a bit wild – of violent temper, but not mad. And a good, crafty trader.

'Yes! Sell him,' said Judah. He pointed to the approaching line of camels and men. 'Look,' he said, 'I know that lot, their main business is in oils and herbs. They do a lot in medicine-roots and skins and wool too. But they'll deal in anything if the price is right – even slaves! Well,' he said – and he grinned like a wolfe, 'why don't we sell them a *slave*, cheap?'

And it was done. Joseph was up out of the pit and stumbling away on stiff legs behind a camel before he knew what was happening. Judah shared out the money and they finished their meal. They laughed a lot and drank a lot and stayed up very late and all felt very clever.

Then, next day, Reuben got back. Judah, swaggering a bit, told him all about the deal and held out Reuben's tenth share to him. Reuben stood still and looked at his brothers. 'Very clever,' he said, 'thank you for telling me. Have you yet decided which one of you will tell our father?' Suddenly nobody wanted to look at anybody else. 'This will just about kill the old man,' said Reuben. 'All right, Joseph was the youngest and the favourite and we didn't like him but this is a terrible thing we've done.'

Judah was now very ashamed. 'Well, not you,' he said, 'you weren't here.' Reuben looked at his brother. 'What difference?' he said. 'Now listen, we won't tell Dad the truth; we'll kill a goat and smear the blood on Joseph's coat. We'll tear the coat too, and we'll tell Dad that we found it on our way back. Joseph left home after we did and travelled alone. Dad will think he was killed and eaten by wild animals.' Reuben looked down at his feet. 'Not far wrong,' he said. And began to say the prayer for the dead.

Well, the news did nearly kill old Jacob. Nobody could comfort him. He sat with the torn and bloodstained coat across his knees and wept and mourned. A light had gone from his life. He didn't know it but the light had not gone out. It had gone to Egypt. Where we shall go too.

Potiphar's Wife

Well, there stood Joseph – in a slave market in Egypt. His feet were blistered and raw. He was filthy and thirsty and exhausted. He seemed to have been walking for days and days. And now he was up for sale. Fairly high price; for he was young, and well-built and intelligent. The traders were offering him as a house-servant, not a field-slave or labourer.

Joseph stood still and as straight as he could. He closed his eyes against the glare for a while. When he opened them again he met the gaze of a handsome tall man dressed in the uniform of a soldier. He was the Captain of the personal guard of the Pharaoh. His name was Potiphar and he was used to judging the quality of men at first glance. He asked the price, paid it, and walked away. Joseph was handed over into the officer's household within the hour. He was fed and he was given a small room and new clothes. He bathed and shaved and slept like a log for nearly a whole day. He was adaptable was Joseph, made of the best of things, always optimistic, always had a strong feeling God was on his side. Wasn't far wrong. God had biggish plans for Joseph and got started right away. Potiphar began to find out he'd seemingly bought a great bargain in his new house-servant. This Joseph could read and write and had a fine logical mind. Left to handle something tricky he used rare good judgment. He could handle men without raising his voice. Soon Potiphar was leaving more and more to Joseph. His household had never been so well run. Eventually Potiphar made Joseph head man. Overseer in charge of everything. He had great affection for Joseph and treated him almost like a son.

Potiphar's wife, however, had rather different ideas. Very attractive woman she was, rather younger than her husband. She also appreciated her beautifully-run household and her perfectly-cooked meals, and her well-trained staff. She also appreciated her overseer.

And who wouldn't? Joseph was now in his early twenties. Tall, dark and very handsome.

He treated his master's wife with perfect manners and deep respect. Which was the last thing she wanted. She didn't want Joseph's perfect manners and respect, she wanted Joseph! She tried every trick she knew, but Joseph was grateful to Potiphar and was a loyal and principled man. Well, the lady turned nasty. She stole one of Joseph's robes, had it found in her room, told a lot of lies about how he'd tried to force his attentions upon her, and how she'd fought bravely for her honour and how he'd fled leaving his robe behind – a very corny story. But often the most unlikely stories are believed and this story, remember, was told by a lady who had not only been spurned but who was also a first-class liar.

Well, Potiphar believed it; every word. And he threw Joseph into prison and his wife into history. So. This chapter leaves Joseph even worse off than we found him. But we shall see.

Dreams Come True

Well, the years have gone by. Joseph is still in prison but it's not too bad at all. Just lately he had been thinking a lot about dreams and their meanings, and about God who seemed to be a lot in his dreams and who seemed to put into Joseph's mind the clear meanings of them. A sort of correspondence between God and Joseph it seemed to be. Mind you, to have God for a close friend didn't necessarily mean it was going to be roses all the way. Look at Joseph. Favourite son of Jacob; good. Ten elder brothers hated him because of it; bad. They'd sold him into slavery; very bad. Bought by a good master he'd risen to be his master's right-hand man; good. Plotted against by his master's wife who wanted him for *her* right-hand man; bad. But not so bad. Joseph didn't waste time looking back. He was young, about twenty-eight. He was strong, fit, and could think clearly and never complained. Also, as I said, he had God on his side and knew it.

It was the King's prison. Not any less a prison but a rather better class of people. Joseph had been in prison quite a long time. Four to five years. There'd been no trial or anything. Unlikely in that prison.

It all rather depended on the King's pleasure whether you came out or not – and the King didn't even *know* about Joseph. It was the King's Captain of the Guard who'd put Joseph away. And as right-hand man to an officer of the King, Joseph was *entitled* to the special prison. All right. He wasn't complaining. The pattern had repeated itself sort of. He was now right-hand man to the chief jailer. He pretty well ran the place. He knew every prisoner and they all liked and trusted him. He had, as my father used to say, time for people. If you were troubled and you spoke to Joseph, the trouble right away got smaller, the frightening dream might turn out to have a quite unfrightening meaning.

Well, one morning there was rather a flurry. Two members of the King's private household were admitted to prison. Pharaoh's chief baker and Pharaoh's chief butler. How they'd offended the King with their buttling and baking we don't know, but there they were – prisoners. Both a bit scared and both turning, as everyone did, to Joseph for reassurance.

Some months passed and Joseph got to know his butler and baker rather well, and from them a very clear picture of the King and his court. The two men came back often to the subject of the King's birthday and of the King's custom of forgiving wrong-doers on his birthday. They were both a bit tight-lipped about what they'd done but were setting a lot of store on getting a birthday pardon. Three days before the birthday both came to Joseph in a bit of a state. They'd both had very vivid dreams and had heard that Joseph could interpret dreams. Joseph listened as always, quietly and sympathetically; he never now questioned the thought that God was handling the dreams department. He waited for the now familiar 'sure' feeling and turned first to the butler.

'The vine and its three branches and the grapes and wine mean that in three days' time Pharaoh will forgive you and you'll get your job back. You will again be in charge of the King's table and the King's wine.'

The butler was overjoyed and promised to put in a word for Joseph to get him pardoned too. 'Leave it to me,' he said, 'I won't forget!'

Joseph now turned to the baker, who was a small man, rather

rat-like, shifty type, about whom the word was that he *had* run a sort of racket with stolen flour and wheat.

'Well,' said the little man, 'good for me too?'

Joseph felt sad. 'Er – no,' he said. 'One thing is the same, your life will change in three days' time too. It will end. There will be no pardon. I don't know what you did to make Pharaoh cross but you are to be hanged for it.' And he was.

More Dreams

Well, the butler forgot his promise. People do. But about two years later God jogged his memory a little. So let us sit a while in the company of Pharaoh King of Egypt. Quite a nice man. Bit of a worrier. Superstitious. Believed in all sorts of nonsense. The palace was absolutely littered with idols and gods. But this particular morning the King was getting no comfort from any of them. He was seated (as is only right) on his throne, and around him were about two dozen of the top magicians and wise men of all Egypt. They all sat in a rather uncomfortable silence. Then the King spoke.

'I brought you all here,' he said, 'at considerable expense; you've been here about a week and a half, and you've come up with nothing. The two dreams I brought you here to interpret I've had twice again since you've been here. There's not one of you that's a penn'orth of help at all. I've given each one of you private audiences and a more contradictory load of rubbish I've never heard in all my life!'

Then the King turned to his butler. 'Stop fidgeting,' he said, 'stand still. What's the matter?'

The butler, who knew the King rather well, came nearer. 'My Lord,' he said, 'I've just remembered something which may help. About two years ago I made you cross about something and you threw me into the palace jail.'

'Well?' said the King. 'On my birthday I forgave you and you got your job back.'

'Ah yes,' said the butler, 'but the baker, whom you'd thrown into jail with me, you hanged. Same day. On your birthday.'

'Well?' said the King. 'He was crooked, you were a fool. So?'

'Well,' said the butler, 'the baker and I were told what you were going to do three days *before* your birthday.'

'No one knew,' said the King. 'I didn't make up my mind until I'd opened my presents.'

'We were told,' said the butler, 'by another prisoner who interpreted our dreams. A young man he was. In charge of other prisoners. A Hebrew. Name of Joseph. I promised to say a word for him but forgot. I feel a bit bad about it.'

'So you should,' said the King. 'Get him.' And very soon Joseph stood before Pharaoh. He stood quietly, waiting for God to help him with the meaning of Pharaoh's dreams.

Then he got that familiar 'sure' feeling and began to speak. 'The two dreams are one dream,' he said. 'Two messages from my God. The real God. There's only one. He has done you a great favour really. He has told you what is coming. It is this. There will be seven years of great plenty and rich crops in all Egypt followed by another seven years of famine.'

Pharaoh sat very still. 'I knew it was bad,' he said. 'Does your God send any other message?'

Joseph went on. 'Appoint overseers in every part of the land to gather and store one fifth of every crop of grain. Build great granaries and storehouses. The good years must create the reserves for the famine years. New planting to be done. Better farming. Every effort made to increase yield. All overseers to be in charge of local area managers. They in charge of state marshals, the marshals responsible to one man. That man Pharaoh shall appoint. End of message.'

Pharaoh, who had not moved, stood up. He took a gold chain from his neck and put it on Joseph's. 'You are the man,' he said. 'Your God is no fool. Stay to dinner. You start work tomorrow.'

Corn in Egypt

Well, another ten years have passed. We are still in Egypt. Everything that Joseph has told Pharaoh was going to happen has happened. There have been seven years of rich crops and now it is the middle of the seven years of famine. The advice given by God to Joseph, and passed on to Pharaoh, has been followed. Great storehouses and reserves have been built up and a first-class rationing system is in operation. Nobody gets fat but neither does anyone starve. Joseph has been in charge of everything. He is now forty years old. He is married and has two small sons. A tall handsome man who lives and looks like what he has become, an Egyptian Prince of the Court. More than half his life now he'd been in Egypt.

Joseph did not often recall the first half of his life. When he did, it was with mixed feelings. He recalled the love of Jacob his father; too much love, perhaps, for it had made his ten elder brothers jealous. He recalled how they had sold him to slavers who had brought him to Egypt. Only one brother dwelt in his mind with real warmth. That was his younger brother Benjamin, the baby of the family and his real brother, the others were half-brothers. Just lately Joseph had been wondering whether the famine was as bad in Canaan where his father and brothers lived. At least he thought they lived, for he'd had no contact with them for twenty years or more. A long way away; three to four hundred miles to Canaan.

Well, that very day Joseph was to find out. Three times a week the storehouses sold grain to people not covered by the rationing system. Border-dwellers, wandering desert tribes and such. Joseph made a point of looking in on these deals. First applications were made to his office at the palace. When he got there on the morning I'm speaking of, a group of obvious non-Egyptians were waiting. There were ten. Joseph knew them at once. They were his brothers. He counted again quickly. No Benjamin. The brother he most wanted to see again was not with them.

The ten brothers bowed low before Joseph. Nothing about this richly dressed Egyptian with his gold ornaments and badges of office and black wig suggested to them the badly bruised seventeen-year-old they'd sold as a slave over twenty years ago. They had come, they told Joseph, to buy grain, a long journey, their families were starving, they had money, they were from Canaan, the sons of Jacob, the ten sons of Jacob. Now Joseph had no reason to love his brothers but neither was he vengeful. However, seeing his brothers made his desire to see Benjamin very strong suddenly. And in Egypt he had great power. After Reuben the eldest brother had finished speaking,

Joseph let the silence go on for a while, then spoke.

'Because I fear God,' he said, 'he gives me special knowledge and I know that there were *twelve* sons of Jacob, not ten.'

The brothers were thunderstruck. Reuben was the first able to speak. 'Lord,' he said, 'our father indeed had twelve sons, the youngest is at home with him, the other ...'

'The other?' said Joseph.

Poor Reuben, who'd not even been there when Joseph had been sold and who was really the best of the bunch, was full of shame, and fear too, of this magical person. At last he said, 'The other ... is no more.'

Joseph left another silence. His mind was now made up. 'All right,' he said, 'fill your bags with grain and pay in silver. Provisions will be given you for your return journey. Provisions for nine. One of you will stay here in prison until you return again bringing your youngest brother with you.' The ten brothers were now pale and afraid.

Joseph rose from his throne and just couldn't resist it. 'I know also from God,' he said, 'that the brother you shall bring back with you is called Benjamin.' Well, you can imagine.

Separate Tables

The brothers went back to Canaan and once again it was Reuben's job to tell their old father of a missing son, and of the strange Egyptian who had kept him as a hostage. 'The top man he was,' said Reuben, 'handsome, tall, dark, typical Egyptian. Gave us all the grain we wanted, food for the journey home, asked a fair price and had good manners. Said that God gave him special knowledge; said he knew you had twelve sons, not ten; said we were to take Benjamin to him when we went back – and put poor Simeon in prison to make sure we did. Said that that would prove we weren't spies. Doesn't make sense. If he thought we were spies why let nine of us go? Fantastic the way he knew all about us!'

When Reuben finished speaking, old Jacob sat quiet. Then he said, 'And you say that when you opened the bags of grain your money was there? It is beyond understanding. I do not want Benjamin to go. Joseph went once on a journey and he was eaten by wild beasts. I cannot risk my Benjamin's life. Who knows what this Egyptian wants of us?'

Well, the weeks went by and at last the grain was all used and the old man called his sons together. 'Famine is in the land,' he said, 'and only from Egypt can we buy grain. If it must be, it must. Benjamin shall go. Take to the man gifts of fruits of the land and take back the money returned to you and more money for the new purchases. And I will pray that God will look after us all.'

When the brothers arrived at the great palace where Joseph lived, they were taken not to the grain-office but to Joseph's own living quarters. They were given fresh clothing and told to get cleaned up because they were to lunch with the master. At noon the master, Joseph, entered the great dining room where his brothers waited – they a group of bearded Hebrews, he the right hand of Pharaoh and every inch an Egyptian. The brothers, convinced of his magic powers, bent low. Joseph told them to rise. Benjamin, who was Joseph's true brother – the others were half-brothers – felt an odd affinity somehow with this splendidly dressed prince of the Court. He was sensitive, was Benjamin, and felt somehow that the Prince was highly nervous, near to tears almost. He wasn't far wrong.

Joseph beckoned him forward. 'You are Benjamin,' he said. 'Tell me, how is your father?'

But before Benjamin could answer, the Prince had gone. The Prince had gone into a small room and was in most unprincely tears. Poor Joseph! He longed to reveal who he was, but somehow knew it was not yet the right time. Yet, seeing his younger brother, he was filled with love. He wiped his eyes and calmed down after a minute or two and went back to his guests. They, uncertain, hadn't moved. Joseph, aware of the many servants, watched himself, and the lunch was served.

Famine or not, it was a splendid meal. Odd in one respect. Separate tables. At that time no Egyptian could eat with a Hebrew. Rather like today. Still it was an agreeable, cheerful occasion. Simeon, released from prison, enjoyed it as much as his brothers.

A Different Judah

When the banquet was over they all set off back to Canaan. But Joseph was not quite finished with his brothers yet. They'd not gone far when they heard the sound of horses' hooves behind them.

'Hullo,' said Judah, 'who's this in a hurry?'

It was a party of armed men with orders to search the brothers' goods for a valuable silver goblet missing from the great dining hall where they'd had lunch. It was the master's own, the men said. The brothers were frightened and when the goblet was found in Benjamin's grain sack they were even more so. They knew it was a frame-up but there was nothing they could do.

The brothers were surrounded by the men and taken back to the city. Soon they stood before Joseph again. Now he seemed remote and strange. Richly dressed, every inch an Egyptian, second only to the King. Summary justice. No trial. Just the sentence.

'The goblet,' said Joseph, 'was mighty Pharaoh's and a gift to me. To steal from Pharaoh is to die. But in this case the thief shall be made a slave to serve me. For ever.'

He pointed at Benjamin. 'This one alone is guilty; the others may go free.'

And Joseph waited. He wondered which brother would speak first.

They all seemed shocked, dazed.

Then Judah stepped forward. It was Judah, a wild, violent Judah who had been the leader in the selling of Joseph to the slavers all those years ago. Now it was a different Judah.

'My Lord,' he said, 'we know that Benjamin is innocent. If anyone is to be punished, it should be us, not him, for long ago we sinned against God and against our father. This Benjamin is the son of our father's old age and the only son left of Rachel, our father's true love. We are the sons of other mothers. Our father would die if we return without Benjamin. We once, long ago, returned without Joseph, who was Rachel's firstborn, and our father mourned for many years. My Lord,' said Judah, 'take me for slave and let Benjamin go.'

At this point Joseph broke down. He told them who he was – and the joy and happiness is impossible to describe. He would not let them look back with shame. He was full of grace. 'It was God's will,' he said, 'God sent me to Egypt. To preserve life, to save you and many others from the famine in the land. God showed me how to make the fat years provide for the lean. God made me equal to the King. Go,' said Joseph, 'and bring your families and all you own here to Egypt. And give my love to my father and bring him too. Tell him that Pharaoh has offered the most fertile land in Egypt for Israel and his children to live in.'

The brothers took the message. Jacob wiped away his tears. 'It is enough,' he said, 'Joseph is alive. I will see him again before I die.' And the great gathering-together began, and at last the huge cavalcade was on its way. Pharaoh had even sent wagons from Egypt. They must have been the most gorgeous furniture vans in history!

Israel in Egypt

Now, Jacob, like many old people, was the most sorry to pull up his roots. And God knew it, and a few nights later God appeared to Jacob and told him, as many times before, not to worry. 'Because,' said God, 'I am going to look after the whole thing. Your twelve sons will become a great nation. You remember how just before Benjamin was born I changed your name to Israel? Now go back to sleep, you've got a great time coming.'

And it was a great time. Pharaoh was happy to welcome the family of his great friend Joseph. 'Give them the best,' he said. 'Let them eat the fat of the land.' First one to use that phrase, Pharaoh was. Very friendly chap. No fool either, this Egyptian. He was fully aware of how many assorted skills this crowd of Hebrews were bringing into his country. They liked him and he liked them. Particularly old Jacob. He observed the loving respect shown by Joseph and copied it. And when, seventeen years later, Jacob died, you would have thought it was Pharaoh's own father. The whole of Egypt went into mourning. And when the body was embalmed and taken north to the family tomb in Canaan, there were thousands of Egyptians in the sad, weeping procession.

The funeral ceremonies went on for weeks. Sorry to go on so long about it; it's the thought of all those Hebrews and Egyptians living so happily together. And they did – and for many years too. God did look after Jacob's sons, and their sons, and their sons too. Joseph lived to a ripe old age. Like old Jacob before him he was close to God and was used by God to show the future. Although the second youngest, he was very much the head of the family, and just before he died, he said a rather puzzling thing to them all. He said, 'The land which God promised to Abraham, Isaac, and Jacob is not this land. One day God will come and take you out of this land to the land he promised. The Promised Land.' And one day God did. As we shall see.

BIRTHPANGS OF A NATION

The years went by and the picture changed. Over four hundred years went by and the original twelve sons of Jacob had become many thousands of people. Not very happy people. For the original Pharaoh's descendant, the present one, was not quite so friendly. In fact he was an absolute horror. He thought of forced labour camps about three thousand years before Hitler did, and used the Hebrews of Goshen (the fertile district which had been allotted to them by his ancestor) pretty well as slaves. They were set to clearing land and making bricks and building a great new city. 'Work 'em to death,' said Pharaoh. 'There are too many of 'em.'

But the outdoor life was a healthy one. And the Hebrew birthrate increased. So one day Pharaoh thought up a new one. A terrible thing. 'From now on,' he said, 'every boy-baby born to the Hebrews is to be killed, drowned in the River Nile.' The order of a madman. But there were plenty of Egyptian spies and secret police to see it done. Great game. Quite enlivened their day for them. Of course not every birth was discovered. No birth certificates or hospitals. Very few doctors available to these thousands of slaves. Women helped each other and the midwives were Hebrew and told lies in their reports to the police. But it was at best a postponement and when, after a month or two, the baby was found (there were frequent raids), it would be worse, much worse.

That was what Amram was thinking as he made his way home from work one night. Back-breaking work, treated like an animal and kept near to starvation like the rest of his people. But Amram was lucky in one way. He could come home at night. A hovel; half a house; two tiny rooms; but home. Thousands of his kinsmen had no home. They lived in great camps up north near the delta, where Pharaoh was building his great new capital, to be called Rameses after him.

Amram stopped at the low door where he lived. 'It will be terrible for us too,' he thought to himself, 'terrible. Lovely baby. Nearly three months old and never seen the sun. Hidden. wrapped up, kept quiet. But now no longer easy to keep quiet.' He looked to both sides and went in. He went through to the rear room. By a small oil lamp sat his family. His wife Jochebed and his daughter Miriam who was eleven and his small son Aaron who was three and fast asleep. Amram glanced upwards at the ceiling. Between it and the roof rafters above it the baby was hidden. He sat down and looked at his wife and daughter. He thought again how alike they were. The same firm jaw, the same steady dark eyes, the same capable hands. Both had the same patience and love of children. Both gave off a sort of warmth. Amram relaxed a little and then paused. He was sensitive to his wife and daughter and tonight they were giving off a different sort of feeling. A sort of suppressed excitement.

Jochebed and Miriam moved closer to Amram. His wife's eyes were bright. 'I prayed,' she said, 'and a plan came. It must have been in my mind for months. Before the baby was born I noticed that many mothers made tiny coffins for their babies. Of reeds. Sometimes they would get caught in the bulrushes. The guards ignore them. I'm going to make one for *our* baby.'

'A coffin?' said Amram.

'No!' said Jochebed. 'Not a coffin, a floating cradle. I'll make it waterproof with pitch and oiled linen and I'll make *certain* it will be caught in the bulrushes – and I know *where* too.'

Amram stared at his wife and waited.

'Miriam, your clever daughter, has made friends with one of the serving-maids of Pharaoh's daughter. She is not like her father. She longs to be married and have children but no suitors are encouraged at the Palace. Every day she bathes in the river not half a mile from here. It is a secluded place about thirty yards long with a screen of tall bulrushes at each end. After she bathes the Princess walks up and down.'

Now Amram was sitting very still.

'In two days' time,' said Jochebed, 'the Princess will find a live baby in the rushes. The most beautiful baby she's ever seen. He will be clean and sweet and she will love him at sight. Who could fail to? Tomorrow I make the cradle.'

'And then?' said Amram.

'Then,' said his wife rather placidly, 'our Miriam, who will be nearby washing clothes in the river, will ask the Princess whether she would like to have a woman look after the baby for her in secret. The Princess will say yes, and Miriam will run and fetch me.'

Jochebed leaned forward and kissed her dazed husband.

'And I,' she said, 'will be the first woman in history to be both mother and foster-mother to the same child at the same time! You'll see,' she said, 'it will come to pass.'

A Prince of Egypt

Well, the plan worked perfectly, and soon Jochebed was being paid *wages* to look after her own baby until he could be taken by the Princess to live at Court. He would be an Egyptian. But that was to come. In the meantime, thought Jochebed, he's mine, and he's *alive*. She brought him up carefully and the Princess visited regularly and secretly.

But a day came when the Princess told Jochebed that the boy would from then on live at the Palace. He would be brought up and educated as an Egyptian. She was no fool the Princess and in some ways a bit like Jochebed. 'It may be,' she said, 'that you have cared for and loved the boy because you yourself lost a son like him; that when I found a baby, you had that day lost a baby.'

The two women looked at each other.

Then the Princess said, 'The boy has been safe with you. I promise he shall be safe with me.'

Jochebed, who was near to tears, said, 'One thing, Princess. We are Hebrews and this house is a Hebrew house and the boy has a Hebrew name.'

'Yes,' said the Princess. 'At court that won't do. I shall call him Moses, which is more Egyptian than Hebrew.'

And that's not a bad description of the boy who grew to manhood at Court. Moses, more Egyptian than Hebrew. He was a quiet sort of youth and inclined to be shy. He was thoughtful and modest. He used to visit Jochebed when he could; and one day, when she was sure of his discretion, she told him what he'd suspected for a long time. That she was his mother; and that her son, the friendly cheerful Aaron, was his brother; and that Miriam, older than both Aaron and himself was his sister.

His father, the quiet Amram, looked at Moses and was proud of this tall, strong young man with the rather serious face. 'Well, my son,' he said, 'so you are one of us. A Hebrew. Yet you live in an Egyptian Palace and an Egyptian Princess is like a mother to you. What you have learned today about us and yourself will not change anything, except perhaps the way you think about us slaves.' A wise man, Amram.

And he was right. Moses began to spend more and more time away from the idleness of the Palace. Dressed in the clothes of an Egyptian, carrying the staff that showed he was of the Court, he could go anywhere and see everything. And almost wherever he went, he saw great cruelty. He trained himself to show no emotion when he saw the appalling treatment of his brother Hebrews. And in his mind he now called them brothers. No emotion. Until one day he found in himself a rage and fury that left him shocked and trembling and left a sadistic Egyptian guard dead at his feet.

Moses was scared; to kill a guard was punishable by death, member of the Court or not. He steadied himself and looked around. No one else was about. Moses lifted the guard's body and carried it to a nearby gully and buried it and went and stayed the night in the poor quarter of the city with Amram his father.

The next day when he returned to Court he knew something was wrong. The Princess was waiting for him. 'You must go at once,' she said. 'My father Pharaoh knows about the guard. In this matter I can't protect you. He cannot make exceptions and he has no love for you as I have. Go at once.' And Moses did.

Midian and Marriage

Moses left Egypt right away. We'll go with him; in fact we'll go a bit ahead of him. To a place far from Egypt. In the country of Midian. A small village. The home of the village priest. A man called Jethro. He was sitting outside his house and waiting for his seven daughters to come home. They looked after his flock for him. Flock of sheep, not people, *he* looked after *that* lot. He was a bit worried, for the girls had used a pasture that day where the water was scarce and the other shepherds all men and rather rough. The last time they had gone there the girls had been treated very rudely and made to wait till last. Jethro dozed a little and suddenly woke in the middle of a great clatter of excitement. His daughters were all round him and all talking at once.

Yes, they said, they *were* back earlier than expected, they *had* gone to the new place, the shepherds *had* been rude – in fact had told them all to go somewhere else! Used bad language. 'One of them,' said Zippora, the prettiest of the girls, 'even tried to lay his hands on me, and then was picked up and talked to by this man.'

'Picked up? Talked to?' said Jethro. 'What man? And all keep quiet except Zippora.'

'This man,' she said, 'he seemed to appear from nowhere. He was dressed like an Egyptian. He stepped between us, held the shepherd's arms tight to his sides and just lifted him about six inches off the ground. This brought their eyes level and then the Egyptian, without temper, talked to him. The other shepherds did nothing, they were afraid. Then the Egyptian gave them back their friend and he and they watered the flock for us. And here we are.'

Jethro looked at his rather flushed daughter, 'Anything else?' he said. 'Yes,' said Zippora, 'he is the handsomest man I ever saw, and his eyes are brown, and his name is Moses, and he's coming to supper.' And Moses did.

Jethro, although proud of his fine bevy of daughters, was very pleased to have another man at his table; and so indeed were the girls. They chattered and told the adventure ten times over till Moses, who was rather a modest man, got rather pink. Jethro shooed his daughters off to bed and he and Moses went out and sat in the garden. Jethro had met very few Egyptians but felt that this one was far from typical. And he was right. The Egyptian was no Egyptian but an Israelite, a member (as Moses explained to him) of a slave race.

'Were *you* a slave?' asked Jethro.

Moses smiled. 'No,' he said, 'I lived in the Palace of Pharaoh and his daughter was like a mother to me.' And he told Jethro the rest of his remarkable story.

Both men sat still and quiet for a while. Then Jethro made up his mind. 'Live with us,' he said. 'Be my son' – then he remembered how Zippora had looked at Moses during supper – 'or son-in-law', he said. No fool Jethro. And that's how it worked out.

The Burning Bush

Moses and Zippora were married and soon had a son and then another. Moses was happy. He liked his wise old father-in-law and his six sisters-in-law. He lived simply. He looked after Jethro's sheep and enjoyed being a shepherd. Often he would go far afield and be away for days. Solitude didn't bother him. On one of these trips he came to a place called Horeb, a pretty sizeable mountain. As the sheep climbed, Moses followed them. Soon he was high above the plain. Suddenly he saw an amazing sight. Not a vision; a real thing. But unbelievable. It was a bush, burning fiercely, with a roaring sound. Nothing near to it was alight but the fantastic thing was that the bush itself stood in the flames unharmed. Not a branch or a leaf changed in any way. Moses remembered suddenly that this mountain was called by people the Mountain of God. As this thought came into his mind, so, equally clearly, he heard a voice. It spoke from the middle of the flames. It said rather an odd thing. It said, 'Take off your shoes.' And then, when Moses just stared, it said, 'Take *off* your shoes. This place is holy.'

Moses did so, and began to have a pretty good idea who was speaking.

He was right. 'This is God,' said the voice, 'don't be afraid, and if you must cover your head with your coat, leave it loose. We have to have a talk and I don't want you to miss anything. You needn't stand so stiff; sit on that rock.' Moses sat down trembling. The bush burned. 'Comfortable?' said God. 'Good. Now listen. I've decided to do something about bringing the children of Israel out of Egypt. They are having a bad time.'

'I come from Egypt,' said Moses.

'I know that,' said God, 'and you're going back to Egypt. I want you to go and talk to Pharaoh for me.'

'I don't want to make excuses,' said Moses, 'but some years ago, as you probably know, I killed a man in Egypt. I'll go back if you say, but Pharaoh may remember.'

'I don't think so,' said God, 'he's been dead for some years. There's a new one. Even worse. The worst yet. I tell you (said God) even with my help you're going to have a hard time.'

Moses said, 'I don't want to question your judgment, Lord, but are you sure I'm the best choice? I'm not a very good speaker, in fact when I'm nervous I stammer.'

'I've noticed that,' said God. 'So I've fixed that your brother Aaron will go with you.'

Moses felt a bit comforted by this – and pleased too – for he'd not seen or heard of his brother since he'd fled from Egypt. He sat quiet and realized that his life was going to be very different from now on. God kept quiet too and then asked Moses what he was worried about *now*.

'Well,' said Moses, 'it's this. If I go to Pharaoh and ask him to free the slaves and tell him the request comes from the middle of a burning bush halfway up a mountain, he's liable either to laugh or to get very cross. Shouldn't I have a note or something?'

'Good point,' said God. 'But not a note. That wouldn't impress him either. Very fond of a bit of magic the Egyptians are. All right then (said God) that shepherd's crook you hold, throw it down on the ground, you've finished being a shepherd, you work for me now.'

Moses threw down the staff, and, as it hit the ground, it turned into a snake. Moses jumped. He hated snakes.

'Keep calm,' said God. 'Take it by the tail.' And, as Moses did, it turned back into his staff.

'Right,' said God, 'that's sign number one. Now put your hand inside your coat and keep it there while you count ten. When you take it out, it will be the white scaly hand of a leper.'

Moses did, and it was. 'Put the hand back,' said God, 'and count ten again and the hand will come out perfectly healed.' Moses did so, and when he saw his own hand back again, he said, 'Thank God' – and then felt a bit silly.

God chuckled and said, 'Perfectly all right. That's number two. Now go home and pack. Get some rest (said God) for you and I have some interesting times coming.'

'Let my People Go'

Well, we are back in Egypt. In Goshen or, as Pharaoh called it, the slave province. Outside a sort of small meeting-hall sat two men, rather depressed. One was Moses and the other was his brother Aaron.

'I didn't even get a chance to show Pharaoh the magic which God gave me,' said Moses. 'Never *seen* a man in such a temper. Pharaoh went crazy. Said he'd never heard of my God and how dare I interfere with all his building work and brick production.'

'What happened then?' said Aaron.

'Well, then he got really nasty,' said Moses. 'He's cut down the food and increased the hours per week.'

'When was this?' said Aaron.

'About five days ago,' said Moses. 'I've just made things worse. I feel I've done it all wrong. God knows what I should do now.'

'If God knows,' said Aaron, 'perhaps we ought to ask him.'

So they sat and waited till God spoke and, when he did, Moses told him all about it.

'Cheer up,' said God, 'I told you this job wasn't going to be easy. Go and see Pharaoh again. This time no matter how rude he gets, you do the magic. Just the first trick this time. See how it goes.'

Well, Moses and Aaron did as God said. They asked for an appointment and rather to their surprise got one.

The day came and Aaron and Moses stood together before the

great throne. Hundreds of people seemed to be present. No Pharaoh. Courtiers, servants, soldiers, priests, officials, and many strangely dressed men with tall staffs of office, each one different. 'They are the court sorcerers and magicians,' said Moses nervously. 'I think we are to be made fun of. Bow your head Aaron,' he said, 'here comes Pharaoh.'

Well, there were great crashings of gongs and blasts on trumpets and music and rose petals thrown about and it all took about twenty minutes, but at last Pharaoh was safely sitting on his throne. There was a silence.

'Speak,' said Pharaoh.

'I don't want to make you cross again,' said Moses to the King, 'but my God said I was to show you a sort of miracle-sign as a kind of credential.'

'Carry on,' said Pharaoh.

Moses took his shepherd's crook and threw it down on the floor. For one horrible moment he thought it wasn't going to work and then the staff turned into a wicked-looking snake. One or two of the women drew back a little. Nobody seemed very impressed. Pharaoh looked a bit bored and then he motioned his magicians and sorcerers forward. They stood in a half circle round Moses and his snake and they all threw *their* staffs down – and all *their* staffs turned into snakes.

Moses could hardly believe his eyes. 'What on earth happens *now*?' he whispered to Aaron.

Aaron said, 'Look, your snake is eating theirs, but it doesn't seem to be impressing the King. I think we're going to be thrown out again.' And they were.

Moses wasn't too worried, he had a strong idea that it was not the end of the matter. He was right. God had hardly started. Three weeks later Pharaoh held a special meeting. All the sorcerers and magicians and soothsayers were there, waiting. Blast of trumpets (rather shorter than usual), and Pharaoh walked in. He got straight down to business.

'As you know,' he said, 'when this Moses first came to me about freeing the slaves I threw him out and made his beloved slaves work harder. Then he did that walking-stick-into-snake thing and you all did the same and I threw him out again. Then he turned all the water into blood and we had to dig new wells for a week. 'Well,' said Pharaoh, 'all these so-called miracles *you* lot have been able to do. Now, Moses tells me, we are to have gnats and flies. Can you match that too?'

The magicians looked at each other and were silent.

'And there's something else,' said Pharaoh. 'Moses said that the province of Goshen where the Jews live won't be affected. He said this God of his will make what he called a "division". Anybody want to say anything?'

The head magician stepped forward and said, 'None of this is possible or *we* could do it.'

Then there was a great buzzing and humming and everyone was madly scratching and swatting. Pharaoh checked up on the division. It was true. No insects in Goshen. He sent for Moses and agreed to everything. The gnats and flies vanished. Then Pharaoh went back on his word and kept *on* breaking his promises. God made the plagues worse and worse and each time Pharaoh said the slaves could go and then when God stopped the plague he said they couldn't. Must have been mad. Well, he was, of course. He brought down terrible things on his people. Their cattle died, they were infected with awful sores, their crops were destroyed by great electrical storms and hailstones as big as fists. And nothing could be salvaged because then millions of locusts came and ate everything up. Then when the locusts passed, a terrible black fog came and nobody could see anyone else and the people just sat in misery for three days.

Every day reports came in to Pharaoh about the division. All said the same. In Goshen where the slaves lived there had been no black fog, no locusts, no lightning and hail, no sores, no cattle death, nothing. When the darkness went away Moses again went to Pharaoh and again Pharaoh went back on his word. The two men looked at each other. Pharaoh's eyes were full of hate. Moses felt sad. He had just received orders from God regarding the next and final plague. He held up his hand. 'I have to tell you,' he said, 'that in ten days' time at midnight all the firstborn in Egypt will die. The firstborn of every single family. Yours too. Whether or not you will let the slaves go is now out of your hands. They leave the next morning.'

Then Moses left the great palace and called together the elders and leaders of the slaves and told *them*. 'And,' said Moses, 'we all have our orders too. Every family is to prepare the same meal that night. Roast lamb. When the lamb is killed some of its blood is to be daubed on the lintel and doorposts of every Hebrew house so that when the Angels of Death pass through Egypt that night they will see the blood and pass over those houses. And this deliverance,' said Moses, 'is to be celebrated every year from now on for ever and will be called the "Passover".'

And at midnight on the tenth night to every Egyptian family came a death and to every Hebrew slave came freedom.

Bread from Heaven

After that terrible night when God sent death to all the firstborn of Egypt, the children of Israel just left. No one stopped or hindered them in any way. They danced, they sang, they laughed. They were full of trust and hope and joy.

It didn't last long. In no time at all they started to complain. First it was the route, into rather bare, unfriendly country. Then it was the food and then the lack of water. The miracle of the deliverance was soon forgotten.

Mind you, pretty soon they had something really *worth* worrying about. An old enemy. Pharaoh, when he rose from weeping over his own dead firstborn son, decided to get nasty. So he called out his thousands of chariots and soldiers and went after the children of Israel. They'd reached the shores of the Red Sea and now there was water in front of them, and behind them, coming up fast, the chariots full of armed men. They were full of panic. God told Moses what to do and he did it. He waved his staff over the sea and the sea parted and the people walked on dry land on the bottom of the sea. On either side of them were great walls of water held up by God. Ahead of them, to comfort them, was a huge glowing cloud set there by God. When they were halfway across the Egyptians reached the shore and went straight on down after them. God waited until every chariot and soldier was below land-level and then let down the walls of water and drowned the lot of them. Ahead, unharmed, walked the children of Israel. Saved by a great miracle.

But in less than a week they were complaining again. The water where they'd camped was undrinkable, the walking was hard on the feet. 'Maybe,' they said, 'we would have been better off back in Egypt.' Moses stood for quite a lot of this nonsense and then had a word with God. God fixed the water right away. He showed Moses a certain tree near the oasis and told him to throw it in. Moses did so and the water became sweet and the people cheered up. Moses didn't hurry them; they were city dwellers after all, slaves or not, and this desert journey was going to be tough.

After a week or two they went on and the complaints soon began again. They now remembered, it seemed, only the *good* things of Egypt, the oven-baked bread, the plentiful meat and fish. *Very* rose-coloured glasses. By the time they'd been six weeks out of slavery they were holding anti-Moses meetings. Mind you, they were all very hungry. The food they'd brought was finished and the country was bare. Then God sent for Moses. 'Tell the people,' he said, 'that there will be poultry for supper and fresh cereal for breakfast. The cereal will have to be gathered from the ground before sun-up, so get everyone up early.'

Moses, who had perfect faith, told the people. Everybody waited to see what 'poultry for supper' meant. The hot sun burned down; lunchtime came and went. Thousands of hungry people. Then, as the sun began to go down, supper flew in. A great flock of quail delivered themselves straight into the camp. There was plenty for everyone and the people ate well and thanked Moses. He told them all to go to bed early. Next morning, just as it got light, he got them all up to gather their breakfast. As the light increased and the dew lifted, the people at first could see nothing. But then they saw that the ground was covered with what looked like fine frosted corn-flakes. A child bent down and tasted it, and said it was like honey but crisp. The people began to gather it, saying to each other, 'What is it?' And that became its name, what-is-it, or, as they said it in Hebrew, *Manna*. And every morning the *manna* was there. It didn't keep, but it was there fresh every morning. Every man gathered his own and everyone had to get up early before the sun got at it.

The Law

Moses looked at the people bent to their task the next morning and thought, 'Early rising, exercise for the back *and* a balanced diet. God must be toning them up for something.' Well, God was. But not right away. The days turned into weeks and the people and their problems kept Moses very busy. He began to look pretty tired. And felt it too. One evening he had a guest to cheer him up a bit. His father-in-law Jethro had come to visit him and had spent the whole day in the great camp and had asked questions and listened to everyone. Moses was fond of him and respected the wisdom of the wise old priest. Jethro looked at Moses with no less affection and began to speak. 'You're doing too much,' he said, 'the people must start to govern themselves. You've done all you promised. You freed them from their slavery in Egypt, you brought them safely across the Red Sea and drowned all their enemies (I wish I'd been there to see it), you arranged the daily arrival of manna from Heaven for them and you've found a way of making fresh water by banging on a rock with your stick. You've even won a battle with the Amalekites for them.'

'Not me,' said Moses, 'not me, God.'

'They can't see God,' said Jethro, 'they can see you. You're easier to complain to than God. You're nearer. Yes,' said Jethro, 'you are doing too much. It's ridiculous that you should have to listen to every grievance and dispute and spend hours and hours on trivialities. Now here's what you have to do. You are to appoint leaders. Honest men who will do all this work for you. You will deal only with great matters. No one but you can talk to God and God is entitled to an uncluttered mind in his head man.'

Moses listened to all this and acted upon it and the people became better organized. It left Moses free to arrange the next part of the journey. This was to the great plain at the foot of Mount Sinai and when the people arrived there they had been three months out of Egypt. 'At this place,' God told Moses, 'on this mountain, I will start to make these children of my beloved Israel into a special people. I will give them through your mouth laws and statutes which will govern every day of their lives. From birth to death. All this will take a long time. Get the people ready.'

Moses told the people to pray and prepare themselves for two days and to be ready on the plain below the mountain on the morning of the third day. Everyone was, and it was something to see. First a sort of hush and then great thunderings and lightnings came from the mountain. It quaked and heaved and great flames and smoke went right up to heaven. Then the sound of a million trumpets began and went on, louder and louder, till the people thought their heads would burst, and then, suddenly it was quiet and still, and Moses began the lessons from God.

First came the ten great rules of behaviour and after these commandments began the lesser rules, in great detail. The people were dazed and frightened. So God asked Moses to go up to the top of the mountain into the great black cloud where they could talk quietly together. It took a long time; Moses was up there nearly seven weeks. God permitted him to take all the notes he needed but God insisted upon writing the first ten commandments himself. With his finger, on two tablets of stone.

When it was time to go Moses turned to God and said, 'You are angry, Lord. Why?'

And God said, 'The people have already disobeyed me. They've broken their promises and are down there worshipping an idol!'

'An *idol*!' said Moses.

'Yes,' said God, 'they put together all their bits of gold and have made an animal idol. A calf. And they are offering sacrifices to it! Well,' said God, 'that's enough. I'm going to wipe them out!'

Moses was afraid but spoke. 'They broke their promise to you Lord,' he said, 'because they are human and fools. How can you break your promise to them? You are God.' And God calmed down and Moses left him.

But Moses was no God and by the time he reached the foot of the mountain and saw the golden calf he was in a violent temper. The drunken, dancing, singing people looked up and there stood

Moses on a rock just above them. He looked ten feet tall. Absolute shocked silence. Then Moses raised his arms and hurled the tablets of the Law down at the calf. They fell short and smashed to pieces. Moses felt that his own life was broken too. He walked down and through the people, who parted for him just as the Red Sea had once parted for them.

Forty Years On

Days passed and still Moses sat discouraged and alone. The camp was very subdued and quiet. The people knew they'd gone too far and kept away from Moses – and from the foot of the mountain where Moses had smashed the stone tablets. The tablets regarding the right way to live. The people were afraid and ashamed. God's own finger had written those laws, it was said, and his revenge was likely to be dreadful. Not so long before they'd seen what he did to the Egyptians.

But God was not thinking of revenge. He was rethinking the whole project of teaching this people to *deserve* to be his chosen. The next day he called on Moses. 'No revenge,' he said, 'the promise about giving them a beautiful land to live in still stands. But they must learn to live humbly and quietly and to obey my laws. I will give you another set of tablets and an exact design for the tabernacle to keep them in. Everyone shall contribute to its making and it will be holy and perfect and called the Ark. It will require many different materials, from acacia wood and goats' hair to gold and onyx. It will be carried from place to place for the rest of the journey and your brother Aaron shall be the priest in charge. At every place it will be the centre of the camp and of the people's lives. Above it reaching to Heaven I will set a cloud. When the cloud moves on the people will move on. Not until.'

All this was done and the people followed the cloud and journeyed on and at last came to the borders of Canaan. God told Moses to send out twelve men, one from each tribe, to spy out the land and bring back reports about it. Off they went all in different directions to spy out the nature of the land which God had promised to the twelve tribes of Israel. Well, the twelve men came back at last and all agreed that the land was rich and had everything, a land they said, 'flowing with milk and honey'. 'But,' they told the people, 'the cities of the land are like forts – like mountains. Many different tribes live in the land, each tribe tens of thousands! And the people of the tribes are huge! Giants!' And every time they told their story they alarmed the Israelites more, who again showed no faith and grew full of fear and anger against Moses who had 'brought them all this way – to be killed by giants!' They held meetings full of madness. 'Let us choose a leader,' they screamed, 'and go back to Egypt!'

Moses wept. But the Lord tapped him on the shoulder. 'Moses,' said God, 'I brought them out of slavery, I drowned their enemies in the sea. I gave them food and drink in the desert. I showed them miracles. And *still* they have no faith in me.'

Moses waited. God sounded more sad than angry.

'Moses,' said God, 'take them all back into the wilderness for another forty years. During that time the lessons will go on, and every person over twenty who spoke against me today will die. Their children shall enter the land, not they.'

And so it was. Not even Moses lived to enter that promised land. But, a little before he died, God gave him a sight of it from a nearby mountain. Even after forty years the Bible says that his eye was bright and his vigour unimpaired. Imagine! Still energetic and clear-headed after all those years in the wilderness training the children of Israel to become fit for the land which God had promised them. It needed a marvellous man to stay with them at all after the way they'd let him down. And Moses was. A marvellous man. In fact never since then, the Bible says, has there been a prophet in Israel like Moses, whom God knew face to face.

The New Man

Now, it's never an easy job to take over the reins from a great man; to have to step into a great man's shoes. Imagine what it must have been like to take over from Moses, the man who had delivered the children of Israel from the power of Pharaoh, who had brought them through the Red Sea and across the desert, who had performed miracles at every turn, who had talked face to face with God, and who had finally led the people for forty years in the wilderness until they arrived for the second time on the borders of the Promised Land.

But Moses was, after all, only a man; he had to die some time, someone had to step into his shoes. And God had marked two possible successors forty years before the appointment would become vacant! Typical. Practical. Like the whole idea of the forty-year delay, during which the people could be made fit for the land which had been promised them. You remember how, when they had first reached the borders of the Promised Land, Moses sent twelve men to spy out the country? And how what they reported frightened the people who, as so often before, showed no faith in God or Moses? And neither did ten of the twelve – remember? Well, one of the two spies who believed absolutely in the promise of God was called Joshua and the other was a man called Caleb. They remained friends all their lives. And, of course, they had plenty of time to get to know one another; forty years in the wilderness.

The great camp of Israel was sleeping. It was the end of a long night and soon the new day would dawn, the day which would mean the end of their wanderings. Only the sentries stayed awake. The sentries and the two men waiting eagerly in the leader's tent. Powerful, middle-aged, prime-of-life men. They were Joshua and Caleb.

They sat in silence. Joshua thinking over yet again all that had happened to him lately. Not just being leader of the people in place of Moses. He'd known he was going to get that job for some time. No, special things had happened, not just the new job. He felt he'd been made over into a new sort of man to fit the job.

It had begun with Moses blessing him just before he died and then, not long after, God himself had spoken; not through Moses, as for so long, but to him, personally, clearly. Orders, plans, encouragement, confidence in him. He'd felt ten feet tall. And now, with Caleb, he sat quiet. Waiting for spies to return and report.

Soon, silently, well trained by Joshua, the spies came in. As over forty years before he and Caleb had returned after spying out the

Promised Land to report to Moses. Joshua's spies, two men, had not gone far. Across the River Jordan to Jericho. The objective, the first place to be dealt with in the taking over of the Promised Land. Not easy, for it was a walled city, like a great fortress. Huge, thick, high walls, so thick and high that many houses were built into the walls. Joshua's spies had known their job; those houses built into the walls had been their way in and their way out.

'A woman helped us,' said one of the men, 'a woman called Rahab. A prostitute; very good-hearted practical person. She hid us, made up lies to cover our escape and told us a great many things.'

'What things?' said Joshua.

'Well,' said the man, 'they're scared stiff of us. The children of Israel are famous! They know of what God did for us recently when we won the two big battles and how he divided the Red Sea and so on. Anyway,' said the man, 'we did a deal with the woman. We promised that, when we take Jericho, neither she nor any of her family will be harmed. Was that all right?'

'Quite all right,' said Joshua and sent the men off to bed.

Making an Impression

Joshua and Caleb talked. Taking Jericho was the second thing; the crossing of the River Jordan was the first. No bridges and no boats; and many thousands of people. He and Caleb, who had absolute faith, didn't waste time worrying. They completed their plans for moving the people down to the plains near the river.

It took about three days and Joshua's officers were everywhere. The people, very different now from the frightened slaves of two generations ago, were fit and excited. The tablets of the Law and the beautiful Ark which contained them were moved to the river bank in charge of priests and of one man from each of the twelve tribes which made up the people.

Then God spoke. 'Joshua,' he said, 'like their fathers before them, the children of Israel will need to be impressed all the time. So as you now carry the staff of my beloved Moses who did miracles for them. I will help *you* do a miracle or two. One of the best remembered is the parting of the Red Sea. Well,' said God, 'as time is short and I want you to make a big impression quickly, you can part the waters of the Jordan for me. We'll start now.'

And it began to be the greatest day in Joshua's life. He had never lacked faith and, as the right hand of Moses, he had seen many miraculous happenings. But never before had he realized how shrewd God is in his dealings with *people*. Joshua, since taking over Moses' job had felt a bit inferior (who wouldn't?) and the children of Israel, although they respected him, had let him know pretty clearly that he wasn't the old man. But now God had decided to show the people that Joshua, whom he'd chosen, was equal to great Moses.

God stage-managed it so beautifully. He'd put the priests and one man from each of the twelve tribes and the holy Ark of the Law down by the side of the great River Jordan in full flood. Well away from them, on rising ground, where they could see everything, the people. Between, Joshua. Instructed by God, he'd raised his staff, Moses' staff, and the priests and men carrying the holy Ark had moved down to the water's edge. As their feet touched the water, the water retreated and, as the Red Sea forty years before had divided for Moses, so had the Jordan halted and piled up in a great glistening wall for Joshua. The priests and their precious burden stopped halfway across and the people passed over in front of them, singing, praying. Then the priests followed and, when the last man was on dry land, the water came down with a roar like thunder.

From that wonderful day Joshua felt like a king and the people treated him like one.

The Walls of Jericho

Soon Joshua's spies told him that news of the children of Israel crossing the Jordan dry-shod had gone through the land like a wind and the many hostile tribes and kings now feared them. Joshua held great prayer-meetings and told the people that God had now forgiven them for their parents' ingratitude after Egypt. The years in the wilderness were over. Clean slate. Fresh start. One more big change, Joshua told them. 'In a day or two,' he said, 'we celebrate the

Passover; from then on no more *manna* from heaven every day. We are now in the Promised Land, a land of milk and honey, and we are to eat the produce of this land.'

All this came to pass and, as so often lately, Joshua saw the wisdom of God.

'He's making them work a little now,' he thought. 'Not too easy. Lot of battles yet. Big things ahead.'

The biggest thing ahead was the city of Jericho. A walled city. Like a fortress. And, since the news of the Jordan, shut and barred and impregnable. By all accounts prepared for a long siege too – as the people of Israel were not.

Joshua spent a lot of time looking at the city of Jericho from some high ground. Alone. Thoughtful. It was a problem. One day he sat thinking of how Moses had told him the story of the burning bush and how a voice had said, 'Take off your shoes, this place is holy'. As Joshua wondered why, in the midst of all his worries, he should think of this particular story, a voice beside him said, 'Take off your shoes, this place is holy.' And he had an inkling that his worries about Jericho were about to be sorted out. He looked round and it was a man with a sword. Good-looking; no wings or anything but pretty definitely an angel. Joshua took off his shoes and listened to the battle-plan for Jericho brought from God by this rather splendid officer. Joshua listened carefully.

After outlining the procedure in detail the angel asked him if he had any questions.

'Well, no,' said Joshua. 'I was going to ask if you were joking. But somehow I don't think that you are.'

'I'm not,' said the angel. 'Goodbye. You're going to have an interesting week.'

He was right. On the first day Joshua had called the people together and begun the first part of the angel's battle-plan. He tried not to feel silly. 'Everyone – priests, army, everyone – we are going to walk round Jericho. Once a day for six days. No talking.'

And it was done. Every day the silent walk right round the great walled city of Jericho had taken place. Silent except for the continuous blowing of seven ramshorn trumpets and the sound of thousands of feet. An odd silence too from *inside* the walls. The people of

Jericho had heard of this newly-out-of-the-wilderness people of Israel with their all-powerful God who parted rivers and seas for them, and they were fearful. But the seventh day was the one. If Joshua hadn't seen it with his own eyes, he wouldn't have believed it. Again the walk, but on the seventh day *seven* times round and then, as signal, a great sustained note on all trumpets and the people began to shout at the tops of their voices. At first Joshua thought nothing would happen but then the earth rumbled almost as if shouting itself, and the great walls of the city split and crumbled and fell in huge clouds of sandy dust, and into that dust, into the city, from all round it the army went. A victory, a massacre, a wiping out of a city already demoralized with fear and terror. No one was spared except the woman Rahab, who had helped Joshua's spies, and her family. Joshua, like Moses his teacher, did not forget promises.

The Hard Way

Joshua, as we have seen, did not forget promises. Neither did he forget that his wildly excited, victorious people were the sons and daughters of a horde of slaves freed from Egypt by God, as famous for their ingratitude and disobedience as for their miracle-laden delivery. Joshua had seen enough of that disobedience and he was a wise and mature man. He called the people together. 'No looting *at all*,' he told them, 'not by anyone. God was very clear on this. The gold and the silver and the bronze is to be collected and put into the holy treasury. It belongs to God who gave us this day and this victory.'

But people are people. God may make us; when we're babies, we are cute; but families develop some nasty habits. And pass them down. So a little private looting went on, and the stuff was hidden, and the parties concerned felt a bit clever.

Hidden? From *God*? Many times in the past Moses had softened God's anger, but now God didn't even consult Joshua. The next battle – a small one – the people lost. And were shocked. None more than Joshua. He prayed and wept and asked why. Then God told him. 'So tomorrow morning,' said God, 'gather the whole people in their tribes and I will show you which tribe, then which family, then which son of that family, stole from me and you will take him and all who share his guilt and the people will stone them and then burn them and raise a great heap of stones over them. The amount stolen was small but the lesson must be huge and remembered – as a big trouble. And the place shall be known from now on as the Valley of Trouble.' And it is. To this day.

Then Joshua had a think about the recent defeat and being a well-trained soldier and a good general he let it teach him. So he took a small force, started a battle outside the city he was trying to take, made like he was running away, then, as the whole city poured out after him, he led them all into a splendid great ambush and the other part of his army finished the job. No survivors. The name of that city was Ai.

This time the people *asked* what they could take.

'Normal spoils of war,' said Joshua, 'and all cattle and livestock.'

Then, to finish the lesson, he gathered the people together in front of the priests and the holy Ark and he read them every commandment and law that God had given Moses. It took time. He didn't hurry.

Gibeon

Well, Jericho and Ai gave the children of Israel a fearsome reputation. But, reputation aside, even after those victories the people were only about twenty miles in. The next place in was called Gibeon. A crafty lot who'd heard about the children of Israel and their all-powerful God and they'd no intention of fighting. But also they'd heard of Joshua's 'no prisoners, wipe-'em-all-out rule. So what they did was they all disguised themselves as foreigners from a far-off land with worn-out sandals and old patched clothes and tired ragged donkeys and dry mouldy bread and they went to meet Joshua to make a 'spare-our-lives' pact. He, a practical man, needing every ally he could get and seeing no saboteurs in this ragged lot, agreed. When he found out the fraud he didn't go back on his word but said that from now on they, the Gibeonites, would be 'hewers of wood and drawers of water' for the people, and for ever.

This place Gibeon was the cause of a happening, a miracle, a favour by God to Joshua, which ought to be as famous as Jericho. A group of kings of various parts of the land were very annoyed at Gibeon surrendering to Joshua, so they decided to band together and all attack at once. Five of them. Joshua didn't mind his enemies coming to him instead of his having to beat the kings one by one. So he prepared. And he and his army went out to meet them. They marched all night and their sudden appearance next morning was a shock. A panic started and the battle became a hunt. God told Joshua he would help with some showers of great hailstones and if he, Joshua, wanted anything else he should ask. Joshua, having chased the five enemy armies into a great valley, was pretty certain he could manage just with the hailstones. But suddenly, at tea-time, it struck him that darkness would certainly help the enemy, a great many of whom were still alive. So Joshua looked at the sun and said, 'Stand still!'

And God arranged it. The sun stood still for about one day – and all the work was done. Never before; never since.

What's in a Name?

You know, it always seems to me a shame that Joshua is most famous for his easiest job. Jericho. A bit of marching, a lot of trumpeting and shouting, down came the walls, and that was it. Yet Joshua, and this is less wellknown, was a first-class leader and soldier who fought dozens of great battles and virtually cleared the Promised Land for the children of Israel. He conquered it, and shared it out among the tribes, and settled them in. A great leader. Successor to Moses and close to God. Who liked him, and helped him a lot. You might say, 'Yes, but the Land was *promised*.' True, but the people weren't just *given* it. They had to deserve it, and *fight* for it. And Joshua showed them how. One of the great loyal servants of God. He brought a people from a wilderness and gave them the dignity of a nation and of a belief. An under-rated man. His name, Joshua, means roughly, 'God saves'. And God did save the nation through Joshua. The people have had other Joshuas since. One, the most famous, lived when Greek was the common language of Europe and the Middle East. Now the Greek alphabet has no letter 'h'; and Hebrew didn't write its vowels at all. Which means that if you take a Hebrew name, write it in Greek letters, and then pronounce it in English, some funny things can happen. Take Joshua for instance; some Roman Catholic Bibles call him Jeshua; and everybody calls his later namesake Jesus.

Gideon Receives Orders

After Moses Joshua. Both great leaders. But after Joshua no great leader of the nation for many years. Only local leaders. Judges. The part of the Bible about them is called Judges. Their work wasn't easy. The Israelites had been a pretty well united people when they were fighting for the Promised Land. But, once settled there in the various parts allotted by Joshua to the various tribes, they drew apart and their enemies lost their fear of this God-protected people. Also, as so often before, the Israelites forgot what God had done and began to worship other gods. So God who had protected them for so long didn't always bother. Nearly two hundred years of this uneasy occupation of the land passed. Long peaceful periods and then new enemies and war and persecution and death. Things don't change much really, do they?

So. Now the enemy are the Midianites and they are a vicious, cruel people and the Israelites are having a bad time. Not surprising; once again they were worshipping idols and breaking their word to God. The bad time had gone on for seven years. Many of the people were living in caves and raid shelters, for the Midianites with their countless fast camels were terrible raiders and laid waste everything they couldn't take away. The people were miserable, oppressed, poor. No leader; there hadn't even been a judge for some time. Enter, much to his own surprise, Gideon.

He was the youngest son of an elderly man called Joash and lived with his wife and family at a place called Ophrah. A bad place to live, surrounded by the enemy and quite cut off from the other larger tribes of Israel. Gideon's tribe was Manasseh, descended from one of Joseph's two sons; a half-tribe really, one of the lesser ones. So.

A son of an unimportant family in a not very strong tribe in occupied and oppressed territory. Gideon was a careful, cautious sort of man who did what the others did. He grew food in secret, hid it, stayed out of trouble and really was not very brave. Old Joash his father would have no truck with idols though, and was rather a fine man. He was very fond of Gideon.

One day, Gideon, rather miserable, was at the back of the house putting away some wheat in a secret place. He felt very humble, very much the youngest son, and very depressed. Very much alone. Then a voice said, 'You are not alone. God is with you, you mighty man of valour.'

Gideon looked round. He was certain he hadn't spoken out loud. Sitting on the ground with his back comfortably against the oak tree was a tall, rather handsome man with very blue eyes. He was smiling. He looked as though he smiled often. Gideon was certain also that the man hadn't been there a minute before.

'I didn't hear you,' said Gideon nervously.

'You didn't hear me arrive, or you didn't hear what I said?' the man answered.

'I didn't hear you arrive,' said Gideon. 'I heard what you said.' And then, as the man smiled again, 'I didn't think it was very funny.'

'Funny?' said the man.

'Calling me a mighty man of valour,' said Gideon.

'I wasn't joking,' said the man. 'Someone has got to lead the resistance and it might just as well be you. You are big and strong and no fool. And the enemy, the Midianites, have had it too good for long enough. Nasty lot, but only men. Get rid of 'em!'

'Me?' said Gideon.

'Well, you with a few others and a bit of help from my department,' said the man.

'But there are thousands and thousands of them,' said Gideon, 'they're everywhere; they're in control, and the tribes of Israel are scattered and apart.'

'They are waiting for a leader,' said the man, 'to pull them together. You,' said the man. 'You are a mighty man of –'

'No, I'm *not*,' said Gideon. 'I don't even know how to start. Even in this town, in Ophrah, they tell us what to do. And they've got that great idol there in the market that they pray to. Baal. One or two of our people pray to it, too, I might tell you. Disgusting.'

'Ah,' said the man, and got to his feet. He was a handsome man with very blue eyes. Unusual. He smiled. 'Ah,' he said. 'The idol. Baal. Start with that.'

'And another thing,' said Gideon, 'the – eh? Start with what?'

'The idol,' said the man. 'Get a few of your friends and one of your father's two bulls and go and harness the bull to the idol and pull it down and smash it up.'

'Just a minute,' said Gideon.

'Next to Baal is the idol of Asherah his wife. Very ugly. It's of wood. Pull that one down too and chop it up for firewood,' said the man.

'Firewood?' said Gideon.

'Yes,' said the man, 'for a sacrifice to God. The sacrifice will be your father's second bull. Your father won't mind. He'll be proud of you.'

Gideon stood still and looked into the man's very clear blue eyes. 'I won't deny,' he said carefully, 'that I've often longed to do what you've just suggested – you seem to know my mind – and I won't deny you probably have some special authority. Would you think me rude if I asked you for some proof?'

'Not at all,' said the man. 'Go into the house and bring out the meat pie and the pot of stew on the stove. And some bread.'

'I'm so sorry,' said Gideon. 'I should have offered –'

'It's not to eat,' said the man.

Gideon did as he was told and put the meat and bread on a flat stone and then, without question, poured the stew over both.

'Stand back,' said the man and gently touched the wet mess with his staff.

There was a great roar and a flash of flame and everything, including the man, disappeared. Gideon was blinded for a moment, then stood looking at the spot where the man had been. He rather missed him.

When the man spoke again from just behind him Gideon jumped.

'All right?' said the man.

'How many men will I need?' asked Gideon.

'Ten,' said the man. 'Strong ropes and the seven-year-old bull. The younger bull is for the sacrifice. Any questions?'

'Look,' said Gideon, 'I'm not used to doing brave things and I'm not really afraid for myself. But what about my father and mother and my own family? Would it be all right if I did the job at night? Less chance of the Midianites knowing who did it. Do you mind?'

'Good idea,' said the man. 'Do it tonight. See you tomorrow.'

Resistance Leader

Well, Gideon had done it. He'd done everything the blue-eyed man had said. He had gathered ten of his friends and taken ropes and one of his father's two fine bulls and they had gone into the market place at dead of night and tied the bull to the great idol of Baal and pulled it down and smashed it to bits. Then they'd done the same to the other wooden idol of Asherah, the female, wife of Baal; they had chopped it up and used the wood for a sacrificial fire to God, using the other fine bull as a burnt offering. Even in that the man had been right; Joash, Gideon's father hadn't been cross, he'd been proud of his youngest son. He was a brave and God-fearing man was Joash and, if his Gideon wanted to be a resistance leader against the enemy occupying forces, good luck to him.

But now, the next morning, Gideon wasn't so sure. The Midianites were no fools and could put two and two together and in every occupied town there are informers and very soon there was a banging on the door and a crowd of Midianites and idol-worshipping townspeople were shouting for Joash to bring out his son. Gideon saw that the thing he'd feared, that his whole family might be wiped out, now looked very possible. He wished that the blue-eyed man were there.

And suddenly he was. 'Leave it to your father,' he said. 'He's being looked after. As you are. Same department.'

Old Joash went out to the mob. They surged forward but the old man was still and calm and they stopped.

'If,' said Joash, 'the god Baal is so powerful, no doubt he will destroy utterly the people who destroyed his image. How can

Gideon escape if he is guilty? Baal will kill him and everyone else who helped smash the idols. How dare *you*,' the old man said to the now silent crowd, 'how dare *you* presume to take over the revenge of a *god*? Let us all be quiet for a minute or two while Baal strikes dead the guilty ones.'

Then the old man stood for a few moments and as the crowd, looking rather sheepish, faded away he went back inside. He expressed no surprise upon seeing the blue-eyed man, whom Gideon now knew to be an angel, and they sat down at the table.

'Right,' said the man. 'Now listen. The Midianites and their friends the Amalekites are massing not far from here for a big new offensive against Israel. Gideon, I want you to send messengers from this tribe to at least three other tribes to gather for a meeting. I will see that this business of the idol is much talked about and the tribes will take heart.'

Gideon, by no means accustomed to being a leader of men, found that people listened to him and got on with it. He, the youngest son, the quiet one, began to feel full of strength and quite soon about thirty thousand people had answered his call. The more the better, he thought. But the blue-eyed man said no.

'God is not all that pleased with the children of Israel,' he told Gideon. 'This last few years there's been quite a bit of back-sliding and worshipping of other gods and rubbish and if this big crowd have any success they'll think they did it all themselves. No,' said the man, 'we'll do the impossible, then God's hand will be seen in it.'

So Gideon sent away two-thirds of them. 'Be prepared,' he told them. 'Everyone has a part to play.'

'Still too many,' said the blue-eyed man, 'ten thousand is still too many. Tell each man to bring his oil jar and all those who have them to carry trumpets of ramshorn or of brass and we are going down to the stream in the valley. Tell the men it is a sort of selection board. It's a fair distance and a hot day and by the time we get there they'll all be thirsty. The men will go down to the stream in platoons and you will appoint watchers. Those men who lie flat and lick the water you can send home; those who kneel and scoop the water into the hand and then drink from the hand are the ones we want. These are not times for the children of Israel to lie on their bellies looking into water, these are times for a non-stop all-round lookout; times to use one hand to eat and the other to fight.'

Gideon got the point but, when only three hundred men remained with him, he was a bit unhappy. There was a huge job to be done. The defeat of a large occupying force in order to start off a great resistance movement throughout the whole land.

'Don't worry,' said the angel. 'You are not alone, any of you. Did you remember to ask the homegoers to leave their oil jars and trumpets?'

'Yes I did,' said Gideon.

'Good,' said the angel. 'When it gets dark I want you to take one man and go down into the next valley where the Midianites and the Amalekites are camped. Thousands of them. A valley full of your enemies. Great opportunity. Take no action. Disguise yourselves, get in, and walk about and listen. You'll be surprised.'

The angel was no fool. He knew that Gideon had almost no experience as a leader and lacked confidence. He sat and waited and at about midnight Gideon got back. The angel smiled; Gideon looked, he thought, a little bigger, a little stronger. 'All well?' he said.

'I was astonished,' said Gideon. 'That whole camp is full of fear. Everybody seems to know there's an uprising beginning. I heard them talking of God. Not *their* God, Baal, whose idol I pulled down, but our God, and how he's on our side. I even heard them talking about *me*!'

'*Did* you', said the angel. 'About destroying the idol and being a man of God and being what I once called you, a mighty man of valour?'

'Well, yes,' said Gideon.

'Right,' said the angel and got to his feet. 'Do it tonight. There's no moon.'

He gave no more orders and left it to Gideon, who went and woke his three hundred men.

'Divide into three companies,' he said. 'Each man will carry a trumpet and some oil jars. We will form a ring above the camp. Watch me. When I smash my jar and set light to the oil, do the same. Then blow the trumpets and shout the words, "For the Lord and for Gideon". Light the jars and roll them, throw them. Fire, noise, confusion, that's what we're after. In the dark they will fight each other in terror. Then they'll run. Let 'em. Thousands of our men from other tribes are waiting for them. I'm not going to ask for any questions. I know it sounds impossible but nearly everything that God does is.'

Gideon turned to the blue-eyed man. 'Did you wish to add anything?' he said politely.

The angel looked at Gideon with great affection. 'Not a word,' he said.

And it all came to pass. A quiet camp in darkness; then, from high above, unearthly trumpeting, shouts of God and Gideon, and rolling, bouncing balls of fire. Panic; pandemonium; men filled with madness and blind, superstitious fear. A headlong retreat into waiting ambushes. Massacre. Victory. As so many times in the past, God had raised a leader when the children of Israel badly needed one, and freed them from bondage.

But still the children of Israel were far from a united people.

Even while the great battle was on and the enemy were in full flight, when Gideon and his small band of guerrillas pursuing them had arrived exhausted at two villages, they had been refused food by their fellow Israelites 'until', said the people, 'the kings of the enemy are actually caught!'

Gideon had straightened up and wiped the sweat from his eyes. 'When I have the two kings,' he said, 'I shall come back to this place and also to the place over the hill who also refused us food and I shall teach both of you a lesson you will never forget.'

And he did. He never questioned the feeling in him that he was guided by God. A sometimes very angry God with many times good reason to be angry with his chosen people. God had picked Gideon, and was making a leader, and a leader had to know how to punish as well as how to reward. The people of both places were shocked at the hard justice of Gideon's punishments. In one place a terrible scourging of seventy men with whips made of briar and thorn twigs. In the other a tearing down of buildings and a mass execution. But the people, seeing a new Gideon, saw in him also the sort of leader they knew they needed.

When the trial of the two kings took place for their crimes against humanity – their oppression and tyranny had been about as long as the last war – the place was packed with the elders and heads of houses sent to see how Gideon would handle things. The evidence was heard and among that evidence was proof that Gideon's own brothers had been slaughtered on the orders of the two kings. Not as an act of war; as an act of murder. The people waited, quiet. Gideon looked at the two kings. Dark, powerful, cynical men with much more experience in cruelty than he had. 'Had you spared my brothers,' he said, 'I should have spared you. I am a man of peace and killing does not come as easy to me as to you. But here in this place you will die as you lived, by the sword.'

The kings showed no fear and in the silence they sensed how the people were judging Gideon. The elder of the two kings smiled. 'Do it yourself, Gideon,' he said. 'Stand up, take your sword, and *you* kill us.' He looked round at the people with contempt. 'You have to *show* them what you are, how strong. So do it yourself,' he said. 'For as the man is, so is his strength.'

And Gideon, recognizing yet another lesson, did so.

Then the people said to Gideon, 'Rule over us, and after you your son and his son too, for you delivered us.'

But Gideon said, 'No, God delivered you,' he said, 'and God will rule you.'

He was a modest man was Gideon and no fool, though the ideal of being ruled by God doesn't always work out so ideally!

In the Bible the whole story of Gideon takes up less than three chapters. Perhaps he'd have been wiser to accept leadership for himself and his family. Anyhow, the way he obeyed God with unquestioning faith gave the people of Israel forty years of peace.

Samson Takes a Wife

'Never took *any* notice of his parents, got into some terrible scrapes, never shaved, wouldn't have his hair cut, had a terrible temper – and was an absolute fool with women! Came to a sticky end.'

If you heard anything like that in the bus or the tavern or the supermarket, you might think it was some middle-aged person talking about one of his neighbours' teenage sons. But before you jump in and take sides, it's as well to remember that the fellow might be talking about one of the so-called judges of Israel. More a resistance leader than a judge really this one. Name of Samson. And what a tearaway! If he lived today, he'd never be out of the papers. *Or* the courts. 'No visible means of support, my Lord, a number of cases of assault. Also of grievous bodily harm, insulting words and behaviour, arson, larceny and quite a lot of manslaughter.' Yes, Samson's parents had a *real* handful.

He was their firstborn. Rather a surprise, for they'd tried many times to have a child but with no success. His mother was beginning to get used to being childless. But one day her husband got home from work and as she gave him a drink before his dinner he looked at her.

'Not drinking?' he said. 'Anything wrong? You look a bit odd.'

'I'm not sure,' she said, 'but I won't drink with you. Not wine or alcohol, this man said I shouldn't.'

'Man?' said her husband.

His wife went a bit dreamy. 'Yes,' she said. 'Wonderful-looking fellow. I don't know where he came from; he wouldn't say – nor what his name was. We weren't together long. When he left me he said I would have a baby.'

Her husband put down his drink. 'Oh yes?' he said.

'Yes,' said his wife. 'It will be a boy and belong to God all his life and no wine or alcohol for me till I've had him.'

'I see,' said her husband whose name was Manoah. 'Yes. Well if he turns up again, dear, this fellow, I'd like to have a word with him.'

And God understood and sent the angel again. Again in civvies. Manoah listened to him carefully. Prophets and medicine men were no strangers in that town. Neither were seducers. His wife was virtuous but this was a marvellous-looking man. Magnetic.

'Wonderful thing to look forward to,' said Manoah to the angel, 'having a son. Always wanted a boy of my own. Offered lots of sacrifices to God in the past. We pray every night. Burnt offerings, the lot.'

'You don't really believe,' said the angel. 'Prepare, while I'm here, one *more* small burnt offering to God. A baby goat.'

Manoah and his wife prepared the gift and the man stood quietly. As the smoke rose it turned pure white and the man walked forward into the smoke and gently, with the smoke, went back up to heaven. Then Manoah believed and was frightened, for he'd had bad thoughts both about an angel of God and about his God-chosen wife.

She listened to his wailing and praying for a fair time and then got fet up. Like any pregnant lady she was very practical. 'Do stop,' she said. 'Nothing's going to happen to *you*. We're going to have a son. We've been allowed to see wonderful things' – she touched her hair – 'and meet a wonderful man. I feel in my heart,' she said, 'that our son will be special. Different from other boys.'

Poor soul, she was right. But that was later. Meanwhile she believed and trusted, and everything that the angel had told her came true. She obeyed his instructions to the letter. No alcohol, careful diet, plenty of rest. And when her time came she gave birth to a fine boy. She, whom the town had long given up as one of the barren ones, now had a real prize-winner. She called him Samson and brought him up carefully. As the angel had said, she made him a Nazirite, a member of a special sect who never cut their hair or beards. But Nazirite or not, God-given or not, pretty soon it was evident that he was going to be a handful. Physically, God gave him everything. Great good looks, a superb physique and the strength of a horse. But he had quite a lot of devil in him too. He had a terrible temper and a great fondness for rough company. He attracted trouble like a magnet and got into one scrape after another.

Apart from anything else they and all the other tribes of Israel were under the domination of the Philistines, who, as the occupying force, kept a tight rein. Samson was quite without fear – as foolish people often are. He was thoughtless and head-strong. Gave his mother a lot of sleepless nights.

'If only he would get married,' she would say to her husband, 'find a nice girl, settle down; if not a girl from our own tribe, from one of the others, a respectable Hebrew girl.' *Very* often she'd say that to her husband and when Samson got home from Timnah one night she'd just finished saying it again.

'We were just talking about you,' she said. 'I'm pleased you're back.' (Timnah was a Philistine place and there'd been a lot of trouble. She was always worried when he went there.) 'Do you want some food?' she asked him. 'Something to drink? Anything you want just tell me.'

Samson looked down at her. 'I want to get married,' he said.

His mother closed her eyes a moment. A prayer answered. God is good. 'A girl of our tribe?' she said. 'Do we know her family?'

'I don't think so,' said Samson the Nazirite, member of a holy Jewish sect. 'She's a Philistine.'

Well, you can imagine. The questions, the arguments, the tears. But mixed marriages have worked before, so Samson's parents, heavy-hearted, agreed to go with him to Timnah to meet the girl's family. Off they went, the parents walking ahead, rather quiet, with not much to say to each other, and some way behind, Samson. They came to the vineyard on the edge of town and, as Samson walked through the trees, a lion roared.

Samson stopped and waited and soon he saw it. He had no weapon but had wrestled in the past with opponents as big as the lion. He had this mad sort of logic, had Samson. And also, remember, he had great strength and a terrible temper. He killed the lion and left it and walked on and caught up with his parents. He was out of breath a little and his robe was torn but they, rather preoccupied, didn't remark upon it so neither did he. Mind you, if your mother asked *you* how you got your jacket torn you *also* might think twice about saying you'd just killed a lion with your bare hands.

But that lion was to make more trouble for Samson dead than it had done alive. Oh yes.

Well, the parents settled all the details and the date was set for the wedding week. (Weddings at that time lasted a week. Big feasting, house guests, happy holiday.) The time came and off went Samson to his bride's town to get married. Once again he and his parents walked through the vineyards on the edge of town, they by tradition ahead, he some way behind. By himself. He came to the spot where he'd fought and killed the lion. There was little left of it; hungry birds, vultures. But there, in among the dried bones, was a nest of bees. A rare thing; and Samson loved honey. He waited till the bees swarmed elsewhere and took a handful of the comb and walked on. A huge bearded handsome man going to his wedding eating candy.

After the ceremony the guests settled down to their week of fun and games. One of the games was the asking of riddles, and Samson, who liked the game – and also liked to gamble – said, 'I've got a riddle. I bet you all thirty weekday suits and thirty Sunday suits that you won't find the answer in the seven days of the wedding.' He chose the number thirty because there were thirty young men at the party. 'All right?' he said.

They agreed and asked for the riddle. So Samson, remembering the dead lion and the honey, said:

> 'Out of the eater came something to eat.
> Out of the strong came something sweet.'

Well, everybody laughed and tried this answer and that but no one got near it – and the bet was huge. Three days went by and the young men no longer thought it funny. Very little is still funny on the fourth day of *any* party. They went to the bride.

'We did not come to your darned wedding to be made fools of,' they said. 'Or to be made poor! You get the answer to the riddle from that Hebrew giant you've married or we'll burn this house down with you in it – and we're not joking!' And they weren't and she knew it.

Well, she *did* wheedle the answer out of Samson – ladies have their little ways – and she told the young men, who gathered round Samson on the evening on the seventh day and in unison jeered at him:

> 'What is sweeter than honey?
> What is stronger than a lion?'

Samson looked at the ring of Philistine faces and, never a good loser, went mad. He went on a rampage worse than ever before and his rages were famous. Next day he delivered the suits of the bet to the young men but they were the clothes of other young men he'd killed. They, terrified, took the shroud garments and fled. He, Samson wouldn't look at his new bride and went back home to his parents.

Exit Samson

As the weeks passed and the time of the harvest came Samson's anger went away and he decided to go to see his wife. When he arrived at her father's house, the dark cynical Philistine smiled up at the huge Hebrew. 'I thought you hated her,' he said. 'I gave her to someone else. Her younger sister is unmarried though, have her.' Samson walked away and looked across at the fields of wheat ready for harvest. He looked at the olive groves too, and decided to burn the lot. And did.

And, as always, bad breeds worse. The Philistine authorities, hunting Samson, burned his wife and her father as a reprisal. Then Samson, in a red rage that made his earlier killing seem like a tea-party, went on a berserk bloodbath that turned him into a dreaded mad-eyed slaughterer. Then he disappeared and turned up again living in a cave high up in the cleft of a mountain.

The Philistines now saw that this wild man, who seemingly couldn't be caught or hurt, was a danger by his example. The Hebrews saw him as a sort of symbol, something to copy. A bad thing. So the Philistines made a plan to have Samson's own people capture him. Not very clever. As we shall see.

The plan was that some of the tribe of Judah, Hebrews like Samson, would go and get him and hand him over. If they didn't, the Philistines said, there would be some killing of Hebrews for a change.

So the men of Judah went to Samson and he listened to them. 'Are you mad?' they said to him. 'The Philistines are the rulers in the land. Because of you many of our people may die.'

Samson got to his feet. 'Swear to me,' he said, 'that you yourselves will in no way injure me. Tie me up with strong ropes and deliver me – which is your part of the bargain with the Philistines – but do not harm me.'

The men promised and Samson let himself be bound and taken from his cave and down to where the force of Philistines were waiting. The men of Judah moved away and Samson stood alone. Tied up. With a great gang of Philistines charging up the slope to kill him.

But God stood with Samson and Samson, with a little help from God, burst the ropes that bound him and looked around for a weapon. Nearby was the vulture-cleaned skeleton of an ass. Samson took the sickle-like jawbone from the skull and proceeded, as so many times before, to lose his temper and kill Philistines. A great many. And, as before, he got away. To this day that place is called Jawbone Hill.

And so time passed and although the Philistines remained in control always there was Samson, the wild man, who lived in caves and always got away, and was a sort of symbol of courage to the Hebrews.

Now although a Nazirite, a man of God, Samson was, as we have seen, an undisciplined character and a bit of a fool with women. Once he was visiting a lady friend in Gaza – after all, caves get lonely – and the Philistine police heard about it. Quick conference; orders given; men stationed here and there; informers; spies; the lot. Knowing Samson they were pretty certain he'd stay the night. 'Tomorrow morning,' they said, 'when he leaves her house a bit sleepy and tired, we'll kill him. Tell the men. We'll do it by the city gates.'

So at dawn the next day they met as planned. By the city gates. Which weren't there. Samson had left at midnight and taken them with him! As always with Samson, the larger-than-life gesture, the over-acted bit.

But enemies in charge are not fools. They never are. They had quite a file on Samson and one thing went like a thread right through it; he was a bit of a fool with women.

All right. The top brass held a meeting. 'There is a woman,' said the man at the top of the table, 'who lives in the valley of Sorek. She has done one or two little spy jobs for us in the past. Very good-looking woman. Expensive tastes. She met Samson once and is prepared to go to a bit of trouble to meet him again. She charges a lot but, if anyone can give that madman to us, she can.'

'Splendid,' said one of the others. 'What's her name?'

'Delilah,' said the man.

Well, the Philistine chiefs of staff went to Delilah and the deal was made. 'We've nearly had him time and time again,' they told her.

'But this Samson apart from being a giant with the strength of ten men is also obviously protected by some god or other. We are not telling you to kill him, it may not be possible, but fix it so that we can catch him and lock him up and we'll pay well.'

Well, it didn't take long. Samson was soon in love and visiting often. Often too she would bring up the subject of his great strength which so many times had saved him and prevented his capture. She was not just making conversation. If she could find out what magic made him so strong, she could maybe break the magic and make him weak, and the men in the next room could rush in and cart him off, and she'd get her money.

Samson would tease her and show off. 'If I'm tied with new bow strings,' he'd say, 'or new ropes never used.' And she would. And he'd burst out of them as though they were cotton.

So she started to nag and withhold a few favours and generally drive him up the wall. And at last he told her. 'I'm a Nazirite,' he said. 'We are special people protected by God. Every hair of my head is my covenant with God, never broken, never cut. If I cut my hair, my promise to God would be broken and his protection of me would stop. My strength is from God.'

And that was it. Delilah drugged his wine and cut off his hair and called in the men. They chained him and they blinded him and they locked him up in a prison and worked him like a mule.

Now, the Philistines made a big thing out of capturing Samson. 'See,' they crowed, 'no superman. Just a man. Broke a promise to his God and became weak. His God was his strength.' So true. And not only of Samson.

They put him on show. A prisoner; blind, weak, with a shaven head. A sight made easy for us to imagine by something not long ago called Belsen. People queued to look at him. National holiday. To be celebrated every year. Samson Day.

The next year, the first anniversary, the celebration took place in a great hall not long built. Much talked about. The only place with a balcony, boxes and gallery. *Very* new. Everything supported by beautiful marble pillars.

The place was packed to the roof. Splendid show. Songs, brave poems, a little play all about how Samson was captured – with a very famous actress playing Delilah. Interval for refreshment and then the main attraction. Personal appearance of Samson himself! Brought from prison by a young guard. No longer bald, still the same huge physique, hollow eyesockets, walking like a king. They stood him where everyone could see him between the two main pillars of the building and they screamed and jeered and threw rotten fruit. Great sport.

Samson stood and seemed to be talking. He was. To God. 'Give me back, O Lord,' he said, 'just this once more, the strength I had. Just once more. Let me pay them back for blinding me. Please.'

And God listened and guided Samson's hands, his left to one pillar, his right to the other. And God helped Samson, the main attraction of the evening, to bring the house down. Hundreds were killed. Samson too. The man who all his life had loved big flamboyant gestures had been allowed by God to make the biggest exit of all.

Ruth and Naomi

Between the great chronicle of the Judges of Israel and the four mighty books of the Kings, which begin with Samuel the Kingmaker and go on to Saul and David and Solomon and all the rest – between the Judges and the Kings comes a quiet little story, the story of two famous women and only four short chapters in the Bible, but with a title of their own, 'The Book of Ruth'. The book, as I said, is called Ruth. She gets top billing. But for me her mother-in-law is the one. A completely unselfish, shrewd, big-hearted woman who saw great tragedy. A mother bereft, a wife widowed. Did God perhaps foresee all the terrible jokes that were going to be made about mothers-in-law and arrange for the story of this one mother-in-law to be written down? Naomi, the mother-in-law of Ruth.

The story begins where another more famous story began. In Bethlehem. In a time of famine. The story moves away to another land across the Dead Sea and then moves back to Bethlehem. Do you know that in the Dead Sea the water is so full of various salts that you can't sink? A person becomes unsinkable; like Naomi.

Naomi and her husband and two sons were of the tribe of Judah descended from Jacob's son. They didn't have much money but they didn't need much. 'With two sons like I've got,' Naomi used to say, 'who needs money?' Fine, handsome young men. Both single, both devoted to Mum, both worried, as was Dad, about this famine – which seemed to go on and on. Living was very hard indeed.

One night at supper, a very poor sort of supper, one of those all-the-family-we've-got-to-face-it discussions took place and Naomi's husband, a good man called Elimelech, said, 'Well, we've just got to face it, people are starving here. And not only here. It seems from what I hear that the whole land is barren.'

The two young men some nothing. They knew their father. If he'd decided something it must be after careful thought.

'We will move out of this land,' said Elimelech, 'across the salt sea to Moab. Our two countries are friendly, and I'm told things are better there. We won't be the first. We'll start tomorrow.' He looked at his wife. 'It'll be a wrench for me too,' he said, 'but what else can we do?'

Naomi got up. 'You are right,' she said and smiled at her three handsome men. 'What can I lose?'

Poor Naomi; in not all that long she was to lose the three of them. It all started so well too. They liked their new home and the people of Moab were kind and the men found work and they managed. Then one day Elimelech came home saying he felt unwell and two days later was dead. A dreadful shock. Naomi was stunned. He'd never been ill, and he wasn't old, a strong man, a loving good man. She thought she would die too. She felt very far from home indeed. As they were. Her sons were wonderful to her and she didn't waste time mourning. They stayed in Moab.

One day she said to her sons, 'Now look,' she said, 'I've been thinking. You are both old enough to get married and we all like this town. I want you to know that if you want to marry Moabite girls it's all right with me. These are good people.'

Her elder son smiled. 'In that case,' he said, 'I'd like you to meet someone. Tomorrow. Her name is Ruth.'

Well, the girl was beautiful. Tall, slim, with lovely hair and eyes and the quietest, gentlest smile Naomi had ever seen.

Naomi and Ruth were friends in five minutes. Naomi's younger son wasted no time either. It wasn't long before he also came home with a local girl for his Mum to meet.

'Mother,' he said, 'this is Orpah.'

And soon the boys were both married and Naomi, who'd thought she would never smile again after her husband died, found great happiness in her fine sons and her daughters-in-law, and the girls found in their mother-in-law a wonderful wise friend. They all lived in the same house; the girls insisted. They wouldn't hear of Naomi living alone or moving from one to the other.

The years passed. Happy years. Life was easy and smooth. At least for the three women; the men were mine workers; hard work, but they made a good living. Naomi used to tease her daughters-in-law about her 'sad lack of grandchildren'. But the two couples were young and there was no hurry. There was plenty of time, they would say.

Then one day Naomi woke up with those words in her mind. 'There's plenty of time.' Something was nagging at her. She remembered that two days before her husband had died he'd said that. Two days before. Big, strong, perfectly fit. 'This is a good country,' he'd said, 'and there's plenty of time.' And two days later he was gone.

Naomi couldn't rest. When her two sons left for the mine that morning she was tense, ill-at-ease. 'Be careful,' she said, 'be extra careful.' The two men and their wives joked with her, tried to break her mood, but she couldn't smile. 'Take every care,' she said, 'every care.'

She was by herself when they brought the news. The two wives were in the market. 'An accident,' they said. 'Awful. Unforeseeable. Despite all precautions. Dreadful thing. Both men killed outright. Instantaneous. No pain.'

No pain. Naomi sat like a stone. Hands in lap. Eyes dry. As the men turned to go, the girls came in, running. They were pale, they'd heard a rumour, the women in the market were saying ... Then Naomi stood up and screamed. Just once; like an animal. Hoarse, from the heart, from the broken heart.

For a second no one moved, then as the girls went forward to comfort her she opened her arms to comfort them. Three widows; all childless.

Back to Bethlehem

After the funeral there seemed to Naomi little reason for staying in Moab in this sad town. So she made plans to return to Bethlehem in Judah. She was silent and very bitter. She didn't pray. 'Go back to your mothers,' she told the girls. 'You are young – and better wives no man could find. May you find husbands that deserve you.'

The girls wept and implored her to stay – or that they could go with her – but she was adamant. First she kissed Orpah goodbye and watched her go, then she turned to Ruth. The tall lovely girl looked into her mother-in-law's eyes. 'Don't ask me to leave you again,' she said. 'I won't. Wherever you go, wherever you live, I want to be with you. Your God will be my God, your people mine.'

'All right,' said Naomi. 'I won't argue.'

They left the next morning. A long journey, and it took them several weeks.

They didn't talk much. At each place they stopped, people were curious but stayed away. Curious to see two women travelling alone: one good-looking, though she never smiled; the other, the younger, very beautiful.

When they arrived in Bethlehem, Naomi had been away ten years. She had left during a famine to try a new land. Now on every side she could see a good harvest. She had left with a husband and two fine sons. Now she was back with one daughter-in-law. Naomi, as she walked with Ruth through familiar streets, streets full of memories, was very sad. But she was grateful for the younger woman's quiet understanding and unselfish sympathy.

They came to the market area near to where Naomi had lived. A woman walked by; stopped; came back. Soon others. 'It is *you* Naomi? You seem different. How long is it? How was it in Moab? We missed you. How's your husband? And your two fine sons?'

Naomi told her old friends the story of the last ten years. They listened with tears in their eyes.

'And this is your daughter-in-law?' they said.

Naomi put her arm round Ruth. 'No. My daughter,' she said. 'No husband, no sons – a daughter. All I have left.'

Her friends, who remembered a smiling happy Naomi, wept and sighed at this sad-eyed grey woman. 'Oh Naomi, oh Naomi,' they said.

'You should change my name,' said Naomi, 'change it to Mara, which means bitter, which by God I am.'

Ruth looked into her beloved mother-in-law's eyes. 'And Naomi means pleasant,' she said, 'which by God you are. Everything, you once taught me, is by God.'

And Naomi, always practical and level, was a little ashamed.

Boaz

In no time at all the whole town knew Naomi's terrible story and people were kind as much as they were able. Ruth and Naomi were poor and not keen on accepting charity. One day Naomi said, 'Ruth dear, on the outskirts of town there's a biggish farm owned by a man called Boaz. My husband was related to him. You never met him. At this time of year, at harvest, there is a custom in Israel that poor people may follow the reapers and glean the corn and barley which is missed. What do you think?'

'I'll start today,' said Ruth, and off she went.

The people at the farm, when she told them who she was, were friendly and she joined the other poor people who walked behind the reapers. Towards the end of the morning the owner of the farm happened to notice her as he toured his fields. Boaz was not a young man. He was a good-hearted, much-liked person.

'Who is that?' he said.

They told him. He'd heard the story of the two widows and he was moved. He called her over.

'Go to no other farm,' he said. 'Glean here every day all day. At midday eat and drink with the workers. Orders will be given that no young man will molest you in any way.'

Ruth felt the tears begin to come.

'I've heard of your faithfulness and devotion to your mother-in-law,' said Boaz, 'and God will bless you for it. It seems to me,' said Boaz, looking at the beautiful Ruth, 'that you are a rare person.'

Well, Naomi was glad to see Ruth safely home that night. It was the first time for a long while that they'd spent so many hours apart. She thought her lovely daughter-in-law looked a bit flushed, and she noticed the size of the bag of wheat and barley she was carrying. Also a little parcel of food. But she asked no questions. She knew that Ruth would tell her everything. When the young woman had washed and tidied herself and they were eating she did.

'I met him,' said Ruth.

'Who?' said Naomi, although she knew.

'Your kinsman,' said Ruth, 'Boaz. You said he was old, he's not old, he's sort of mature, distinguished, adult. We spoke together. He knew about us and how I came back with you from Moab when poor Mahlon died and I became like you, a widow. He asked if I felt homesick for my own land and did I miss my mother and I said you were my mother and that seemed to please him.'

'It pleases me too,' said Naomi. 'Did he say it was all right to glean in his fields?'

'He said more,' said Ruth. 'He said I was to glean nowhere else, and I heard him tell the reapers to tie the bundles carelessly so that there will always be enough for both me and my mother. He asked me to join him for the midday meal and gave me too much and insisted I brought the food I couldn't eat home. Said that all this was the least he could do for a kinswoman. I suppose he meant you.'

'Not altogether,' said Naomi and felt a long-dead matchmaking urge begin in her for her beautiful steadfast daughter-in-law. 'Not altogether. Here in Israel the laws of kin and family are clear and strict. The land belonging to my husband, his inheritance, also as it were includes me and, as the widow of my son, you too. So my relatives are also yours in a way.'

Ruth smiled. 'So I'm sort of related to that man,' she said. 'That's nice.'

Naomi began to gather dishes. 'Yes,' she said. 'That's nice.'

Harvest Home

Every day Ruth went to the fields and worked hard and one night when the harvesting was nearly done she came home rather excited.

'Tomorrow night,' she told Naomi, 'there's to be an end-of-harvesting party for the workers and although I'm only a gleaner I've been invited.'

'By Boaz?' asked Naomi.

'I'm not sure,' said Ruth. 'I don't see him often. Is it all right to go?'

'Yes,' said Naomi, 'it is. Be home early tomorrow.'

The next evening Naomi had a cool bath waiting for her daughter-in-law and helped her to dress and do her hair. They dipped in boxes and found a little jewellery and some good perfume. When the job was done Ruth was a sight to see.

'Now listen,' said Naomi, practical. 'A while back I told you a bit about family custom here in Israel. Widows like us can ask a kinsman to buy the inheritance of our dead husbands and we go with the property. The man gets land plus goods plus, if he wants, a wife or extra woman of his house. Some fine marriages have come out of such deals. Boaz is a close relative, I think next-of-kin in this law. Tonight, ask him his advice on this matter.'

Ruth, rather shy of the rich Boaz, waited till late in the party and then stumblingly spoke to him. He, knowing the laws better than she, told her that another man was of closer kin and that he would ask him if he wanted to take over the inheritance of the two women.

'If he does, well and good,' said Boaz. 'If not, as the Lord lives, *I* will do the part of next-of-kin for you. You have honoured me by asking me. The whole town knows you to be a woman of worth. You are not of Israel, yet you are an example to us all.'

And there they sat, Ruth and Boaz, and they talked long into the night and found much to say. When Ruth got home Naomi was awake and when the girl had finished pouring it all out Naomi said, 'I know Boaz. He will settle this matter. Tomorrow.'

And he did. He was now sure that he loved this girl from Maob, this beautiful girl Ruth. But he knew that he could still lose her. So he felt a bit tense as he took his seat, accompanied by ten elders of the community, at the town gate, the traditional place of open-air discussion. Together they waited for the man whom he'd spoken of to Ruth to come by.

Before long the man came down the road. As he was about to pass, Boaz said correctly, 'Turn aside, friend. Sit down here.' The man did.

Boaz began. 'Naomi,' he said, 'kinswoman to us both, has, as you know, now returned from Moab with her widowed daughter-in-law. Her other son also is dead and also Elimelech her husband. She offers for sale the parcel of land belonging to her dead husband and sons. By family law you are the next-of-kin and have first option.'

The man pondered. 'I'll buy,' he said.

'If you buy,' said Boaz, 'understand that by the family law of Israel you also buy Ruth of Moab, widow of the firstborn, thus restoring the name of the dead to his inheritance.'

The man pondered again and Boaz could hear his own heart beating.

'No,' said the man. 'I won't buy. The arrangement impairs my own inheritance. I pass my right to the next closest of kin. Is that you?'

Boaz smiled. 'Yes,' he said.

Then with all due ceremony, with the elders as witnesses, he bought the parcel of land. The transaction, by tradition, was sealed by the giving of a sandal by the party of the first part to the party of the second part. All was correctly done and when the day of the wedding came the whole town turned out and the good wishes were genuine.

Boaz was a generous man and it was a great party. Naomi, mother-in-law extraordinary, moved among the guests and many remarked how she looked as she did ten or so years before when her menfolk were all alive. Naomi cried a little – mothers do at weddings – and turned often to look at Ruth and Boaz standing together in a glow of happiness.

The months passed and one day Ruth went to Naomi. 'You once joked with me about your sad lack of grandchildren,' she said. 'Well, I'm attending to it.'

When the baby was born, Naomi became its nurse, grannie, sitter-in, taker-out for walks, the lot. Ruth didn't mind; in Naomi's hands *she* had been safe. The baby, beloved grandson of Naomi, was named Obed. Obed who was the father of Jesse, who was the father of – But before we go on to Jesse and his sons, one of whom was to be King of Israel, we must become acquainted with the last of Israel's judges, the great prophet Samuel. Samuel, the King-maker, who gives his name to the first two books of Israel's Kings.

Birth of a Kingmaker

As with the stories of Isaac and Jacob and Joseph and Moses and Samson, we begin the story of Samuel at the beginning – with our hero's birth.

Samuel's father lived at a place called Ramah, not far from Jerusalem. His name was Elkanah and he had two wives – most men of his income-bracket did. Their names were Peninnah, who had lots of children, and Hannah, who had none. And not for want of trying, it was just hard luck. She longed for a child. Her husband Elkanah, who loved her, used to say to her, 'Why weep? Why be sad, and go off your food? Am I not more to you than ten sons?' (Nearly as tactless as me whose firstborn came into the world on May 1st. 'Ah,' I said to my wife about two hours after she'd had him, 'Ah, Labour Day!')

Poor Hannah. Very much Number Two wife. And Number One wife, Peninnah, made certain she remembered it, especially each year when the whole family went to Shiloh for thanksgiving. Shiloh, where the holy Ark was kept and the sacrificing and praying went on for days. All in charge of old Eli, High Priest and one of the leaders of the people. The leaders called *Judges* in the Bible.

At Shiloh each year Hannah was very sad. Year after year she prayed and hoped, but no baby. Only a lot of nasty remarks from Number One wife. Hannah would fast and grow faint and would look unsteady and sick. She would sway and rock back and forth and in a low voice implore God to make her a mother. And one year old Eli noticed this dazed-looking woman who looked so pale and who muttered and wept. 'You drink too much,' he said, 'you should try to give it up. Be strong.' Nearly as tactful as me!

Hannah explained to the old priest. She poured it all out. 'I told God,' she said, 'that if he gave me a son I would give him back to serve God all his life.'

Old Eli was moved. This was a good woman and this was true love of God. 'Go in peace,' he said to her. 'I also will pray for you and God will answer your prayer. You shall have a son.'

And it all came true.

Hannah had waited so long, prayed so hard, hoped so much, and now she had a fine baby boy. 'I shall call him Samuel,' she said. 'God promised and kept his word. And I shall keep my word to God,' she told her husband. 'Samuel will serve God all his life. In a year or two I shall take him back to Eli and he will be the smallest, youngest helper in the house of God. Each year I shall visit him and I shall take him new clothes. Each year a bit bigger. He will live in the sanctuary and become a priest like good Eli.'

Elkanah didn't argue. He had other children by his other wife and also he felt that this God-granted son might well be a sort of special person. He wasn't wrong.

So the day came and Hannah took little Samuel and gave him over into the kindly hands of Eli. Who was very pleased to have him. You see Eli had two grown-up sons of his own who worked with him in the sanctuary, but they were no good. Violent, dishonest men. Great sadness to Eli who knew he'd been rather weak with them. But in Samuel Eli found great joy. The boy learned quickly and was sensible and good-mannered and he showed the old priest great love and respect. God did not leave Hannah lonely. She had other children; but every year she went to Shiloh, to the sanctuary, to see Samuel her firstborn.

The years passed. Samuel was very observant and he saw and understood many things. He saw how Eli's two sons used the service and sacrifices offered to God to commit every kind of sin. They ignored their father, who *was* rather old. He in turn drew closer to Samuel. Once he said to his wicked son, 'If a man sins against a man, God can help. But, if men sin against God as you do, who then can help?' But they still ignored him.

Then one day a man called on Eli. The old priest knew the type right away. Gaunt, poorly dressed, eyes with an oddly unfocussed look; the visionary, the bringer of messages, the holy man. The man refused both food and drink and delivered his message. From God. About Eli's two sons and their evil practices – and their punishment to come. 'They will die,' said the man. 'Both on the same day. And your house, the house of Eli, will grow weak. Poverty will come, poor health, early death, sadness. For in allowing your sons' wickedness you have shared in it, and will share their punishment.'

Poor Eli was shocked.

'And,' said the man, 'God will raise up for himself a faithful priest who will be strong and will *not* permit wrongdoing, and a time will come when the remnants of your house will go to his house to beg for a crust, a job.'

Poor Eli. He seemed to lose heart after that. His eyesight, not good for a long time, grew worse. A big man, he seemed to shrink a little, to sag. He looked a bit lost. And leaned more and more on his young helper Samuel to whom he told everything. 'All will come to pass,' said the old priest. 'It was the word of God. How rarely in this land is God's voice heard any more. I do not hear or see visions, nor does anybody else.' Eli looked at Samuel. Handsome, clear-eyed, quiet. 'Perhaps *you* will hear the voice and see the way,' he said. 'You were given by God, perhaps *you* are to be his faithful priest.'

The old man was not far wrong.

Samuel Takes Over

Meanwhile Samuel looked after old Eli with great care. Stayed near him; even slept near him, in a little room just across the passage.

One night Samuel had seen the old man to bed and tucked him in and had gone to his own bed. He had prayed as usual and had settled down. He was tired. He'd had a long day. He dozed off.

Suddenly he was awake, wide awake. He ran in to Eli. 'Here I am,' he said. 'What do you want, father?'

The old priest said, 'I did not call you my son, go back to bed.'

Samuel did and lay still. It was very silent.

Then again the voice, 'Samuel,' it said, 'Samuel.'

Again Samuel went in to Eli who again said he had not called. The old man, nearly blind, sensed a strangeness in the night. 'Go back to your bed,' he said gently, and he waited.

Sure enough, Samuel came in a third time. 'Here I am, father,' he said. 'Are you playing a game?'

Eli was now sure. 'The voice you heard,' he said carefully, 'was not mine but God's. Go back again to your bed and when the Lord calls you again, answer, *Speak, Lord; your servant hears.*'

Samuel did as he was told and the voice did call again and spoke clearly and at some length into his mind. The voice told him many things, all of the future. Samuel, boy priest, was now a boy prophet. Chosen by God.

His life did not change much. He grew into a fine young man and took over many of the duties of the sanctuary. He preached and people listened. He became famous from one end of the country to the other. Man of God, prophet, leader. A leader however whom not all the people followed. Many still worshipped idols and forgot God. So some years later, when the Philistines attacked, God didn't help. Even though the people took the holy Ark to the battlefield and prayed extra hard, they lost. And worse, the Philistines captured the Ark itself and took it away.

The people of Israel were shocked, forsaken. Many thousands were killed in the battle. Among them Eli's two sons. On the same day, as was foretold. A dreadful day. The old priest, who had not wanted the holy Ark to leave Shiloh and his care, was deeply anxious and ill-at-ease all day. He sat on a seat by the road waiting for news. He could not see but could hear and feel the defeat all round him. And when the messenger came from the battle and told the awful news of the loss of the Ark, poor Eli felt that God was lost to him too.

The messenger poured out his news and then stopped in the middle of a sentence. Eli sat still. Poor Eli. He was nearly a hundred years old. 'And what of my sons?' he said.

And the messenger told him.

The old man closed his blind eyes and toppled backwards like a tree falling. His neck snapped. Old Eli, teacher and father to Samuel was dead. All foreseen; all told to Samuel by God. Samuel who now took over the reins.

The Ark of God

Samuel's beloved teacher was dead; his beloved Shiloh without its Ark. Now, you might say, 'Well, the Ark of God didn't win the battle for Israel, it didn't do them much good, did it?' True, but for some time, remember, Israel hadn't been very true to God.

Mind you, it didn't do the Philistines much good either. They took it first to a place called Ashdod, and the five Philistine lords met and decided they would put it in the great temple of Dagon, their Number One god. Half man, half fish. Huge stone statue in the middle of the floor. They put the Ark next to it. Next day, the huge victory ceremony. Prayers outside, then a song or two, then the great temple doors were opened and the people poured in. Dagon was flat on his face with a chipped nose!

Volunteers were asked for and they stood him up again and postponed the second half of the ceremony till next day. Next day they found him flat on his face with his head and arms broken off.

And that wasn't the end of it. No, quite soon a plague of boils and awful tumours began. Thousands were afflicted, people died. Then a plague of mice started that ate everything in sight. Millions of them.

The five lords called an emergency meeting. 'It's the holy Ark,' they said. 'Powerful magic. Belongs to a God who once used *ten* plagues. Who can part seas and rivers. He must hate Dagon. Get the Ark away from Ashdod, take it inland to Gath.'

It was done and in no time at all the tumours and mice were all over Gath too.

The Lords met again. 'All right,' they said, 'up to Ekron with it.'

But the people of Ekron had heard all about it and were full of panic at the thought of receiving the great honour of having the Ark in their city. They refused. It didn't help. At Akron the plagues arrived before the Ark. Even worse.

That was it. 'Send it back to Israel,' the lords decided, and called the magicians and soothsayers in as to how best to do it.

'On a specially-made cart,' the magic men said, 'and by its side a box full of golden statues.'

'What of?' said the lords.

'Tumours and mice,' said the magicians.

One or two of the lords started to object.

'Don't be stupid,' said the wise men. 'What do you want, the full set of ten plagues? Do you want to be clever like Pharaoh of Egypt? Let the cart be drawn by cows, not oxen, cows with new calves, but lock the calves away. Then send off the cart. Let it go where it will. No driver. If the Israelite God is in this, the cows will forget their new calves and go straight to Bethshemesh. That's the nearest town within Israel's borders. The people will be out in the fields harvesting. So they can't miss seeing it coming. They'll know what to do with it.'

And it was done. The cows, against nature, undriven, looking neither to right nor left, took the Ark of God straight back home. The Philistines had had it for seven months and they wished they'd never set eyes on it.

Samuel in Command

In Israel the rejoicing went on for days when the Ark of God came home. Samuel watched everything and listened to God. He knew that a great lesson was starting.

You know, when God chooses a man to speak for him, to prophesy, to lead a people, he chooses very carefully. Abraham, Moses, Joshua, all of them special men. Men who could think big and learn from the past the lessons of the future, and Samuel was no different.

Of all the leaders of the people of Israel, the leaders called *Judges* in the Bible, Samuel was the last, and in many ways the greatest. He had grown up serving God in the sanctuary of Shiloh where the Ark was. A priest, but very much of the people. He knew about people. He knew that the people of Israel were as big enemies to themselves as the ever-present Philistines. Saved by God, protected by God time and time again, often they forgot God and raised up other gods and idols. They always suffered for it but didn't learn.

So Samuel called the people together at a place called Mizpeh. 'There is one God only,' he said, 'only one. If you throw away all the other idols and rubbish and if you all return to the one God to whom you owe so much, and serve him only, you will live free, not in fear of the Philistines, all your lives. You will defeat the Philistines.'

The great meeting went on a long time. But spies are everywhere and soon the Philistines knew all about this vast multitude, many unarmed, ready for slaughter, ready for a surprise attack, a massacre.

Samuel led the people in long services of prayer, in fasting, in sacrifice. The Philistines gathered and drew near. As Samuel was preparing a burnt offering, one of the far-off lookouts saw the approaching Philistine armies and the word spread like a bushfire. The people began to panic. Samuel went on calmly with his duties. Then against the skyline, all round, the enemy appeared.

Samuel looked up and spoke to God.

The Philistines began to descend the slopes, then they stopped. Then a great noise came from the sky; it roared like endless thunder. To the people it was not loud; to the Philistines it was an unbearable head-splitting vibration that brought chaos and confusion. The noise could not be kept out, it was *in* the head. They staggered and stumbled into each other. The people went up the slopes at their enemies and it was a rout, a great victory, a sign of forgiveness, a promise from God. A promise kept. Never again during Samuel's lifetime did the Philistines win. All they had taken was won back. They were subdued, they stayed away. So did other enemies.

The people looked up to Samuel, paid him great respect. He wasn't too much impressed. He knew this people well. Neither did he stay in one place, a great figure that people went to. He went to them. Place to place, a regular tour. The first circuit-judge in history. Often he thought back to his beloved teacher so long dead. Old Eli – and his two bad sons. Samuel would smile rather sadly to himself at those moments. He too had bad sons. He didn't know it but neither would succeed him. No more judges. From then on, kings. He, Samuel, would anoint two. And that must be our next story.

The Lord's Anointed

Samuel, when he was old, was one day sitting in his garden and thinking yet again what a great disappointment his two sons had been to him. Maybe they'd had in him too much to live up to but certainly they weren't much good. Like him they were judges but they were not honest men. They took bribes. And yesterday's visit from the elders of the people hadn't helped either. 'Your sons are no good,' they'd said, 'and you, Samuel, are old. So give us a king to govern us. No more judges. A king like other nations.'

Samuel closed his eyes and told it all quietly to God and after a while God replied. 'First of all,' said God, 'understand that the people are not rejecting *you*. No, as so many times before, they are rejecting me. To have *me* for king would be enough, you'd think, but no. All right,' said God, 'let them have a king, but tell them first what having a king entails. They will be his soldiers and servants and factory workers. Their best farms and cattle and possessions will be his by right. Anything he wants they will have to give him. He will have power over life and death. They will be hit hardest where it hurts most. In the pocket. To have a king is very expensive. Tell them.' And Samuel did tell them.

But the people refused to listen, so Samuel went where God led him and chose a young man who was tall and broad and handsome and anointed him king. His name was Saul. As a king he turned out to be no great bargain. And that's why Samuel was out looking for a replacement fairly soon, and that's where this story really begins. It begins, like the story of Ruth, in Bethlehem, where another story, more famous than either of them, began. It begins about a thousand years before that other story. One thousand years BC. It begins with a rather puzzled man, Ruth's grandson Jesse, a farmer, now middle-aged and with eight sons. It was to his eldest son, a soldier called Eliab, that Jesse was speaking.

'It's all very puzzling,' he said. 'Out of the blue there comes to Bethlehem the prophet Samuel, whom we haven't seen since we all went to Mizpeh for the crowning of King Saul and you got excited and joined the King's army.'

'I know,' said Eliab. 'I'd heard that Samuel had retired or gone into excile or something. Seems that he was very cross with Saul after that battle with the Amalekites and regretted making him king. The story was that Saul disobeyed the rules given by God to Samuel for kings to follow. I don't know the details,' said Eliab, 'but we did win the battle. Saul knows how to fight even if he does break rules.'

Jesse hadn't really been listening to his son. 'Samuel comes to Bethlehem,' he said, 'to make a sacrifice to God. He even brings a young heifer with him for the offering. He is met by the elders who are nervous of him and no wonder. Samuel the great judge, the prophet, the king-maker. Then the sacrifice is arranged to take place in our big field and *we* are invited. "Jesse and all his sons," Samuel said. One or two of the elders were a bit jealous, I'm told. Ah well,' said Jesse, 'let's get cleaned up. It's quite an honour really. A special day.'

It was indeed. At noon the field was full of people and the elders had got everything ready. A lot of noise and excitement for this was the great prophet Samuel, chosen by God while still a child. Maybe some great prophetic announcement was to take place.

Well it did, but quietly, in Jesse's own home, later. Jesse never forgot it. He was an observant man was Jesse and when Samuel had arrived for the sacrifice and the crowd became silent he'd noticed the great horn of oil at the prophet's belt. Chased with silver with a golden lid and handle. It was the anointing horn used by Samuel at Saul's coronation. A *special* sacrifice, thought Jesse? But the horn stayed, unused, at Samuel's belt.

After the service Samuel turned and walked over to Jesse, who was a bit over-awed by this bearded patriarch with the shrewd eyes. 'Come, Jesse,' said Samuel, 'let us sit awhile in your garden and let me meet your sons and then we can eat a little food.'

Jesse sat next to Samuel under a tree and introduced his sons one by one. He felt a great tension and stillness in the prophet.

'Eliab, my eldest,' said Jesse. 'Next, Abinadab; next Shammah.' And so on.

The young men came forward and bowed. Samuel looked into each face intently and his head was tilted as though listening. The seventh son stepped back from Samuel and joined his six brothers.

The prophet turned to Jesse. 'Are these all your sons?' he said.

Jesse said, 'No. One more, David the youngest. He is with the sheep.'

'Send for him,' said Samuel and did not raise his eyes till the boy stood before him, a handsome well-built boy with a friendly smile.

Samuel looked into the boy's eyes and again seemed to listen. Then he rose to his feet and took the great horn from his belt. 'Jesse,' he said, 'this boy, David the shepherd, your youngest son, will be the next King of Israel. A great king, greater than Saul, who will reign many years yet. But after him; David. Who will know great love and great danger, but God will protect him because,' said Samuel, 'God has chosen him.'

Then Samuel anointed David, and David, who didn't much like oil on his hair, went back to his sheep. And Samuel went back home, leaving poor Jesse very puzzled indeed.

Giant Killer

The weeks passed and one supper time Jesse looked across the table at his youngest son and again tried to work it out. This boy, David, was one day to be King of Israel. All by order of God, Samuel had said. Jesse was very fond of his youngest son but quite honestly couldn't see anything very kingly or even princely about him. Certainly a very good-looking boy; beautiful eyes, like his mother. Her love of music too; good singing voice. Made up songs; poems too. Could play the small harp very well. Surely, thought Jesse, a king needs a bit more than that.

Then the old man remembered that on a number of occasions, to protect the flock of sheep he looked after, the boy had shown himself quite fearless. No songs or poems then. A fighter strong and swift, and a dead shot with a sling. Many wild animal skins to prove it.

David looked up from his food. 'Any news about the battle, father?' he asked.

Jesse came back with a bump to his other worries and his other sons. 'No,' he said, 'I know nothing; only rumours. So tomorrow morning early I want you to go again to Azekah where your three brothers are stationed and take food for them.'

'What rumours?' said David.

'Oh, a crazy story,' said Jesse, 'that the Philistines have a great giant in armour who stands on their side of the valley and roars in a great voice for King Saul to go and fight him – or choose someone to do it for him. No battle going on at all, I'm told. Just the two armies face to face and all our lot rather scared of the giant.'

'What a marvellous story,' said David. 'I hope it's true, I've never seen a giant.'

It was true. When David had given over the food to his eldest brother Eliab, the big soldier took him down to the valley. 'He makes his challenge every hour,' said Eliab. 'You'll see him in about ten minutes.' While they waited, he told David that King Saul had offered a huge reward and his daughter in marriage to any man who would kill the giant.

Then there was a great brutish roaring and a clanking of armour and there was the giant. Huge. Marvellous sight. Covered in bronze from head to foot. 'One man,' he roared. 'If he kills me, the Philistines shall serve Israel; if I kill him, Israel will be *our* servants.'

David looked up at Eliab. 'He's only big,' he said. 'Take me to the King.'

Eliab, very much the elder brother, told him not to be big-headed and to go back to his sheep. But David went to the King. And there was something about this handsome boy who called the giant 'an uncircumcised Philistine' and Saul's soldiers 'the army of God'.

'All right,' said Saul. 'Try it. No one else has offered. Use my armour and my sword and shield.'

They dressed David, who was not very big, in all this stuff and when he went to stride out to do battle he couldn't move. So they took it all off again.

'Look,' said David to Saul, 'with God's help I've killed a number of quite large wild animals. And God's on our side. Also,' said David, no fool, 'between the giant's helmet brim and his nose-piece he is uncovered. I shall challenge him from the narrowest part of the stream in the valley and I'll do it with a stone.'

'A stone?' said Saul.

'Yes,' said David, 'from a sling. I can't throw a spear.'

King Saul looked down at this mighty man of valour. 'And then?' he said. 'What will you do then, my young friend?'

'I shall cut off his head with his own sword,' said David, and walked out. A moment later he came back – 'You needn't worry about the reward,' he said. 'And I'm too young to get married.'

Saul watched the whole thing. The calm small figure of the boy, the stone slung like a bullet, the great metallic crash as the giant fell, and the beheading with the absurdly large sword that the boy could hardly lift. Then the terror of the Philistine army and the quick victory for Israel.

That was the first time that David and Saul met. In some ways, battle or not, giant or not, it was their happiest meeting. And they were to see a great deal of each other.

David and Saul

After David had killed the giant his life changed completely. He stopped being a shepherd and went to live in the King's household and was treated almost like a son by King Saul who was very grateful to him. One of the King's sons was called Jonathan; he and David took to each other at sight and as the years passed they became like brothers. And, as the years passed, David the boy who killed the giant became David the soldier who killed *many* of the King's enemies. In the ceaseless battles with Philistines David's skill and complete lack of fear soon made him noticed and Saul made him commander-in-chief.

Saul was a strange man. Very moody. Emotional. Unbalanced. Given to sudden rages and dreadful fits of depression. As David grew to manhood he came to know this dark side of the King very well, for often Saul would allow no one but David near him during his times of what the court doctors called the evil spirits. The King would send for David, who could play upon the small harp and who could make up songs, and David would sit sometimes for hours making music to calm the King.

But as I say, as David became a man, he became a great soldier, and was often away when the King's evil spirits attacked him. It was noticed at court that news of a victory for David would first please the King and then bring on a great rage and deep depression. David, famous since a boy as the giantkiller, was now, as a handsome broad man in bronze armour, the hero and champion of all Israel. They made up songs about him and Saul heard them and the dark moods changed their character. He became convinced that David was trying to steal the throne from him. He began to plot ways to kill David. He would send him on dangerous missions with too few men, he would put paid assassins among David's troops. But God, who had chosen David for a special purpose, looked after everything. Saul was right; the next king *would* be David. But David would not need to steal the throne, he would be put on it by God. Much later, though; meanwhile Saul plotted and was filled with jealousy and fear.

Not all the time; when he was normal Saul treated David as a son, heaped honours upon him, gave him, as he had promised, one of his daughters in marriage. But it was an atmosphere that could not continue. On two occasions when David was playing upon the lyre Saul, far from being soothed by it, had suddenly hurled a spear. David's reactions were fast as a cat and both times he'd ducked, but it had been close.

One day Jonathan went to David and told him that Saul was scheming yet again. 'Take my sister Michal, your wife,' said Jonathan, 'and find a house. Live away from the palace and the King. It's safer.'

David took the advice and things were a bit easier for a while. He lived quietly, when not away with the army, and gave orders that he wanted no parades or banner-waving or conquering-hero stuff as it only annoyed Saul. He behaved, as always, in a loyal and principled way. But he was dealing with a man not quite sane.

One night he got home and Michal looked very worried indeed. 'Jonathan was here,' she said. 'Father has given orders that you are to be arrested in the middle of the night and charged with treason and killed tomorrow morning. No trial. By the King's order.'

David stood still. He had the feeling that a new chapter was beginning.

Michal looked up into his face. 'My father has spies everywhere,' she said. 'I've made a sort of dummy and put it in your bed. It's got a goat's-hair wig. We'll have supper and retire early. We'll leave a dim light in the bedroom and the dummy will fool anyone looking in. When the house is quiet you can escape through the garden. Don't worry about me,' she said. 'My father will be angry but he will not harm his own daughter.'

David looked into his wife's eyes. 'I shall go to see Samuel,' he said. 'He is old now but he is God's prophet. He will know what God wants of us all.'

And Samuel did, though it was some days before David found the old prophet.

Samuel told him, 'All this was foreseen. King you shall be and Saul now knows this, but the path to your throne will be hard. Assassins sent by Saul have already followed you here but were made powerless and dazed by God. Saul too came and fell into a fit and tore off his clothes and lay for a day and a night like a beggar under a tree.'

David felt sad. He was a simple good man and felt himself to be surrounded by great forces. Also he knew the other Saul, who was generous and good company – and indeed his father-in-law. 'What of Michal my wife who helped me escape?' he said.

Samuel paused. 'She has been sent to Gallim by Saul and made wife to a man called Phaltiel. One day you will get her back. Not yet. Now you must go from here. To my friend Ahimelech in the town of Nob. He will give you shelter and also the great sword of Goliath the giant. It is yours by right. Go then to the cave of Adullam, where I will see to it that your seven brothers and your parents will join you. Also others. Four hundred. They will be your first force. Go now.'

David did as the old man said and all this came to pass and he felt better. Then he heard that Saul had killed Ahimelech for helping him and had wiped out the town of Nob in revenge.

David now saw that Israel must be split into two, those for him and those for Saul. He knew it to be a bad thing, for Israel had enemies enough without civil war. But it had to be. Now he and his four hundred were outlaws. Soon they were six hundred. David trained his men and they lived off the land. Saul hunted and hounded them without rest. There was one fantastic occasion when Saul, tired at the end of a fruitless day of searching, took shelter in a cave and went to sleep. Further back in the cave were David and a small band of his men. They wanted to kill Saul, but David stopped them. 'He was like a father to me,' he said, 'and he was anointed king by Samuel. Anointed by a prophet of God.'

Then David quietly cut off part of Saul's robe and he and his men left the cave. When Saul awoke and came out into the open David called to him from across the valley and told him how near he had been to death. 'But not by my hand,' he said. 'You hunt me to kill me but I will not harm a hair of your head. See I cut only your robe – with the sword which could have cut your throat. God will judge between you and me.'

Saul stood still. David watched him and recognized the sign of a calm, sane period in the King.

'David,' said Saul, 'you are better than I am; you have repaid my evil with good where I try only to repay your good with evil. Now I know that you will surely be King of Israel, a strong firm Israel in your hand. I ask only that my descendants and my name shall not be destroyed.' And David swore it.

The Last of Samuel

David knew better than to think that the King's sanity would last, or that the war was over between them. And when, a few months later, news came to him that Samuel was dead – Samuel, the great prophet of God, who had anointed both Saul and himself with holy oil – David knew that nowhere in Israel was he any longer safe from Saul. There was one place, though, where Saul might not follow him. David and his six hundred men went to the city of Gath, where the giant had come from. The city was deep in Philistine country, enemy country to Saul. David went to the prince of Gath, who, Philistine or not had a high regard for David the fighter, the soldier, the leader. David was frank and asked for refuge as now he too, like the prince, was an enemy of Saul. The prince gave David some land and he and his men settled in. The prince, rather crafty, had chosen land on the Israelite border, knowing that David's men would live by plunder, and hoping to increase the enmity between David and Saul. But David, just as crafty, plundered the Amalekites to the south of Judah leaving no survivors to point out the difference. Over a year passed and Saul stayed well away. The prince of Gath, believing that David was now a firm enemy of Israel, made him his bodyguard, but his generals who were preparing for a big battle with Saul did not trust David and on the day of the battle sent him and his men back behind the lines.

Saul had heard of these battle preparations and he too had made ready. When he saw the huge Philistine army he was shocked and scared and sadly missed David who had been his commander-in-chief and a great soldier. Saul asked God for advice but God, who was not very pleased with Saul, wouldn't answer. So Saul did something that pleased God even less. He went to see a witch. The witch of Endor. He went disguised but witches know and she recognized him. She was frightened, for Saul had forbidden all mediums and wizards and witches. But he told her that this was a special job.

'Call back from the dead,' he said, 'the prophet Samuel, who made me king and is a friend of God, who won't talk to me.'

The old witch, who knew her job, got busy with her bits and pieces and, sure enough, fairly soon there was the spirit of old Samuel. And not very pleased about being disturbed.

'If God won't speak to you,' he told Saul, 'it is because he has turned from you, as I told you he would after you disobeyed him. Israel's next king will be David whom you hunt like an animal.'

'I've somehow known that for a long time,' said Saul, 'but what about the battle?'

Old Samuel paused. 'Israel will suffer a great defeat,' he said, 'the Philistines will live in Israel's cities and many of your soldiers will be killed.' He paused again. 'Your sons will be killed also,' he said, 'and you Saul also will die.'

Saul was terrified and threw himself at the spirit's feet. When he looked up the spirit had gone.

And it came to pass; the defeat, the massacre; the killing of Saul's sons, Jonathan and two of his brothers. Jonathan the great friend of David. And lastly the death of Saul, who, wounded and afraid of capture, had himself killed with his own sword.

When the news was brought to David he wept. He felt again that he was part of a huge design. How God had arranged that he would have no part in the battle, no part in the death of the King he was to replace. The King who had loved him and hated him. Who had honoured him and degraded him. Who had been at first a great king, then mad, now dead. David, great soldier and leader, knew that his own exile would soon end. But for Saul and for Jonathan he wept. All his life a musician and poet, David made a great lament. He addressed it to the mountains of Bilboa beginning, sadly, *'The beauty of Israel is slain upon they high places. How are the mighty fallen.'*

THE KINGDOM OF DAVID

Even after the death of Saul and Jonathan, David did not become King of Israel right away. No, God, who had chosen David to be King of Israel, was going to make quite sure first that Israel would appreciate a good king when they got one. So David first became king of only part of Israel, he became King of Judah, the southern part, where the tribe of Judah lived, to which tribe he belonged by birth. He lived in Hebron as King of Judah for over seven years. The rest of Israel was governed by one of Saul's surviving sons. He was not very good at it, but he had a good commander-in-chief, a sensible man called Abner, and he it was who finally brought the civil war to an end and united all the tribes under one king, David. Another thing he did was to restore David's first wife to him. Michal, daughter of Saul. Mind you, when she came back David had a few other wives, as was the way then (Multiply, God had said), and a fair-sized family. But she was made very welcome.

So: Israel was now united, and David, more experienced now in kingship, took over and made Jerusalem his capital. The years of tribal war seemed now at an end. One of the saddest of the last incidents was the ill-judged murder by one of David's men of Abner, who had done so much. David, a wise man, made the funeral a great lesson in the stupidity of war and strife.

Then David decided to bring the Ark of God, the scrolls and tablets of the laws and commandments, to Jerusalem. For twenty years or more the Ark had been looked after in a small village not far from Jerusalem. David made it a great day of joy. A great feast. The people danced and sang, and none more than David. Michal, who hadn't been too happy about all the other wives and children was rather sour about David's dancing and singing in the streets till all hours. 'So *vulgar*,' she said. 'I am a king's daughter, and your prancing, I assure you, is not very kingly.'

David pointed out without anger that he was not trying to be kingly, he was paying homage to God's word. 'God,' he said, 'who chose me above your father.'

God listened and decided that perhaps Michal should stay childless. And she did.

The Ark stood, as always since the time of Moses, in a decorated and beautiful sort of tent. And David, who lived in a handsome palace of stone and cedar and gold and silver, was bothered by this. He felt that the Ark should have a palace too, a great temple, a house to live in. He spoke of this to a prophet called Nathan, an elderly and respected man.

The next day Nathan went to David with words given to him by God in a dream. 'God said he understands your feelings,' said Nathan. 'But the tent will do for the time being. Certainly a great temple will be built for the Ark but by your son, not by you.'

'Which son?' said David. 'I've got lots.'

'God didn't say,' said Nathan, 'although I rather gathered he isn't born yet. He will be wise and a credit to you. If you like,' said Nathan, 'you can start gathering building-materials but don't start work.'

David listened, prayed his thanks to God, and started gathering. Another thing he did round about this time was rather fine, bearing in mind he was a rather busy king. He found out that Saul's son Jonathan, his own great friend, had left a child, a boy in his teens, with crippled feet. The boy lived far off with an old servant. David had them both brought to Jerusalem and to live in the palace. 'Your father was like a brother to me,' he told the boy, 'and you shall be like my son.'

A Real Big Sin

Very human man, David. A man of principle, a brave man, a man blessed by God, and indeed chosen by God, as we've heard. But a human man, and subject, as we shall hear, to human weaknesses. What is a king after all but a man? A man who sits in a rather more fancy chair than the rest of us. Kings have burnt cakes, and tried to stop the tide coming in, and abdicated for love; they have been fools and gamblers and great sinners. And King David also was a great sinner. Not regularly, just once. But a real big sin. He was punished by God and forgiven. Poor David, a man in a fancy chair. The fancy chair was on the flat roof of his palace.

David had been King of Israel for some time now and he loved to sit in the evening and look out over the hills and skyline of Jerusalem. He was by himself. Earlier that day the prophet Nathan had come to lunch and they'd talked about things in general and David had been pleased at Nathan's approval of his careful leadership of the nation. The people loved him and Israel was united as never before. The Ammonites were the enemy now and many battles took place, indeed there was one going on now, but in general things were going well. David got to his feet and stretched. Joab his commander-in-chief could handle this battle, he thought; capable fellow, Joab. David strolled to the handsome balustrade of the roof and looked down. And that was it. In a small roof-garden of the house next door, glowing in the pink light of the evening sun, a beautiful woman was rising gracefully from a white marble bath.

Now David was not a boy, middle forties; and not a fool. He was married to a number of wives and had a fair-sized family. But it was bonnet over the windmill. He was a very handsome and virile man and the lady got carried away too. Her name was Bathsheba and her husband was an officer in David's army and away at the war. Convenient. But quite soon she was pregnant and it was months since she had seen her husband. David had him sent home on leave for a few days but the gallant officer had foresworn all women till the battle was won. He wouldn't go near his wife. David tried everything; gave him presents, got him drunk, had the dancing girls in, sexy music. Nothing. The officer went back to war.

Then the whole thing went really bad. David told Joab his commander-in-chief to put the officer in the sort of danger that would kill him. And it did. Bathsheba mourned for her husband and then went and lived in David's house and he married her.

Weeks passed and it was nearly time for her baby to be born. Then Nathan the prophet went to David. No approval this time. No, a strange-faced Nathan with an odd question. 'Ponder,' he said, 'a rich man with many sheep who steals the only sheep of a poor man, for pleasure's sake. Does he sin?'

'He most certainly does,' said David, 'and shall be punished for it. Who is the man?'

'You are the man,' said Nathan, 'and you are to be punished by God. In a number of ways.'

Then Nathan left and David prayed for forgiveness, and when the baby was born weak and sickly he prayed for its life. But the baby died and Bathsheba wept. She was not a bad woman any more than David was bad. Such things happen. But there are rules. Called commandments. Given to Moses by God. They hadn't been out all that long and God wanted them obeyed, especially by the man he had chosen to be an example to others.

Absalom, my Son

David in his comforting of Bathsheba gave and found great love in her and when she again told him she was going to have a child he prayed differently. For *her*. That *she* should have joy. And God was pleased and sent a message again through Nathan the prophet. 'It will be a son,' said Nathan, 'and he will be king after you, and he will be gentle and have great wisdom. His name will be Solomon which means Peaceful. And God will be his friend.' Nathan paused. 'I must tell you however that your punishment is not complete,' he said. 'As one son shall bring you joy so is another to give you grief. And God will raise up evil against you out of your own house.'

As the years passed and David and Bathsheba enjoyed the growing up of their son Solomon, old Nathan's words were almost forgotten. Then the thing began.

Apart from Bathsheba David had, as we've seen, a number of other wives, all of whom he'd met and married before Bathsheba. And by them he'd had quite a large family. His firstborn was a young man called Amnon who fell in love with his half-sister called Tamar. He behaved very badly and her brother, called Absalom, swore revenge and waited his chance. He waited two years and then killed Amnon. And fled. King David, who lived his fine family and handsome sons, grieved terribly. He wept both for the death of Amnon and for the loss of Absalom, the most handsome of them all.

Then Joab, David's commander-in-chief and old friend, saw that the King's heart was not really in the banishment of Absalom and he found a way for David to forgive and Absalom to return. But after his son's return to Jerusalem, for two full years David wouldn't see him and this set up in Absalom, already an arrogant and ambitious young man, a great bitterness. He began to plot and scheme to win the affection of the people. It wasn't hard. He was the King's son, and in line for the throne, well known, one of the best-looking men in all Israel. He created a whole network of spies and supporters and the conspiracy grew strong and dangerous.

Four years passed by and David, who was no fool, put some twos and twos together and decided to abdicate and he and his family and household left Jerusalem and Absalom moved in. But it was not that simple; it never is. Not everyone wanted a new king, and David was much loved, and as he walked into exile many thousands decided to walk by his side.

David now saw Israel was divided and vulnerable. A country at war with itself is anybody's prey and Israel had no lack of enemies. Surrounded by them; like today. So David mustered the thousands with him into an army and, as so often in the past, Joab and his brother Abishai commanded them.

Soon all the espionage and counter-espionage and preparation for the big showdown began, though David gave strict orders that Absalom was on no account to be killed. Not that Absalom had any such scruples. He had the throne and many spies and a huge force of trained men and no feelings at all about killing his father. He tried a number of times but David got away, warned by *his* spies.

And the day came. A terrible day – when tribe fought tribe and Israel killed some of its finest sons. A great many. Twenty thousand men died that day. The battle was won, if such a battle can be won, by David's army.

And Absalom died that day in a way that was almost farcical. He'd fought all day and watched his men and his hopes beaten into the dust. All was lost. He turned his horse and made for the nearby forest of Ephraim. As he entered the forest he was snatched from his horse by the forked branch of a great tree and there he hung, by the neck, helpless, wounded, dazed. Soon along the same track came some of David's men and recognizing Absalom they told Joab. He, who less than five years before had arranged the forgiving of Absalom by his father, now ordered – he valued the rough justice of those times more highly even than the King's command – that Absalom be killed as a traitor. So Absalom was speared to death as he hung, and his body taken down and buried in the forest. The last death of that terrible day.

The news was brought to David and the people saw no triumph, no elation, just a heartbroken man who'd lost a son. 'O Absalom,' they heard him say. 'Would to God, I had died instead of you. O Absalom, my son, my son.'

Choosing a Successor

But soon David put aside his grief and got busy. There was much to do. Tribes had to be made friendly again; the army, split in half, had to be completely re-organized. He knew that this civil war, begun by one of his sons, was part of the punishment God was giving him. 'Out of your own house shall come evil,' God had said. And more was to come too. Later, another son was to try to steal the throne, and there was to be famine, and pestilence. Poor David, who sinned for love and killed for love, was to suffer much. But Bathsheba, for whom he sinned and killed, was worth it. She became his favourite wife and a loyal and splendid mother to their son Solomon.

The son who tried to steal the throne the second time was called Adonijah. Like Absalom his brother he was in line to be king anyway but, as David grew to be rather old, Adonijah got impatient and started to undo all the careful unity that his father had built up in Israel. He talked some of the higher-ups of the army and religion into joining him and held a sort of 'I-hereby-crown-me-king' ceremony. Word came to old Nathan the prophet, now *very* old, and he told Bathsheba. Who went to see David. 'Once you promised me,' she said, 'that our son would be *King* Solomon. Now I hear that Adonijah has declared himself your successor. Solomon is much liked by the people and the city is full of rumours and confusion. All Israel waits to be told the real truth.'

David wasted no time, he sent for the prophet Nathan and gave clear orders. 'Go to Gihon,' he said, 'and take Solomon, who shall ride upon my horse and wear my crown. And take also Zadok the priest; at Gihon you shall anoint Solomon king. You and Zadok. Then the great trumpets are to be blown so that Adonijah will know by hearing them that Solomon is the new King of Israel and not he. Let there be no rumours and confusion, only joy, for Solomon is God's choice as well as mine.'

All this was done and the people were pleased. It was done at roughly the same time as Adonijah was having a big party to celebrate *his* taking over. Very big affair. He had many supporters, who thought they were onto a good thing. But when all these guests and friends found out what all the excitement in the streets and all the trumpeting and music meant, they got up and one by one made excuses to leave early. Not because they were at the wrong party. They'd backed the wrong horse. Eventually their host was all by himself. Packing. He didn't live very long, that one. Rough justice in those days.

But David's story ends on a quiet note. It ends, as many old men's lives end, with the old man passing on some advice and a few thoughts to his son. The handing over of the reins. David was about seventy when he died and his mind was clear to the last. Early in his reign when he had wanted to build a great temple to God, God had said it would be built by his son but that David could prepare the plans. So David gave to Solomon to the last detail the plans for the Temple, and told him where the great stores of precious metals and rare woods and fine marbles were waiting in readiness.

'God has chosen you to do it,' he said. 'A great task; but be strong and of good courage. Fear not, be not dismayed, for God is with you.'

Then there was a great ceremony where David gave into the temple building fund his great personal fortune; and all the tribal leaders and the heads of houses and anybody else who wanted followed suit, freewill. And David, who was a great king, because he could put things simply, said to God, 'All this that we give you, you first gave to us.'

And David died, the Bible says, *in a good old age full of days, riches and honour. And Solomon his son reigned.*

The Wisdom of Solomon

Now, when King Solomon took over the throne of his father, King David, he wasn't after all very old. Early twenties. He had a good head on him and a good education. He was interested in everything and possessed a marvellous memory. Strong-minded; like his mother, Bathsheba. He was remarkable and rare. More sophisticated than his father, who'd begun life, you remember, as a shepherd-boy. Solomon for *all* his life had been the son of a *king*, the first great King of Israel, and maybe, even counting Solomon, the greatest.

The most important gift left to Solomon by David was a united and peaceful people. The twelve tribes close and happy together as never before. Missing their beloved King David but seeing in Solomon a new David. And Solomon was aware of the huge responsibility but not daunted by it. It's no fun being the son of a great man. People compare.

But Solomon, as I said, was a different sort of thinker. He was a planner. Enormous breadth of mind. He sat down and looked at the country and people he was to rule. He saw clearly and with admiration what his father had done but was not over-impressed. Very little did impress the young King. He saw a largely peasant people with not many skills. Happy to be at peace and willing to work to remain so. They were proud of him and trusted him. He also knew the value of peace, especially with the old enemy, Egypt.

So the young King, who was a great realist, decided to test the people's trust in his judgment. He announced that he would take as his number one wife the daughter of Pharaoh, King of Egypt! The Elders were shocked, but then saw Solomon's good sense. In one blow the enemy was now a father-in-law, and import–export could begin. Solomon was to marry into other countries many times in his forty-year reign. It made for trouble eventually but that was later.

Not long after Solomon became King, during a big religious meeting, God appeared to him in a dream. A sort of vision-dream, and God asked Solomon how he could help. Solomon was honest and told God how very much aware he was of his young shoulders and that he could do with a really wise head on them. 'An understanding mind,' he said. 'Clear knowledge of good and evil. This is a huge people. I don't know much.'

God was pleased. The humility and modesty pleased him. It always does. 'Right,' he told Solomon, 'you shall have wisdom and discernment as no one before you and as none who come after you. Also you shall have things you didn't ask for, riches and honour and possessions. Great power, and peace.' And it was almost from the next day that Solomon began to be called 'the wise'.

Part of his new God-given wisdom was a great knowledge of people and how they think. One day two women were brought before him for judgment. A nasty case. One woman accused the other of swapping her dead baby for her, the accuser's, live one. In the night. Both babies only days old.

Solomon listened. Both ladies very upset. Lot of screaming and crying. 'Bring a sword,' said Solomon. 'Cut the live baby in two. Each lady to have half.'

Silence. Then the real mother begged it not to be done. 'Give her the baby,' she said. 'Don't kill my son!'

Solomon did nothing of the kind. 'Keep your son,' he said. 'Next case.'

This judgment went through the land like lightning. Everything the King did or said was news. His laws for full employment. His division of the country into equal tax and supply areas. The people were involved, interested, alive. Solomon had big plans for them; the building of the great Temple in Jerusalem. His father David had begun to collect materials and left detailed instructions. Now it was time to put those plans into execution. It was a holy, special task.

The Building of the Temple

For nearly five hundred years, the Ark of the Lord had travelled and wandered wherever the people of Israel had travelled and wandered. Now they had a King and a King's capital city. And in that city, Jerusalem, the Ark was to have a permanent home. The foundations were dug in the fourth year of Solomon's reign. He supervised every detail. Only the best was good enough. And if the best was not obtainable in Israel, then he would import it. The timber for the great Temple was a good example. The local stuff wasn't good enough so Solomon asked a great friend of his father's called Hiram to help. He'd known this Hiram all his life, almost an uncle, but his deal was businesslike. So much timber plus so many skilled woodmen per year in return for wheat, oil, foodstuffs, and some land. Hiram agreed to everything gladly. He'd loved David and saw in Solomon all that was best in his old friend. His forests were in Tyre, north of Israel, on the coast. A long way to go, but they worked it out and the cutting began. Great rafts of the finest cedars and cypresses of Lebanon were brought down the coast and then inland by camel-train. Thousands of men were put to quarrying stone and thousands more to dressing it into squared blocks – a very new thing in those days. Joiners and carvers and metalworkers were brought from other lands. Every kind of expert. Time and money did not matter. It was gorgeous. Whole rooms were lined with pure gold. Fine marbles and precious stones were everywhere. Beautiful winged figures of cherubim stood against exquisite tapestries. All the work in gold and silver and bronze, in stone and wood, and the weaving and dyeing was in charge of one man called Hiram – yes, same name as David's old friend Hiram, King of Tyre, who supplied the wood from Lebanon; probably named after him. And loaned by that Hiram. Rather confusing.

This Hiram was the son of a widowed Jewish mother who had married a craftsman in Tyre. Both he and his master, the King of Tyre, were dead keen on the building of the Temple. All right, you'll say, both were well paid. So were all the other workers. But this wanting to join in the great work was remarkable. Like David before him Solomon had this drive, this ability to get people going.

A marvellous, unique man. Yes, Hiram, the genius, could *work* in copper and bronze, but it was Solomon who created the huge mining and smelting plant far south in the hot, windy desert. He even *used* the hot wind and built his furnaces in its path. Blast-furnaces three thousand years ago! Metal was cast in moulds made of local clay and taken north for Hiram to finish and build in.

The Temple took seven years to build. It employed thousands and developed many new crafts and techniques which Solomon noted and used in other ways. He learned from everything. In any age he would have stood out. A genius, vastly gifted, and a dynamic human being.

Solomon in his Glory

But one thing Solomon was not. He was not 'the man of the people' his father, King David, was. The people were staggered by Solomon. Impressed, overawed, overpowered. But no *love*. David they had loved. He'd had the 'common touch', the warmth. Not Solomon.

Solomon performed miracles of planning, created great buildings, works of art, gardens vineyards, huge business deals. But forced labour was known in the land. No choice. One month in three many, many thousands of workers left their farms and homes in what was a sort of draft call-up. It rankled. One leaves home to fight for it, not to be reminded of the slavery of one's forbears in Egypt.

And then there were the taxes and the vast supplies demanded by the court and the army. Full-size army kept up; Solomon took no chances. Indeed he created a chariot corps that was huge. Housed in stables of a size and magnificence never known before. Famous, talked about. As Solomon meant them to be.

Jerusalem became, under Solomon, the centre of a vast import–export organization. Solomon had a fleet that included ships able to go on trading trips lasting three years. And the things they would bring back! Apes, peacocks, ivory, the rarest woods, gold, silver. Mind you, silver during Solomon's reign was not counted very valuable. Rather common. Solomon wouldn't have it in the place. He preferred gold. He drank out of it, ate off it, sat on it, and slept on it. No statesman or prince or King visited without bringing valuable presents. Always including gold. No vanity on Solomon's part. A currency backed by gold is no new idea. These days we bury it in mountains or forts or banks. The only differences is, he let you *see* it.

Solomon was to *intelligent*. Even having so many wives had good sense behind it. He married into the ruling families of many nations who might otherwise have got jealous or unfriendly. Every King for miles around was an in-law! No raiding parties, just parties. Why go to war with Solomon if you could go for the weekend? Especially if your weekend might show you wonders you'd never seen before. The glorious Temple like a great golden jewel. The palaces with their fountains and gardens. The great camel-trains that went off in every direction. Heavy-laden, valuable, important.

This building of a huge freight service using camels was pure Solomon. These especially bred and tamed beasts that could ignore the water-holes which mules and asses absolutely depend on. Far down into Arabia they went, these trains; into the Yemen; even to Sheba, nearly fifteen hundred miles. Their drivers spoke of King Solomon. So did the seamen of Solomon's fleet who brought ashore the rare goods and fine cargoes from Solomon's land.

The ruler of Sheba was a Queen. She ruled well. Shrewd, logical, a good Queen. But also a woman. And curious. She listened to the stories, allowed for the boasting and exaggeration, and was still left with something that, being a woman, she really had to go and see for herself.

So she went. Fifteen hundred miles. With a tremendous retinue of servants in gorgeous array. Camels weighed down with gifts of every description. Not only gold and precious stones but vast quantities of rare spices and perfumes – which were the riches of *her* country. Nothing was forgotten. She was prepared to be impressed but, womanlike, she also intended to do a little impressing herself.

Well, she made an impression. But what she saw and heard at the court of Solomon left her speechless. There were no secrets. Solomon answered her every question and showed her everything. The way the court was run, the various ministries, the religious life and, most impressive of all, the frequent conventions, where thinkers from many lands would sit together to talk – and to listen to Solomon who seemed to be able to speak with knowledge about everything. Kings and princes would travel long distances just to talk to him. She was staggered and said so. And when it was time to go back home to Sheba, Solomon matched her gift for gift, and anything else she desired was freely given. Not marriage – he normally married princesses not queens! Not even romance, as far as I can make out from the Bible. With seven hundred wives it's maybe a little difficult to find room for romance. Some of these wives, mind you, Solomon had married for political reasons, as we've seen. Good thinking. But seven *hundred*? And three hundred *concubines*. He needed to be rich.

Idols at Court

Solomon was a civilized man. Threse women were of many different beliefs and he didn't insist that they should give up their religions. He built them idols, told them to bring their gods and other rubbish with them. Gave them incense-accounts and sacrifice-allowances. And, I'm sorry to say, as he got older and not so wise, got rather interested himself. Eventually he built a huge sacrifice-stadium to some of these gods not far from Jerusalem. Within sight of the Temple.

Well, that was it! God was angry. There are too many commandments forgotten for 'political reasons'.

'For the sake of your father David,' God told Solomon, 'your kingdom will remain intact till you die. Then it will be broken in two. Part will be given to your son and the rest to your servant.'

God didn't name the servant and Solomon didn't ask. He knew that all the rest God said about not keeping faith and so on was true. And Solomon, because he was a man of vast knowledge and achievement, knew that for the people of Israel the party was over. The forty years of peace, the prosperity, the unity as a nation was at an end. He also knew, special God-gifted person though he might be, that it was his fault.

This perhaps is the less well-known part of the Solomon story. How the wonderful gifts of wisdom and wealth from God gave him the sort of absolute power which corrupts. Solomon was after all human, and you've got to be very careful with great power; Solomon wasn't careful enough.

The Kingdom Divided

When God told Solomon that one of his servants was to rule over part of what had been Solomon's kingdom, he didn't mean one of the grooms or the footmen. But a very able man with a high position in Government called Jeroboam. He was told he was to be a king by an old prophet who met him one day on a country road. The old prophet showed Jeroboam the new order of things in a rather costly way. He tore up his new coat. Into twelve pieces. Then the old man, in his shirtsleeves, told Jeroboam his fate. 'The twelve pieces,' he said, 'are the twelve tribes. You are to be king of ten. God said so.'

When Solomon got to know, he tried to kill Jeroboam. Understandable. So Jeroboam fled to Egypt and didn't come back till Solomon was dead and his son was on the throne. A very stupid man, this son of Solomon. Often the way; clever men have stupid sons. He had grown up knowing that one of the least popular laws his father had made was the one about forced labour. The people for a certain period of each year had no choice; and they hated it. Solomon was a realist, and hard, and the law got many things done, but the people hated it. So when this stupid son, after his father died, had a chance to remove the law, to 'lighten the yoke' – and he was advised to – he did the opposite. And with no tact either. 'My father chastised you with whips,' he told the people, '*I* will chastise you with scorpions! A *heavier* yoke,' he yelled.

Idiot! An immediate general strike. The Minister of Forced Labour was killed. And the people all went quietly home. 'To your tents O Israel,' was the slogan. 'This is not what King David meant for us.'

God looked on. Sadly. But it had to be, and soon Jeroboam was back from Egypt and the old prophet's words all came to pass. The ten tribes in the north of Israel asked him to be their king and he said yes. And almost overnight the people, whom King David had unified for his son Solomon to rule as one nation, broke into two. The north, the ten tribes, kept the name Israel; the south, mainly of the large tribe of Judah, called itself Judah. (The other tribe in the south was Benjamin, descendants of Joseph's younger brother.) Stupid son reigned over the south. Stupid son had a name; it was Rehoboam. So similar to Jeroboam that I have purposely avoided using it. It seemed less confusing to be rude to him. But that idiot reigned seventeen years, the Bible says, going downhill the whole time. Other books say seven; quite long enough in my opinion. Anyway, he and his kingdom went to the bad. Idol worship worse than ever and shocking decadence of every kind.

Jeroboam's ten tribes up north were a bit better but not much. He started well. He was shrewd and was soon aware that his people were going to miss Jerusalem and the great Temple, the centre of their religious life, the house of God's Ark. Jerusalem was now in Judah, the 'other country'. So Jeroboam got busy. He chose two places in the north, both of them rather holy places in the minds of his people, and he built at each site an altar, a place of worship. Good idea. But he got rather carried away. He appointed his own priests, invented services, and even created new feast days.

'I will even give you,' he told his people, 'in each place, a feature as good as the great Temple.' D'you know what he put up? Golden calves. Honestly, people never learn. It would be comic, if it weren't so sad. A tragic sequel to the greatness of Solomon and David. But one thing they had done. They'd left Israel with a picture of the greatness that might be hers – a happy people, powerful, prosperous and united; at the centre of it all, the great Temple of God in the Holy City of Jerusalem. They would hang on to that picture through all the years that followed. So much trouble was to follow. As we shall see.

PROPHETS, PRIESTS AND KINGS

Well, king followed king in the two kingdoms of Israel and Judah. None of them much good in those early years. Some good prophets, though. The first were Elijah and Elisha, who did a great deal to keep up faith in God among the people of the north. They needed to. For we are now to meet a new King of Israel. Ahab, son of Omri, an army commander, who had come out on top after another army commander had wiped out Jeroboam's grandson and his family. This Ahab was a real stinker. Who did evil, so the Bible says, more than all who went before him. And as if this wasn't enough, says the Bible, he took for wife one Jezebel who was worse than he was! They both of them just ignored God and worshipped Baal and built idols and temples to him. And not only the King and Queen but all the court too. The corruption spread down from the top and the whole people rather went to the bad.

Right. God had now had enough and as before looked around for someone to speak for him. He chose a man from a place called Tishbe, a Tishbite, gave him certain instructions, and sent him to see King Ahab. The Tishbite's name was Elijah.

Always a bit cross was Elijah. Mind you, he always wore a shirt woven of camel's hair, which couldn't have helped much. Anyway he went to see Ahab and came straight to the point. 'No more rain,' he said, 'until further notice. Goodbye.'

Well, the weather started to get a bit dry, so God thought Elijah had better go where Ahab couldn't find him. 'Go east,' said God, 'to the brook of Cherith. Very barren, but the water is pure.'

'Any food?' said Elijah, who didn't each much but liked a little.

'Food will be brought to you morning and evening,' said God.

'Won't the bringers be able to tell Ahab where I am?' said Elijah.

'Not these bringers,' said God, 'they will be birds. Ravens.'

So off went Elijah and settled in and twice a day, sure enough, the food arrived; bread, meat, all he needed.

Then the brook began to dry up (no rain, you see) and God moved him again. 'North,' said God, 'I've arranged your food.'

'More birds?' said Elijah, who'd come to like his beautiful blue-black friends.

'No,' said God, 'a poor widow.'

Elijah found the place – it was a little town just outside Ahab's kingdom. Just as he came to the gate he saw a poorly-dressed woman gathering sticks and somehow knew that she was his new landlady. He sat down on a stone. 'I am tired and very dry,' he said. 'Could you bring me a little water and perhaps some bread?'

'I will bring the water with pleasure,' she said, 'but I've no bread. No food at all except a little flour in a bowl and a little oil in a jar. And that's all. I suppose,' she said, 'you could say we are starving.'

Elijah got up. 'I will gather some sticks for your oven,' he said, 'and I will live in your house and, until God sends us back the rain, there will always be flour in the bowl and oil in the jar.'

She started to say something.

'God said so,' said Elijah.

And it was so. The poor widow was a very puzzled woman.

Then one day her son became ill, and got worse, and then died. She said to Elijah, 'What have I done? What have you against me? You say you are a man of God. Did he send you into my house to kill my son? He's all I've got.'

Elijah knew her to be a good woman and he himself was puzzled. 'Give me the boy,' he said, and took the child up to his room. He laid the body on his bed. Then he talked to God.

'I know, Lord,' he said, 'that there are many wicked people in Israel and that Ahab and his awful wife Jezebel have got to be punished for all the idol-worship and so on and that's why you've stopped the rain. And I know, Lord,' said Elijah, 'that you are very busy. But I'm sure you didn't mean this poor woman to suffer such a blow.'

He looked down at the body. A good-looking boy whom he'd been very fond of. He knelt beside him and laid his own head on the boy's chest.

'Lord,' he said, 'make his heart beat again. Such a cheerful little spirit. Give it back.'

The body remained lifeless.

'Give it back,' said Elijah, his head still pressing on the boy's chest.

And then again, 'Give it back, Lord, please.'

And the heart began to beat.

Soon the boy opened his eyes and looked into Elijah's face. 'Hullo,' he said, 'I'm hungry.'

'So you should be,' said Elijah. 'It's supper time.'

And they went downstairs.

Elijah versus Ahab

Well, Elijah lived just over Israel's northern border with the poor widow and her son for about two and a half years until one day God told him to go down and see King Ahab.

At roughly the same moment King Ahab was talking to his chamberlain, a good man called Obadiah who was rather afraid of the wicked King and of his wife Queen Jezebel who was worse.

'This famine is all that prophet's fault,' said the King, 'that Elijah in his hair shirt! Ever since he turned up over two years ago and said, "No rain", there's been none. People are dying like flies. We've had to cut the palace banquets down to five a week! The Queen's livid. My race-horses are losing weight! Obadiah,' said the King, 'go and see whether there are any springs or grassy valleys we may have overlooked.'

So off went Obadiah and was soon back with bigger news. 'I met Elijah,' he told the King. 'He wants you to go and meet him.'

'We've had this nonsense before,' said the King. 'Hoaxes. I've searched this country top to bottom for him. I've even sent messages to all the neighbouring kings. He's disappeared off the face of the earth!'

'It's not a hoax,' said Obadiah. 'I *know* him. And he *will* be there. It's about bringing the rain back.'

When Ahab saw Elijah, he found it a bit difficult to meet the prophet's hard unforgiving eyes. So he started to blame *him* for the drought and famine and Israel's trouble.

'Not me,' said Elijah. 'You and your false gods Baal and Asherah, and your wicked ways. All right,' said Elijah, 'the rain is to come back, but on condition that all the hundreds of priests of Baal and Asherah meet me up on top of Mount Carmel and all the people are there to see the meeting. Don't argue,' said Elijah, 'you have no choice.' And it was done.

Elijah looked down at the thousands of silent people. 'How much longer,' he asked them, 'are you going to limp along with two opinions? Either Baal is the true god or God is.'

The people were silent; listening.

'I say that God is,' said Elijah, 'and here are four hundred and fifty priests who say that Baal is. So let us both, they and I, prepare a fine bull for sacrifice, on dry wood. Then let us both call upon our gods to send down the fire to light the wood. They can go first. Is it fair?'

And the people said yes. And it was done.

Well, the priests of Baal nearly went berserk. They prayed and shouted and walked round and round and cut themselves with sharp knives and went into fits and frothed and raved until nearly tea-time. Not a word. Not a spark. The meat started to go off a bit. Hot day.

Elijah rather enjoyed it. He even rubbed their noses in it. 'No one at home?' he asked them. 'Perhaps he's out the back, or upstairs asleep, or maybe,' he shouted, 'like always, there's no one there at all! All right,' he said to them. 'Get yourselves bandaged up. It's my turn.'

He turned to the people. 'Come nearer,' he said. The great multitude surged up the slope. Then Elijah drenched the meat and wood with water and then did it twice more. Then, in silence, alone, he prayed. One voice. 'Show them Lord. They need miracles. They always have.'

There was a pause and then a great roar of flame and the soaking mass went up like a firework. Nothing was left. Not even the great stones of the altar. Marvellous sight. The people fell back and then prayed to the one and only God. Fervently. Elijah watched them, not too impressed. He knew about mobs, did Elijah.

He raised his voice and pointed at the priests of Baal. 'See that they do not escape,' he said, 'for they are wicked and led you wrong.'

King Ahab looked at Elijah with no affection at all. 'I ought to kill you,' he said. 'Two years ago you walked in, said that there would be no more rain and then disappeared. Today you turn up and do this trick of burning up a sacrifice without making a fire and everybody's impressed and the people are all now going to believe in your God for five minutes as they've done before so many times. Also you've let the people loose on nearly five hundred of my wife's holy men. They're sure to kill the lot and my name will be mud. Jolly good day's work! I hope you're satisfied.

'Well, my old enemy,' said the King. 'I'm not impressed. If you want to impress *me*, bring back the rain.'

Elijah straightened up. He tilted his head as though listening. 'I hear a sound,' he said, 'like the falling rain. Come, we will go back up the mountain and you shall eat a little meal and by the time you've finished the rain will have begun.'

The King looked up at the absolutely clear sky. There hadn't been rain or a cloud in that sky for over two years. Drought and famine. 'Right,' he said.

When they got to the top the King's servant fixed him a snack and Elijah's servant waited for orders. Elijah sat down and lowered his head between his knees. The servant waited. The King chewed a date.

'Go,' said Elijah, 'to the very top and look toward the sea.'

The servant did and came back. 'Nothing,' he said.

Elijah didn't raise his head. 'Go again,' he said, 'and again. Seven times.'

By the seventh time the King was at the toothpick stage.

'There is a cloud,' said the servant, 'small, no bigger than a man's hand.'

Elijah got up and he smiled. A rare thing. 'Get in your chariot,' he said to the King, 'and go and don't stop till you get home. Because there's going to be the biggest rainstorm you ever saw.'

'Want a lift?' said the King.

'No,' said Elijah, and hitched his robe up to his knees, 'I'm going to run. I haven't run down a hill since I was at school.'

'Horses are faster,' said the King.

'Not this time,' said Elijah, 'I shall beat you all the way back to the Palace.'

And he did. About thirty miles. Not bad for an old prophet! Mind you, for that sort of performance you *need* to be a friend of God.

The Still Small Voice

King Ahab got home drenched. As soon as he'd changed he told Queen Jezebel all about it. 'Really?' she said. 'So Elijah killed nearly five hundred of my holy men. Well, you send a little message to that filthy old prophet to say that by this time tomorrow he'll be where they are!' Terrible woman. Scared everybody. Elijah too. Friend of God or not he was only human. He cleared out that night. South to Beersheba and then into the desert. Very depressed and exhausted. 'Lord,' he said, 'it's all too much. I'd be better off dead.' And he fell asleep.

When he awoke he was parched and hungry. 'Ready to eat?' said a voice and Elijah was aware suddenly of a wonderful smell of hot bread. He turned and there it was. On hot stones with a glowing fire below them, and a jug of sweet water near his hand. In charge, a friendly-faced youngish man in white.

'I'm staggered,' said Elijah. 'No one knew I was here.'

'Well, God knew,' said the young man. 'Please help yourself.'

Elijah was starving and ate well. It seemed a special sort of bread. Wonderful taste. Elijah reached for the water, smiled at the young man and took a good drink. When he lowered the jug he was alone. Under a single tree in the middle of a desert. He lay down, much comforted, and slept all day.

He woke after dark. 'Ready to eat?' said the voice.

Elijah sat up.

'Eat a lot,' said the young man, 'for you have a long journey ahead of you and you'll need all your strength.'

And it was a long journey. Forty days and forty nights. To the mountain called Horeb, where Moses saw the burning bush and received his orders from God about freeing the Egyptian slaves. Well, God had sent for Elijah to tell *him* a few things too. Also God knew that Elijah was feeling low. Always rather cross, remember, and just now he had some cause to be. He'd done miracles for the people and preached and healed the sick and the people still worshipped idols and were wicked. Elijah felt that as a prophet of God he was a failure, that he still walked alone.

Well, the days passed and at last he was on the mountain. He'd told it all to God and now he waited for God to speak. Which God did, but not right away. First Elijah was given a sort of show. A great wind began, which moved huge boulders as if they were cotton-wool and lifted mighty trees out of the ground. Then the mountain heaved and split and a great crack ran along the valley like a tear. Then every tree and bush burst into flame with a great roar. In the middle, quite safe, Elijah. The noise was tremendous, deafening, yet suddenly, in his mind, quite clearly, Elijah heard a still small voice, which spoke quietly and told him many of God's plans for the future including the news that quite soon he, Elijah, was to have an assistant who would take over from him when he died. There was nothing vague or mystical about the message. God supplied Elijah with the full name and address. The name, Elisha. Rather like his own, easy to remember. The place, a village near the Jordan not far from his own home town. Elijah went there right away.

He found his new assistant in a ploughed field. Elisha was a ploughman. Middle-aged, strong-looking man. Elijah talked with him and then formally put his cape for a moment across Elisha's shoulders. A bit sadly, for he knew how hard a prophet's life is. Far harder than a ploughman's. Elisha said his goodbyes and off they went. Two men of God.

Naboth's Vineyard

Now you might say, what does a prophet *do*? What sort of life did Elijah – and after him Elisha – live? Did they sit around and prophesy all day long? Five-day week? Working hours?

Well, no. They travelled around a lot; they were judges; they had wide knowledge of the great list of laws given by God to Moses – upon which all law is based. A sort of unofficial theocratic government over against the government of Israel's idol-worshipping kings. They gave advice; were healers; were respected, held in awe. They were 'men of God' and had devoted disciples.

Meanwhile the King and Queen and Israel went on with their nasty ways. Next door to the palace lived a man called Naboth; quiet-living man, who was a farmer and specialist in wine-grapes. Naboth's vineyard was famous. One day the King decided he wanted that vineyard next door for a vegetable garden so he told Naboth he would offer him either money, or another vineyard as good elsewhere. Reasonable.

But Naboth refused. 'The God *I* believe in,' he said, 'the *only* God, gave us a law which forbids the selling of an inheritance.'

The King, who hated to be crossed in anything, was made even more angry by Naboth saying 'the only God'. He and the Queen spent a fortune on other gods. The palace was *littered* with idols. So he swore at Naboth and went home very put out. Went off his food. Told the Queen all about it.

'Poor darling,' said his wife, 'just you leave it to your little Jezebel. She'll get your vineyard for you.' Terrible woman. She got busy and wrote lying letters on palace notepaper, and used the royal seal, and bribed and corrupted and threatened and brought false witness. In the end poor Naboth was accused of treason and sacrilege on a trumped-up charge in front of dishonest judges and he was found guilty and taken outside the city and stoned to death. Disgraceful business.

Jezebel went to the King. 'Naboth is dead,' she said. 'You wanted his vineyard. You're the King. Go and take it.' So Ahab had his supper, his appetite fully restored, and went next door to the vineyard. Very satisfied with himself and his clever little wife.

First person he met was Elijah, sent by God with one or two messages. 'I won't stay long,' said Elijah. 'This vineyard. To steal it you broke just about every commandment in the Book.' It was nearing dark and the prophet seemed to grow taller. 'I am instructed to tell you,' he said, 'you know who by, that where Naboth died, there shall your blood flow. Evil will come upon you and your family and nothing can stop it. It will be arranged that nobody belonging to you will get a funeral. Jackals and vultures will eat their bodies.'

The King was now terrified. 'It wasn't me,' he said, 'it was Jezebel.'

'Jezebel,' said Elijah, 'will die by violence and her body also will be eaten by wild dogs. Goodbye. We won't meet again.'

It all came true, of course. In God's good time.

In fact the first part, the death of King Ahab, happened very soon.

He and the King of Judah had struck up an alliance against the King of Syria. But after what Elijah had told he him didn't go into battle without special precautions. Had the King of Judah go into battle in the royal chariot while he, Ahab, was disguised as an ordinary soldier. A lot of good it did him! You may think that the phrase 'If it's got your name on it' is modern. King Ahab, in disguise, in the middle of a great army, was killed by an arrow shot by an enemy archer who, as the Bible puts it, *'drew his bow at a venture'*. An arrow which found a chink in Ahab's armour. It had his name on it all right. Meanwhile the King had built new stables in what had been Naboth's vineyard. And it was there that they washed down the chariot in which the King had bled to death. God has his ways of doing things. Some sooner. Some later.

Elijah's Mantle

Meanwhile there came a day when Elijah told Elisha that he had to go on a journey. It would be his last journey and he knew it. He didn't tell Elisha. But Elisha knew. Prophets do. So did the sons of the prophets in all the townships of Israel, through which they went together. 'You stay here,' said Elijah in one town after another. 'You stay here while I go on to such and such a place.'

'Not me,' said Elisha. 'That's a long way. I wouldn't rest. I'll come too. How *can* I leave you?'

They came at last to Jericho where they were met by fifty young men, all of them from god-fearing families who revered Elijah. The old man was tired.

'Here?' said Elisha. 'Have we come far enough?'

'No,' said Elijah, 'further east, over Jordan. You stay here.'

'Not on your life!' said Elisha. 'Take my arm. I *can't* leave you. We'll *all* go.'

It was meant. God meant the young men to be witnesses. Not of everything but of enough. They saw the two prophets go down to the river. Then Elijah took off his sleeveless coat, his mantle, and he struck the water with it. The water parted and he and Elisha walked across the dry riverbed. As they reached the other side the water came down again. The young men were goggle-eyed.

The prophets walked on till out of sight. They stopped. 'Here,' said Elijah, 'I am to be taken from you.' Elisha looked sad. 'What shall I do for you?'

'For years,' said Elisha, 'I've known I am to follow you. To wear your mantle. I've known I'm to have a share of your spirit. It will be hard to take your place. Give me a double share. I shall need it.'

Elijah understood. His eyes took on that unfocussed visionary look that Elisha knew so well. 'I am to be taken from you in a special way,' he said. 'If you *see* this miracle you will know you are in my place, with double share. If not, not.'

Then he walked away a little. Elisha saw everything. And it was a sight to see. A sort of glow began high in the sky above Elijah's head. It began to descend, turning, swirling. It was white and gold, shimmering. It hurt the eyes. Warmth came from it. Then it took shape and became a chariot and six white horses, all incandescent like white heat. It circled, coming down. Then Elijah was in the chariot and it circled, going up. And up. The noise of a whirlwind began and grew louder, then died away. The chariot and horses became again just a glow. The glow faded.

Elisha was alone. A bit lonely. He turned and at his feet was Elijah's mantle. He picked it up and walked back to the river. The young men hadn't moved. Elisha felt a bit nervous. 'Oh well,' he said to himself, 'I can only try. And I did see the miracle.' And he banged the water with the mantle. It stopped and parted and he walked across and up the other bank and as he passed through the young men they all bowed their heads to him. They had witnessed; now they knew. And through them soon the whole nation would know that Elijah the great prophet was dead. Dead and gone; leaving nothing behind except his cloak, his mantle. And Elisha, the young men would say, chosen by God, now wore that mantle. Also, as time went on, they would learn that he was just as blunt and honest as his master, and just as fearless.

Elisha in Shunem

Elisha in his work travelled a *great* deal and with his servant, a much young man named Gehazi, came one day to a place called Shunem. First time. They stopped at a rather fine house to ask the way. The woman of the house, without knowing who her tired dusty poorly-dressed callers were, had them in, showed them where to clean up, and gave them a good meal. Gehazi wanted to tell her who his master was, but Elisha, rather amused, wouldn't let him. 'I – er – travel,' he told her, 'a teacher of Law, a sort of judge.' When they had finished, she made them promise to call any time they were passing. And they did.

One day when they arrived she said to Elisha, 'I hope you won't think it a liberty but we've built a sort of bed/living-room for you to use when you come. It's given me great pleasure to do, and my husband too. We knew you to be a man of God before we found out your name and we are much honoured that you eat at our table.'

Elisha was touched. The little room was charming. She was a wealthy woman and had good taste. As time went on, he found out that the one sadness in her life was that she had no children. She'd married late and her husband was quite an old man, much older than she was.

So one day Elisha had a word with her. He'd come to admire and like this sensible friendly woman. 'One way and another,' he said, 'you've gone to a lot of trouble. I've been thinking of how I can repay you in some way. As you now know, my work brings me into contact with some very important people and I only have to ask. But I've often heard you say you need nothing. That you are content. This is rare, and good. However,' he said, 'one thing you do not have is a son. Build another room. A nursery. He will be born a year from today.'

And he was. And grew into a handsome boy with all his mother's gentleness. He loved to be among the workers on his father's large farm. A fit strong boy. Never a day's illness. But one terrible morning he complained of a bad headache and by lunchtime he was dead. His mother was frantic and rushed to Elisha who was at Mount Carmel about twenty miles away. She was distraught, beside herself, sobbing, hardly making sense. She threw herself at Elisha's feet, clutched his robe, Gehazi moved forward. Elisha waved him away. He was shocked. Stood still. Waited.

She looked up. 'Did I *ask* you for a son?' she said. 'You *gave* him.'

'God told me to,' said Elisha.

'Has God told you that he is dead?' said the woman.

Elisha helped her to her feet. 'No,' he said. 'Come on.'

The boy's body was on Elisha's own bed in the room the woman had built. Small body, pale, cold. Elisha was tense. His beloved master Elijah had once given back life to a child, but could he? He took the boy's hands and put his mouth to the boy's mouth. Nothing.

Her got up, walked about, prayed, *demanded* God's attention for a minute, and tried again. Time passed. The child's hands became warm, then his lips. Elisha sat back. The boy's eyes remained closed. And then, into this holy silence of a miracle, the boy sneezed. He sneezed seven times. By the seventh his mother was at the door with a hankie.

An Unprofitable Servant

Now, when Elisha took over Elijah's mantle he also took over fifty disciples, you remember. The fifty young men who witnessed. As the years went by they became a hundred. It was a good life; even in famine. If there was nothing for the soup but wild roots, bitter, maybe poisonous, Elisha was there to put in a pinch of flour and it would taste marvellous. He could make a little food go a *very* long way. If you were chopping firewood and your iron axe-head flew off into the river, the Master would make it float back to you. A good life. But you learned not to take advantage, or you were in *real* trouble. Like Gehazi, Elisha's servant. It happened like this.

The King of Syria had recently won a big battle against Israel – who didn't win them all by a long way. And he was very pleased with his C-in-C, a man called Naaman, who deserved it. But Naaman, poor chap, was a leper. Early stages, but positive. Rather unsightly. One day his wife said to him, 'My little maid, who was one of the prisoners brought back from this last war with Israel, tells me that there's a prophet there who she's sure could help you. She's a nice truthful girl. Nothing to lose. Go and see the King.'

Naaman did and the King said, 'Right, I'll give you a letter to the King of Israel asking him to arrange your cure. You go and pack your bag and take a nice present.'

So off went Naaman with a few servants and when the King of Israel read the letter, he – the King, that is – got very bothered. He thought it was a plot to start up the battle again.

'Am I *God*?' he said to his Prime Minister. 'Can I perform miracles? How can *I* cure leprosy? I can't even win a *war*.' He went on and on.

Now the Prime Minister was no fool and he went and told it all to Elisha. 'Tell the King to calm down,' said the prophet, 'and send Naaman round to my house.'

When Naaman arrived with his servants and chariots Elisha didn't invite him in, or go out to him. He sent Gehazi out. 'My master says go down to the Jordan,' said Gehazi, 'and wash yourself all over seven times and you'll be cured.' And went back inside.

Naamen felt like a brush-salesman, and lost his temper. 'I didn't come all this way to be told to go and wash myself,' he shouted at his servants. 'The least he could have done was to have come out to me himself. Done a bit of praying to this God of his. A burnt offering or two. Bit of magic; laying on of the hands; all that stuff. If I'd wanted to wash in a river I could have stayed at home in Syria. Our rivers are a damn sight better than any here in Israel. Come on,' he said, 'I'm fed up.'

But his oldest servant said to him, 'Why not try? If Elisha had asked you to do something complicated and costly, you would have done it without question. As Mrs Naaman said, what can you lose?'

So Naaman did. Seven times. Obedient as a child. And by the seventh time his skin was as clear as a child's. He went back to Elisha, who this time was waiting for him outside the house. 'Your God is the true God,' said the soldier. 'I'd like to change to him. Is it too late?'

'Never too late,' said Elisha and when Naaman offered payment for the cure he wouldn't take a penny.

But Gehazi was greedy and when Naaman and his party left he went after them and caught them up. 'My master sent me to say,' he told Naaman, 'that he does after all have a use for some of those bags of silver and so on.'

'Delighted!' said Naaman and lent him a couple of men to carry it all.

Gehazi hid it. Didn't do him much good. 'I know all about it,' said Elisha. 'The soldier was to be shown God, not a liar and thief. So, Gehazi,' said the prophet, 'as you've taken over a fair amount of Naaman's property, you'd better take over his leprosy too. As from now.'

Man of War

Now, it might seem to you that Elisha was a bit hard on his servant Gehazi. But, make no mistake about it, Elisha *was* hard. He had to be. You might think that because a man is a prophet of God, he must therefore be a man of peace. Not a bit. Elisha was a very useful man to have on your side in time of war. And in Israel at that time the war never seemed to stop. Syria was the main enemy just now and the King of Syria used to get in a terrible state. His most secret plans seemed to be known to Israel almost before he finished writing them down. 'Elisha, the prophet,' he was told. 'Special powers.' So he sent a large army marching off to kill him. Elisha met them, made them all blind, kept them marching right into captivity, gave them back their sight and a good feed and sent them all home. After this the Syrian king got rather discouraged for a while. Understandable.

Then he tried a new idea. A siege. A huge army, with supplies and equipment enough for a year, went and surrounded the city of Samaria, capital of Israel. No one went in or out. Before very long things were very bad indeed. People would eat anything, eventually even each other. Such things happen. The King of Israel would walk along the ramparts of his besieged capital and look out, and to every side he could see the enemy and their mouth-watering heaps of stores. His name was Joram and he was the son of the wicked King Ahab. Joram was a bit better than his father but not much and Elisha didn't have too much time for him. Or he for the prophet.

So, when the people cried out to the King to deliver them, he blamed God for the siege, and soon was blaming Elisha, God's representative. Then he decided to kill Elisha. He screamed and shouted at the old man about what people were forced to eat and the huge prices that were being charged for almost any kind of food – even corpses. 'A man is worth more dead than alive,' he yelled and he wasn't joking.

Elisha got up. 'Keep quiet,' he said, 'and hear the word of the Lord. By this time tomorrow every kind of food will be on sale in the city and at the right price.'

The King nearly frothed at the mouth but decided to delay Elisha's execution for a day or two. He'd been made to look silly before, had the King, and in addition he was hungry.

Well, Elisha prayed and God arranged it. He arranged it that evening just as it was getting dark. Suddenly the Syrian army, camped round the city, began to hear from all around them the full sound-effect of a much larger army. Chariots by the thousand, a million marching feet, bands, horses, the lot. Nothing to be seen. 'Reinforcements for Israel,' someone said, and in five minutes a mad panic was under way and the Syrians dropped everything and just ran.

Into that deserted camp later that night wandered four lepers from the city. They were starving and had worked out that they had nothing to lose by going over to the Syrians. They couldn't believe their eyes. To every side piles and heaps and boxes and sacks of everything. They went mad. They ate and drank and sang and looted and hid things and dressed themselves up in finery and armour. And then calmed down. 'This is not right,' said one of them. 'This is a day of good news. Let's go and tell the King.' And they did.

The King at first thought it was a trap to entice the people out of the city, so he sent out scouts on some of the last few horses and they followed the trail of stuff abandoned by the Syrian army right to the Jordan. They reported back and the people left the city and gathered up every single thing. A wonderful day!

During that afternoon Elisha went down to the main market where it was business as usual. Crowded. Very cheerful. He bought one or two things and as he turned he met the King.

'Shops seem well stocked,' said Elisha politely. 'How are the prices?'

'Normal,' said the King – and could have bitten his tongue. But he came to a bad end. Like his father. He was one of Ahab's sons remember.

Elisha the Kingmaker

Let us go back for a moment to the day when old Elijah was told about his new assistant, Elisha, on Horeb, the mount of God. He was told other things too. About happenings and changes that would take place among the ruling families in Israel and Syria. New kings to be anointed for both places. Also, soon after that, you remember, Elijah told Ahab what he and his family could expect after the way they'd behaved over Naboth's vineyard. 'Where Naboth died, there shall your blood flow,' Elijah had said. 'And your wife Jezebel and all your male descendants will be wiped out. Not one of them will get a funeral. Jackals and wild dogs will eat their bodies.'

Ahab had died soon after that, remember. Killed by 'a bow drawn at a venture' in one of Israel's many battles against Syria. Now it is time for the rest of those prophecies to be fulfilled. Not by Elijah himself, of course, but by Elisha.

The King of Syria, we've noticed, in spite of the fact that their two countries were nearly always at war, was not above sending messages to the man of God in Israel. This time the man he sent was called Hazael, and his errand was to enquire whether his master, the King of Syria, would recover from a sickness which had laid him low.

Elisha looked at the King's messenger. 'Your master will recover,' he said. 'But God has shown me that he will never have a chance to do so. That he will die soon.'

Elisha looked unseeingly, unblinkingly into Hazael's eyes until the younger man felt very uncomfortable. Then Hazael saw a great sadness come into the prophet's face and the unblinking eyes fill with tears. He felt himself in the presence of huge forces.

'Why do you weep, my Lord?' he said.

'Because,' said Elisha, 'God has shown me also that *you* are to be King of Syria and that you will bring death and destruction to the people of Israel.'

It all came true. The Bible tells us little of Hazael, but the day after he got back and gave the King the message about his certain recovery he killed him and took over the throne. And he *did* become a terrible enemy to Israel for all the long years of Elisha's life. Fifty more years nearly.

Well, now that they had a common enemy, the kingdoms of Israel and Judah had begun to draw together a bit. Also King Ahab and Queen Jezebel had married their daughter to a prince of Judah and one of *their* sons was the reigning King of Judah and nephew, of course, of the reigning King of Israel.

And now it was the turn of the King of Israel to be sick, and his nephew the King of Judah was visiting him. Well, the King of Israel, Ahab's son, had an officer called Jehu, who one day was in the mess with a crowd of his brother officers when a messenger from Elisha asked to see him outside.

The messenger was brief. 'I am to anoint you King of Israel,' he told Jehu, 'and you are to clean things up generally. Also you are to wipe out every last one of the family of Ahab including his widow Jezebel, the worst of the lot.' Then he anointed Jehu and left.

Jehu went in and told the mess and rather to his surprise they believed him and joined him. Off they all went to find the King. As I told you, he was poorly and the King of Judah was visiting him. So Jehu paid his respects and killed them both. Both of them descendants of Ahab, remember.

Then Jehu went to attend to Queen Jezebel. 'Driving furiously,' the Bible says. Apparently it was a habit of his. Anyway by the time he arrived at the Palace, Jezebel was waiting for him. Painted and powdered and dressed to kill. She looked down at him from a high window screaming insults. Behind her were two or three of her eunuchs. Now these fellows were no fools and they could see that Jehu was the new man. So when he invited them to throw Jezebel down to him they did. Very nasty mess indeed.

Jehu then attended to her entire family, to all the idol-worshipping priests, and everything else on Elisha's list. Needless to say, not one of Ahab's family was given burial. Jackals and vultures, as Elijah had prophesied. All, as I said, in God's good time.

Elisha lived a long time. Right through the thirty years of Jehu's reign, and the seventeen years his son ruled after him. He made many prophecies and performed many miracles. Even on his deathbed he told a rather worried King of Israel, Jehu's grandson, that the next three wars against Syria were going to be all right. Even *after* he died, he helped to bring a dead man back to life.

'A double portion of your spirit,' he had asked from his master Elijah. Certainly he seems to have had it.

Another Kingmaker

We heard how after Solomon the children of Israel split into two kingdoms. Israel in the north and Judah in the south. And we have heard about Elijah and Elisha and how they stood out against the wickedness of King Ahab and his family. Now, all these happenings took place in the northern kingdom, Israel. So it's time we had a look at the southern kingdom of Judah and the city of Jerusalem, where David had set up his capital and where Solomon had built the great Temple for the Ark of the Law.

King had followed King, as in the north. None of them particularly good, but none so bad as Ahab. One other difference, though. None of this throne-stealing by other families which was such a feature of the north. Jeroboam, then Omri (Ahab's father), then Jehu, were army commanders who had seized the throne of Israel. In Judah the family of David still reigned. There had been bloodshed, though. Most of it arising out of the marriage of Joram, prince of Judah, with Athaliah, the daughter of Ahab and Jezebel. Tried to bring her parents' idolatrous ways to Jerusalem with her. And her husband, who ought to have known better, didn't. This Joram was an ugly customer. As soon as he came to the throne, he killed off all his own brothers – and anybody else who might be expected to cause trouble. But he didn't last long. He died of a horrible disease. And not before the Philistines, those old enemies of the Israelites, had invaded the country and killed all *his* sons except the youngest. It was this youngest son, now King of Judah, who was killed by Jehu together with his uncle, the King of Israel, on the day that Jezebel and her sons and grandsons were put to death.

Well, when the news of all this came to Jerusalem and Athaliah, now an old woman, heard that her only surviving son was dead, she decided to kill all *his* sons and reign herself. Odd sort of grandmother. Mind you, the death of her own sons may perhaps have turned her mind. Anyway, she was Jezebel's daughter and she arranged it.

But *her* daughter was a god-fearing woman and married to the high-priest of the time, Jehoiada, and she managed to steal the baby of the family away. And she and her husband hid him in the Temple, where they brought him up carefully and kept him out of sight.

For six years Queen Athaliah reigned and then Jehoiada could stand it no longer. He called the Temple and Palace guards together and introduced them to the real King who was now seven years old. 'Get your coronation drill brushed up,' he told them. 'We've had a mad old Queen long enough.' He issued to them the spears and shields that had been King David's and set the day and it was a splendid ceremony.

The old Queen, when she saw the boy with his crown on and the guards at attention and the trumpets blowing and the happy rejoicing people, screamed, 'Treason! Treason!' But the people remembered murder, murder, and Jehoiada thought it best that she were put to death. 'Not in public,' he said, 'nor here in the Temple, but at home.'

Jehoiada had great wisdom and gave that wisdom to the teaching of the boy King. The boy's name was Joash, and the high-priest taught him everything. Above all, a love for God and a love for God's great Temple where, after all, he had spent all his early childhood. He grew into a fine young man and indeed not since his ancestor Solomon had Judah had a king who cared so much for the Temple and its worship.

When King Joash was about thirty years old he said to his old foster-father the high-priest, 'A great deal of money comes into the Temple one way and another, yet not a penny gets spent on repairs or maintenance. I know that the priests have to live off the money that they are given, but the place is looking very shabby. I've spoken to the priests but they won't cooperate. Any ideas?' The high-priest had a think and invented what we now know as the collection box. The priests got some, but less. The box was by the door and when it was full it was emptied by the King's Secretary. He used most of the money to pay for a crowd of carpenters and stonemasons who soon had the beautiful Temple built by King Solomon looking spick and span again. Joash and the high-priest were determined practical men. They knew that the people had to be involved; that if your religion costs you a little you appreciate it more. Like anything else.

Never Kill a Prophet

Joash, brought up and taught by Jehoiada, was a sound practical ruler. But Jehoiada died when Joash was about forty. The middle years, when a certain silliness is known, even in the wisest. The old priest was buried like a king. Among kings. He deserved it. People remembered him – and his words. Pity they didn't take more notice of them. The rot began to set in right away.

After the funeral ceremonies came the entertaining by Joash of all the various powerful men who ruled the rest of his country for him. Not quite so well brought-up as he'd been. But persuasive; and as I said, powerful. In no time at all the restored Temple was being ignored. Idol-worship began. There were men who stood fast in their love of God, the only God, but there were plenty of the other kind. It would be pleasant to say that Joash, bred and taught by a man of God, emerged as a hero and brought his straying people back to the Law. Well, he didn't. There *was* a man; not unexpectedly the son of Jehoiada. He and Joash had known each other all their lives. He was called Zachariah, and it was to him, not to Joash, that God spoke when things had really got rather bad.

The next day Zachariah went to the Temple and climbed up till he was high above the people. He was known and a vast crowd gathered. Someone went and fetched Joash. Zachariah stood silent, looking down. His eyes were glowing, odd, unfocussed. He raised his arms and the noise of the huge mob died away.

'From the time of our fathers' fathers,' he shouted, not loud but every word could be heard, 'from the time that great Moses gave us the Law of God, we have known that to keep that Law was *right*, and that, if we did right, we, God's people, would grow and prosper. It was promised, spoken, written on stone. If we break the Law we are punished. If you forsake God, he will forsake you. Prepare then for punishment; you have forsaken God, now he has forsaken you.'

No one moved. Deathly quiet. To the idol-worshippers, the Temple-forgetters, this was the enemy. One of them bent down, picked up a stone. 'Does he think he is an angel of God?' he shouted. 'Stone him!' And the mob went mad – as mobs do. Zachariah was dragged down and beaten and the mob stoned him to death in front of the Temple doors.

Now Joash could have stopped it, but he didn't. He let the son of the man who'd been a father to him be killed for telling the truth. His own brother, near enough. After the stoning, the mob drew back and the King went forward to the battered, bloody body. As Joash halted, Zachariah's eyes opened. Joash was transfixed. It was like looking into the eyes of Jehoiada who'd taught him all he'd forgotten about honour.

Zachariah's bruised and broken mouth moved. 'May the Lord see,' he said, 'and avenge.'

The Lord did. Quite soon too. Before a year was out the country had been invaded by the Syrians and all the powerful, persuasive rulers were dead. King Joash, wounded in battle, was killed in his bed by servants who remembered Jehoiada, the priest buried among kings. But not before he'd given away most of the gorgeous treasures of the Temple to try to buy off the Syrian king. Sensible, you might think? Practical? A king who'd spent all his childhood in the Temple should have known better. Joash was not even buried among priests. He wasn't good enough. He was only forty-seven. Nothing sadder than when a promising man goes to the bad.

'The Rod of God's Anger'

King Joash was succeeded by his son. Twenty-five years old. Rather like his dad. Bit weak. Allowed the old trouble, the idol-worship, to continue; took no account of the value of God's help and thought he could do it all himself, just because he was a king. He thought that a king makes gods. Wrong. God makes kings. And everything else. Anyway, the new King of Judah made a big army. You might have thought he'd get his own back on the Syrians but instead he decided to take on the other kingdom of Israel in the north. The King of Israel wasn't keen but had no choice really. This was the king whom Elisha had encouraged on his deathbed to make war against Syria. And so he did. But here he was attacking Jerusalem, breaking its walls, and taking reparations from the Temple treasure. Surprising Elisha didn't turn in his new grave.

Anyway king followed king in both kingdoms. As the kings were, so were their subjects. Always the way. For a time Syria continued hostile, as Elisha had prophesied, and attacked both Israel and Judah many times. (Still is a bit troublesome, by all accounts!) But Hazael was dead now and Syria soon had troubles of her own from the north – the new and terrible empire of Assyria based on Nineveh. A much more powerful and sophisticated enemy this – in spite of the way one of their kings is said to have repented at the preaching of Jonah! Hard, cruel, unstoppable. Soon, having disposed of Syria, the King of Assyria was looking on past it to the divided nation of Israel with its two kingdoms and beginning to lick his lips. 'The rod of God's anger,' as the prophet Isaiah would soon be calling him.

He set to work on the northern kingdom of Israel first and demanded a crippling amount of gold and silver to stay away. It was collected by heavy taxation and paid. But this taxation bred a discontent, then a sort of revolution, and over the next few years the country nearly destroyed itself. Then the Assyrians, like a great cloud of locusts, swept down and the kingdom of the north was no more. Ten of the twelve tribes of Israel lived in the north and they were taken away in their tens of thousands. Slaves, prisoners of war, refugees, displaced persons. And they'd had so many warnings. Been given so many chances.

Samaria, the capital of the north, fell after a brave fight and its story was the same as the rest of the country. It was depopulated; its people captured and taken away. The Assyrians knew about killing resistance. They moved other people into Samaria. Beaten people, captives from other conquered lands. Many cultures, many religions, many idols worshipped in many tongues. The city, once great and important, became the place of discouraged and demoralized people. People with no status, no position, no standards. Eventually despised. The word Samaritans was coined for this motley lot. A term of abuse. Excuse my dwelling on this, but it makes the practical charity shown by a later 'good Samaritan' an even more valuable story.

Enter Isaiah

Well, the people of Judah had not always been on the best of terms with their fellow-Israelites of the northern kingdom. We've noticed that. But never can they have wished them a fate like this. Besides, there seemed every prospect that Jerusalem and its lovely Temple would go the same way as Samaria.

It is twenty years now since Samaria fell. And the King of Judah, like his father before him, has become accustomed to doing much as the Assyrians tell him. He pays huge tribute, shows respect, does as he's told. His name is Hezekiah. A sensible good man. At present rather worried. He had been led into joining a coalition of armies to try and stop the Assyrians and it had gone wrong. He'd done all this against the advice of a man who'd always counselled him well. A man called Isaiah. A shrewd careful man whom today we call 'the prophet Isaiah'. Who now stood before him, listening carefully.

'They demanded a fortune in gold and silver as a sort of punishment tribute,' said the King. 'I even had to strip the gold facings from the Temple doors. All the lovely silver things from inside the Temple too.' Isaiah said nothing. He was not the sort of man to say, I told you so.

'And now that I've paid it and apologized,' said the King, 'it's all for nothing. There's a tremendous army massing outside the city walls. Jerusalem will fall and it's all my fault.'

'It will not fall,' said Isaiah. 'I've told you dozens of times. This is God's city. Where the Tablets of Moses are kept. Where the Ark lives, where the Temple stands. I tell you again. Have confidence.'

But the great armies settled down all round the city. The King of Assyria sent high officers who told the frightened people lining the great walls in their own language exactly what they could expect. 'And forget your God,' they shouted, 'this Lord you think will help you. Did he help the north? Did he help all the tens of thousands of your brethren?'

King Hezekiah was worried sick. He went and talked to Isaiah. Described the huge forces, the thousands of archers, the great battering rams.

'Not one arrow will come into the city,' said the prophet. 'No soldier, no shield; no siege will happen. The Assyrians will go back the way they came. God said so. God will defend this city. It is his. God, and the Angel of Death who helped that time in Egypt.'

And it was so. The next morning nearly two hundred thousand of the Assyrians were dead. The great camps were silent. Cemeteries. The survivors were soon gone. They didn't come back. Jerusalem was left alone.

But good Hezekiah was succeeded by a son who was as evil as his father had been good. A terrible fellow. He even built idols *in the Temple*. God had him taken by the Assyrians, in chains, and brought near to death for a while. That taught him. He changed his ways quite a lot. But during his wicked time Isaiah grew very worried that the true ways of God would be forgotten entirely. Not many books in those days; even the Law of Moses handed down by word of mouth. So Isaiah and his disciples started to collect the Law in a book. Jews, and Christians too, have been people of that book almost ever since.

Jeremiah and the Fall of Jerusalem

We have seen how Isaiah and his disciples collected God's Law in a book, and with it a prophecy of the disaster that was in store for the people if it were neglected.

Nobody knew of this book at the time. It was found nearly seventy years later when a very good king was on the throne – Josiah, grandson of the wicked one. He was busy restoring the rather neglected and shabby Temple, and this old book turned up in an odd corner. It was like a bombshell. Josiah saw it as a sort of message from God and he began a clearing out of every idol, image and false god in the whole country. The people loved him and gladly turned again to the true God.

Well, as might be expected, God was pleased at this turn of events. And so was one of God's prophets. A man called Jeremiah. A wise shrewd man, Jeremiah. He knew that the things that had happened to the children of Israel were, to a large extent, their own fault. The old trouble. Idol-worshipping; God-forgetting.

'Good,' said Jeremiah to the people. 'Pay tribute to the Assyrians, and busy yourselves finding God again. The enemy is strong. Don't depend on miracles; you haven't deserved a miracle for some time.'

But Josiah, when he was about forty, decided to have a go. He was killed in battle. A sad loss. The people felt more than ever surrounded by their enemies. Like today.

Then, among these enemies, over the next few years huge shifts of power took place. New nations grew, the Medes, the Babylonians. Great battles raged around Judah. Egypt and Assyria joined forces and were both crushed. Assyria's great city of Nineveh, where Jonah went, was utterly destroyed. The Medes and the Babylonians shared the spoils. Judah became subject to Babylon. Left alone and at peace, so long as she kept up the payments.

'And so you should,' said Jeremiah. 'The new King of Babylon, Nebuchadnezzar, is not soft. Live as God said you should. Obey his laws. Babylon is a punishment. Do *not* revolt.'

But the King, Josiah's son, made the same mistake as his father. His attempt failed too.

Nebuchadnezzar took heavy toll. 'All the nobility to be taken to Babylon,' he said, 'all the artisans and skilled workers, and all the soldiers. *I'll* choose Judah's new king. Josiah's second-born. And I'll name him too. Call him Zedekiah. Easy work for a twenty-one-year-old. Very few people left to rule.' Then he left, with his huge army and the thousands of prisoners.

Jeremiah stayed by Zedekiah. Gave the same advice. 'Do not oppose,' he said over and over again. 'You can lose everything.' And for nine years the young King took heed.

Then, having raised and trained a few fighting men, he barricaded Jerusalem and shouted a defiance. It was a walled city and withstood the Babylonian siege a long time. But the time came when people were starving, so Zedekiah and his men went at night through the wall and made for Jordan and help. They were captured. Zedekiah was tried by Nebuchadnezzar and his punishment was dreadful.

His sons were killed one by one before his eyes: then he was blinded and led away to Babylon together with nearly everyone else left in Jerusalem. Then the Babylonian army moved in and smashed down the walls. Then they pulled down the great Temple. It was the end. Or so it seemed. The end of the Temple, of Judah, of the nation.

So sad. Mountains of rubble, which glowed golden when the sun went down. So sad. And odd. For the Babylonians were a people from Ur of the Chaldees, where Abraham came from. Where it all began. And where the people of Judah were soon to experience a new beginning.

Ezekiel Foretells the Return

In Babylon the two tribes which had formed the country of Judah were given a new name. It took too long to say 'People from Judah' or 'Judahites', so they were called 'Jews'. Their religion, which they took with them and were allowed to practise, Judaism. Nebuchadnezzar, King of Babylon, allowed his thousands of Jews more than their religion. He was no fool the King. They had many skills, these Jews, many scholars, many fine families. They were a valuable addition to any empire. They could show him much.

Mind you, Babylon had plenty to show the Jews. They were goggle-eyed. A wonder of the world. The great hanging gardens, the gorgeous buildings with their towering bronze gates, the wide avenues, the endless riverside embankments with their palaces and villas. The wonderful bridge over the Euphrates, and, even more fantastic, the Tower of Babel, heard of since the oldest times and now restored by the King. A great wedding cake of brick and stone in seven tiers nearly three hundred feet high. A wondrous magical city. Department stores, banks, huge markets, hundreds of temples and chapels and altars to every kind of god and goddess.

So the Jews remembered what Jeremiah the prophet had taught them. He had stayed on in Jerusalem and wept over it. But not for long. 'Don't weep,' he had said, 'don't look back. Establish yourselves, put down roots, make the best of it. Ignore their gods; you have your own religion; practise it.'

And the people did make the best of it. Very few doors were closed to them. Business, the law, industry, even the court – as the story of Daniel shows us. A boy from a good family in Jerusalem who rose to be right hand to the King of Babylon. And translated some writing on the wall for that King's successor which pleased him not at all. *And* all came true. We shall come to that story later.

Well, the years passed. Another prophet appeared among the people. Younger, harder than Jeremiah. Ezekiel. He had made the seven hundred mile trek from Jerusalem to Babylon and his eye was clear. He knew that the Jews now had to find God within themselves; not look for signs, portents, miracles. They'd had those, and turned away to other gods so many times. Now they had no Promised Land, no kings, no leaders. Only their religion and one, the only, God.

The people were discouraged, they felt forsaken. They thought that God lived in Jerusalem, in the Temple. Well, the Temple was now destroyed. Even if God still lived there, it was a long way for him to come. Ezekiel didn't rest. He had to teach that God is everywhere, that the exile was only a lesson, it would end one day but when didn't matter. 'God is here in exile with us,' he taught. He was a visionary and a magnetic preacher. And the people listened. They made a new life, they prospered, they turned out to be the good investment that Nebuchadnezzar meant them to be. But more important, their faith grew strong. In exile, far from the Promised Land, surrounded by every kind of idol and belief, they stopped the nonsense that had gone on for so long and brought them so much trouble, they served one God, and God was pleased.

Now Ezekiel began to prophesy a return. God granted him a vision and he translated it for the people. 'If you think of yourselves,' he told them, 'as a dead nation, a dried and scattered skeleton, a pile of dry bones, then hear the word of the Lord. Each bone will be connected to another bone ...' There's a lovely negro spiritual about it.

And of course it all came true.

Home Again

Now, let us for a while move our story from Babylon, where the Jews have been in exile for nearly fifty years, to Persia. And let us meet a remarkable man called Cyrus. He was the son of a King. A King who ruled over a small place. Cyrus was what today we might call a princeling. I suppose people called him that in those days too, when he was young! They were sorry. For Cyrus was not only a highly competent man with ideas of government far ahead of his time, but he was also ambitious. First he took the huge Median Empire from his own grandfather, then he moved north and west, conquering a vast area, the whole of Asia Minor near enough. Everywhere he brought a firm, humane rule. He removed one cruel despot after another and put his own men in. Even the King of Lydia, called Croesus, whose name still means untold wealth, was conquered and removed by Cyrus. He created new laws everywhere and gave the word law a different meaning – 'the laws of the Medes and Persians, which alter not'.

Then Cyrus, who created the Empire of the Medes and Persians, looked south, at the Babylonian Empire. Nebuchadnezzar, who'd taken the Jews into exile, had been dead for twenty years now and Babylon was ruled by a much weaker man, Belshazzar, who'd allowed his country rather to go to seed. He was the man who saw the writing on the wall and had Daniel in to tell him what it meant. Well, what it meant, Daniel told him, was that Babylon would fall to the Medes and Persians. And it did. Mind you, you didn't have to be too much of a Daniel to see that it probably would. After all, the great armies of Cyrus had been digging this huge trench right round the city for months.

The people, led by Belshazzar, had laughed at first. Theirs was the most important city in the world; mighty Babylon, with food stocks for twenty years of siege. The soldiers in the trenches would starve first. Their city, on the great River Euphrates, was protected by superb fortifications. It would last for ever. Also, they'd heard a story about Cyrus taking revenge on a *river* for drowning his favourite horse! He'd spent a whole summer cutting the river into nearly four hundred channels. The Babylonians laughed even more. 'All this power's gone to his head,' they said. 'Gone a bit mad. Trying to teach a river a lesson!'

Well, not quite. Maybe, as it worked out, Cyrus was trying to teach *himself* a lesson, about rivers. For when he took Babylon, on the night of the writing on the wall, he did it by diverting the Euphrates into the great trench, and he and his army went into the city along the river bed. They broke down the city walls here and there from the *inside*. And the overflow from the trench created havoc and confusion. Special man, Cyrus. In no time at all he got the river put back and the place dried out and some good government going.

The people were staggered. No killings, no marching-off of herds of captives, no interference even with the various religions and Babylonian idols. Cyrus, an Emperor, thought in terms of a commonwealth. With everyone benefiting by peaceful trade and shared knowledge.

Cyrus then looked at all the various peoples of Babylon, captives from so many lands. 'If you want to,' he said, 'you can all go back home. Government grants. Cheap fares.'

Well, this meant the Jews too, who had become very much a part of Babylon. Fifty years is a long time. Very few of the original captives still alive. New generations, new ways. Not everyone wanted to return to the Promised Land; where living, by all accounts, was much harder than in prosperous Babylon. But the Jews themselves were now different. Their *religion* called them back to Jerusalem. Their belief in God was strong. Isaiah and Jeremiah and Ezekiel had all been right; the exile was to punish and to teach. Now they had begun to learn, they were forgiven, and God's Temple must be rebuilt. In David's city, in Jerusalem.

So thousands gathered together and a great caravan of horses and mules and camels. Cyrus was generous. He gave the Jews all the vast treasure of gold and silver that Nebuchadnezzar had taken from the Temple so long before. Everything to the last bowl and chalice and candlestick.

It was a long way. With detours for water places, nearly nine hundred miles. It took a long time. Once back in the Promised Land people went off in all directions to try to trace family, but the Temple was begun. A simple altar, and regular sacrifice to God. The first big gathering of the people was the Feast of Tabernacles. Very apt. It was at Tabernacles, the Harvest Festival, that Solomon had dedicated the first Temple.

The Second Temple

The rebuilding began well enough. A good feeling everywhere. The returned exiles with their new strong belief in God, their careful practice of his Law, put their brains and their money together and chose their priests and their builders and got the work started. But then a lot of the local people, people descended from the various nations brought to Israel by the Assyrians as captives in the past, asked if they could join in. 'We believe in the same God,' they said. 'We have done since our fathers and grandfathers were brought here from other lands. All right, we may have intermarried a bit and have some different customs, we may not be the pure Jews you are, but still.'

It was a chance for a tolerance, an integration. But the exiles said no. They were jealous of their new letter-of-the-law Judaism and maybe afraid a bit also to let outsiders in. Anyway, the people not allowed to help decided to hinder, and there were a lot of them. The exiles built houses for themselves, schools, factories, even some synagogues, but no Temple. The building got no further than foundation level. Whenever the Jews attempted to return to it there were threats and trouble.

The years passed. Cyrus, founder of the Empire of Medes and Persians, died. Good Cyrus, by whose edict the exiles had returned to build their Temple and put back in it the glories and treasures that Cyrus had given back to them. Cyrus had even promised them, in the same edict, money and supplies. A witnessed document. An emperor's order. But now he was dead. So was his successor, his son. Now there was a new emperor, Darius, whose low opinion of the power of God had been radically changed when Daniel, now rather old, had walked, unharmed, out of the lion's den.

Enter now, as so often before, a prophet. In fact two. Haggai and Zechariah. They'd got rather tired of seeing that unfinished Temple and began a sort of What-have-we-got-to-be-afraid-of campaign. They prophesied that all would be well. They pulled up their sleeves and started work themselves. Soon there were others.

Well, the trouble-makers were soon busy and the Governor of the province turned up. 'By whose order are you building?' he said. 'What are the names of the people in charge? Whose servants are you?'

The elders of the Jews were polite. 'We are the servants of God,' they said, 'and we build to honour our God, and by edict of Cyrus. A witnessed document.'

Well, the Governor asked them to stop the work till he could write and get a reply from King Darius, but the elders said gently that they thought God would like them to continue. 'But write anyway,' they said. 'We don't tell lies.'

So a report was sent and Darius looked through the files and sure enough he found the document. He wrote back right away. 'Leave them alone,' he told the Governor. 'The edict is of the Medes and Persians, it must be honoured. We pay the full cost of the work and all sacrificial supplies. Everything from the meats to the wine and oil.' He then added some unpleasant details of what would happen to anyone who interfered. And signed his name.

It took about four years. Not as beautiful as the first Temple (which after all had had Solomon, a great connoisseur of the arts, in charge) but a splendid and nobly-appointed place of worship. About seventy years from the destruction of the first Temple to the dedication of the second. Almost exactly as foreseen by Isaiah and Jeremiah and Ezekiel. The voices of the prophets go through the Bible like a golden seam of common sense.

The Temple was finished in time to celebrate the Passover. When Jews remember their freedom from slavery in Egypt. It was a wonderful, heart-warming, emotional occasion. All the exiles and those of the land who'd joined them in their new, true Judaism made the eight days of the festival a joyous happy time. Among the huge sacrifices of bulls and rams and lambs was a smaller offering of twelve goats, to recall the scattered twelve tribes. A sad reminder of how fortunes can change for people. Now though, with their new Temple, the Jews felt that all was well. Their small country, Judah, was not their own; it was a province of the mighty Persian Empire, but their ruler, King Darius, was an enlightened and tolerant man. After the years of exile and the hardships that marked the first few years of their return, it seemed that a new age had dawned.

Ezra and Nehemiah

With the rebuilding of the Temple it seemed that a new age had dawned for the returned Jewish exiles. But it wasn't to last. Kings die. Time passes. Things change. After Darius, his son called Xerxes, or in the Bible Ahasuerus. This was the King with the rather bad temper who got rid of his first wife because she didn't like his boozy parties. And set up a sort of beauty competition to get a new Queen. He was lucky; he got Esther. Who managed to stop the mass-murder of countless Jews at the last minute. We could have used an Esther during the War. Marvellous story, Esther. We will have it a little later. Meanwhile, let us stay with the fact that Esther was a Jewess. The King didn't know it when he married her, but didn't mind when he found out. Wise king; labels don't matter, it's the person. The point is, there were a great *many* Jews in Babylon and Persia. Not all had wanted to go back to the Promised Land. The Jews had suffered *many* invasions and occupations. They were scattered now across *many* countries.

Well, Esther's husband died and his third son became King. Another odd name, Artaxerxes, sometimes called Longimanus or 'longhanded'. Complicated, isn't it? We'll call him 'the King'. He took over a huge empire and a magnificent court. The leaders of the various peoples living in Persia made their visits of homage and their oaths of loyalty. Soon the various sects and factions came with petitions to the new King.

The Jews sent one of their leading priests, a man called Ezra. He'd heard things about the Jews living in far-off Jerusalem he wasn't happy about. 'Also,' Ezra told the King, 'quite a number of your Jews here in Persia *would* like to return to the land of their ancestors.' Well, Ezra nagged at the King and at his flock, and eventually, about seven years later, the King let him lead about seventeen hundred Jews back to Jerusalem. He had the King's authority to examine affairs at all levels, both civil and religious.

Ezra wasn't pleased at some of the religious backsliding he found in Jerusalem, and said so forcibly. His reports to the King were clear, strong, to the point. He spoke of intermarriage and various other bad lapses among the people of Judah. He was a powerful preacher, Ezra, and he shook the place up. Eventually called a vast meeting in Temple Square and, whilst the thousands stood chilled to the bone in heavy winter rain, Ezra took his time and showed them the error of their ways.

The years passed and the King used often to mention at dinner to his guests the nagging he used to get from Ezra. He respected loyalty and single-mindedness, did the King. And such people he would raise to high office. He was no fool. One such person was Nehemiah, an important and trusted official of the court and cupbearer to the King. He saw the King at every meal. The King was used to him, and liked him. So, when for a day or two Nehemiah seemed a bit sad, the King asked him why. 'You're not ill,' said the King. 'What's troubling you?'

Nehemiah began to tell him and the King decided he would avoid, if possible, another nagging. He listened carefully. '... so you see,' said Nehemiah, 'the city of my fathers, Jerusalem, stands among rubble. The walls and gates broken down by your predecessor Nebuchadnezzar have never been repaired. They remind my people all the time that they are a conquered people. A fine city, with a loyal populace, a splendid Temple, surrounded by a waste of smashed stone and brick ...' He went on a while.

'Right,' said the King not wasting any time. 'Go to it. You can have letters of authority, requisition-forms for materials, and an escort of cavalry. Try not to take too long. Good cupbearers are hard to find.'

When Nehemiah arrived in Jerusalem, he could see that the

reports were not exaggerated. There was much to be done. Also he saw right away that there would be trouble with the Governor of the province.

In those days a walled city was an *important* city and the Governor of the province, a Persian Empire man, did not want a lessening of his own authority, either by the upgrading of one of his cities or by Nehemiah, who had arrived from the Persian court with powers equal to his own. Nehemiah didn't waste too much time with him. He surveyed the work to be done, at night, in secret. Then he called a big meeting, took over the governorship of the city and told the people his plan. His enthusiasm caught on. Volunteers and donations poured in. The work started.

Neighbouring gentile tribesmen, egged on by the deposed Governor, did their best to hamper the work, first by jeers and derision and then, as the walls began to grow, in more violent and threatening ways. Nehemiah was a realist. 'The work will continue,' he told the people. 'But every builder and labourer will be protected by an armed man. In one hand a tool,' he said to them, 'in the other a weapon.' Much of today's Israel has been built in the same way.

The people, reassured and protected, worked with a will. They knew from Nehemiah that *God* wanted this work done – and they did the whole job in fifty-two days! There was a great ceremony of thanksgiving. With their grand new Governor himself a Jew, and with Ezra the priest to declare and interpret God's Law to them, they had indeed a great deal to be thankful for. Advised by Ezra, Nehemiah made many good laws, carried out many reforms, especially concerning the financing of the Temple and the conduct of its worship. The people practised their religion, kept themselves to themselves and hoped the neighbouring countries would stop molesting them. And they did. For almost three hundred years. A happy ending to this section of our story.

IN FOREIGN LANDS

Jonah the Prophet

Now once or twice in the last few pages, I've found myself mentioning stories which needed to be told at some length but which we hadn't time to stop for if we were to get a proper picture of Jewish history. The Bible doesn't stop for them either. It tells them separately. The first of them, Jonah, is to be found among the books of the prophets. Not that Jonah wanted to be a prophet. He wasn't even very good at being a prophet, and was very cross about having to be one. Mind you, some of the things that happened to Jonah would have made anybody cross.

Jonah was quite an ordinary man. Not rich; not poor. Rather inclined to argue – with anybody. Hard-headed, obstinate sort of man. Even when he received a message direct from God he argued. Suddenly, straight into Jonah's mind God had spoken. Unmistakably God; and there was no mistaking the message either. God spoke clearly. 'Jonah,' he said, 'I have an errand for you. I want you to go to Assyria, to the great city of Nineveh, and tell them that I know how wicked they've all become and that in forty days from your arrival the city will be destroyed and the people will perish.'

Jonah thought for a minute and then decided to argue. 'Look, God,' he said, 'Nineveh is a long way and it's not the time of the year for long journeys – it's too hot. But the main point is I don't want to be made to look foolish. Look,' he said, 'you're not the kind of God that destroys cities and wipes out thousands of people. You're gracious and kind and slow to anger and merciful, and everyone knows it. I'll go all that way, make a lot of speeches and nothing will happen, and I'll look silly.'

There was a little pause and then God, who was rather used to people like Jonah said, 'Leave first thing in the morning.' And Jonah knew that he'd better shut up.

The next morning, very bad-tempered, he packed a few things together and started the long hot walk to Nineveh. He was cross when he set off and by the time he got to Jaffa he was even *more* cross.

Now the fact that Jaffa was a port gave him an idea. He said to himself, 'I won't go to Nineveh at all. I'll get a ship and go to Tarshish – in Spain. I'll hide. Who wants to be a prophet, and be made to look daft?' He found a ship that was going to Tarshish, bought his ticket and went aboard. Very silly. As he was soon to find out. He went below and very tired from his long walk he dropped into a deep sleep. The captain ordered the anchor lifted and they set sail. A hot calm day with a slight breeze. Very pleasant. Jonah slept on.

Now God, who was a little surprised at Jonah's disobedience, decided to take a hand. The skies became grey and leaden. The breeze stopped. Everything grew still and close. And then, suddenly, from nowhere, the hurricane struck! Panic was everywhere. Passengers and crew screamed and shouted and were full of fear. Jonah, below in a corner of the hold, slept on. The captain ordered everyone to pray to their various gods to find out which one was cross. Vows were made, sacrifices were promised. But of course nothing happened. The great roaring wind did not lessen one bit.

Then the captain came upon Jonah fast asleep and woke him roughly. 'Ah,' said Jonah, 'are we there?'

'*There!*' said the captain. 'The only place we're likely to be is at the bottom of the sea. Never known a storm like it. Sea's gone mad! Come on,' he said, 'up on deck. I've got everyone praying to their different gods to try and stop it. Up you go,' he said, 'get started.'

When Jonah came out on deck into the screaming wind and among the weeping, praying people, he knew at once what was up. He took the captain to one side. 'Look,' he said. 'It's my God. I'm a Hebrew and we only have one. There *is* only one. And he looks after everything. I've done something I shouldn't have – or rather I haven't done something I should have and this hurricane is all *my* fault.'

'Well,' the captain said, 'do something about it. Start praying.'

Jonah said, 'I don't think it would do any good. If I were you I'd have me tossed overboard. I've got a very strong feeling that's the only solution.'

The captain said: 'Have you tossed ... I couldn't do a thing like that! Had my own ship thirty years and never lost a passenger yet. I can't go tossin' – it's against the regulations! Besides it may not work and in these seas I couldn't guarantee to fish you out again. Also, quite frankly, I don't really believe there *is* only one God. Seems a lot of work for just one. Try praying. I'll come back.'

But the storm grew worse and somehow the word got round among the terrified people that it was all Jonah's fault. So, when the captain came back followed by the crew and passengers, Jonah got to his feet, apologized to the captain, and allowed himself to be dropped over the side.

Immediately the sea became calm and the hurricane died away and the sun came out and the sky became blue. As Jonah floated away from the ship he could hear the captain leading prayers to the one and only God.

A Second Chance

Time passed and now Jonah was all alone. Calm blue sea. Clear blue sky. Silence. He floated on his back, looking up to heaven and thinking, 'Now what?' Suddenly he was aware of being caught in a current. He turned over and looked ahead. He saw an odd sort of small island. It had no trees and seemed quite smooth. The current was swifter now and was carrying him towards what seemed to be a cave. As he drew nearer, he looked up. Above the cave, at either side, were small bad-tempered eyes. It was a whale! As Jonah opened his mouth to yell, the whale shut *his* mouth with a snap with Jonah inside. He was cold, wet, very frightened and he didn't like the dark and never had. There he sat inside the whale, he didn't even know what he was sitting on, and started to have a think about things.

'All right,' he said to himself, and his voice sounded echoey and spooky, 'all right, I disobeyed, but God could have sent someone else. *I'm* nobody. The message could have been given to someone important, a priest or a prince or something, not to me, I'm nobody.' And the words 'I'm nobody' went on echoing and ringing round the great vaulted inside of the whale for far longer than the other words until Jonah's head was banging. And then suddenly all was deathly quiet. Jonah was now looking at himself very honestly and seeing himself very clearly – as of course you can when it's pitch dark – and he saw that he was really at a very low point, the lowest ever, lost, alone, very unhappy – and all really his own fault. Maybe this down-into-the-depths-and-then-being-saved is what the Jonah and the whale story really means. But let's not get too theological. We must get on with saving Jonah. He now felt very humble and very wretched. He asked God to give him another chance. He promised to do as he was told. He remembered, and was grateful for, all the good things in his life given to him by God and spoke quietly and sadly into the vast listening silence for quite a while. When he'd finished he felt better. Of course!

Well, nothing happened for a time. And then, far off, Jonah began to see a golden glow. After the darkness it hurt his eyes a bit. It got no bigger. Jonah got up, stretched his cramped legs and walked forward. The glowing shining spot drew larger. Jonah walked faster and along the whale's tongue and out through the whale's open mouth and on to dry land! The glow was God's sunshine and the gold was the yellow sand.

Jonah stood and wept with relief and joy. As his clothes dried in the hot sun they began to smell a bit fishy, but he kept his mouth tight shut about it. He offered up a heartfelt prayer of thanks and waited for God to speak. He waited quite a while. Not a word. So Jonah thought that perhaps the subject ought to be broached by him. 'Er – God,' he said, 'I haven't forgotten the message. Not a word. You said I was to go to Nineveh and tell them that you know all about their wickedness and that in forty days after I get there the city will be destroyed and the people will perish. That's what you said. I was to go and tell them. And God,' he said, 'I'll go right away.' And he did. Straight from that empty beach to Nineveh. His steps were guided and his journey safe.

In Nineveh

Very impressive place Nineveh. For those days a big city. A hundred and twenty thousand people lived there. And God was right. The people *were* wicked and cruel and they *had* forgotten him. At first they all laughed at Jonah and were rather rude, but there was something about this cross little man and eventually Jonah was brought before the King. The King told him to stop shouting and to tell his story quietly. Which Jonah did. The King listened in silence and realized that it was all true. He *had* ruled badly and the people *had* all gone to the bad. He had a long serious talk with his government and then issued a great proclamation. He said, 'Everyone is to fast; you are to pray to God for forgiveness; you are to dress in sackcloth and you are to stop the violence and evil ways.' Then the King himself dressed in sackcloth and began *his* fast.

Jonah watched all this without saying much. He'd told his story and delivered the message. If this huge city had got themselves into this highly dangerous position it was their lookout. Mind you, in his heart of hearts Jonah didn't really believe that God would do it, but he said nothing.

In the course of a few days he saw a whole city change its ways. The gambling and the debauchery and the cruelty and the evil and the selfishness disappeared. The people walked in fear of the Lord, silent, fasting, praying. One day the King, who was now very pale and thin and wasn't a bad chap really, said to Jonah, 'Who knows,' he said, 'who knows, Jonah? Perhaps God may yet forgive us all. Perhaps he will lose his fierce anger and change his mind so that we don't all perish. Who knows?'

Jonah had, as we've seen, his own ideas as to how likely the all-merciful God was to wipe out a hundred and twenty thousand people. 'Ah,' he said, 'who knows?'

Now the time was nearly up. The people were hollow-cheeked and weary. Even the most hardened evildoers had mended their ways. There was no gossip, no rumours, no lies, no slander, no raised voices. Truth and honesty had come. People rediscovered simple values and they blamed only themselves and repented and prayed, from the heart, for forgiveness.

And of course God did forgive them. You cannot imagine such joy. It was like V-day and New Year's Eve and a great noisy wedding rolled into one. Every single person was filled with joy. Except one. Jonah. Jonah, who all the time had been pretty certain it wouldn't happen, when it didn't happen, went very strange indeed. He was so cross, so angry, that he rushed out of the city and sat on a stone in the hot sun and sulked. Meanwhile the city went mad with joy and God smiled down upon them. It was some time before God noticed that Jonah was not among the dancing, happy people and asked him what was wrong.

'Well,' said Jonah, who was now right back to his old argumentative self. 'Well, I was *right*! When you spoke to me at home about coming all this way with that all-wiped-out-in-forty-days message, I knew you wouldn't do it. I *know* you. You're *not* vengeful. You forgive people. I told you then that I didn't want to come and be made to look silly. That was why I disobeyed you and caught a ship to Tarshish instead. And all that business with the hurricane and that great smelly whale! I've frightened a lot of people half to death and I've had some very nasty experiences and all for *nothing*. So, if you don't mind, I'm going to sit here in the hot sun till I *die*.'

God said gently, 'Do you think you are *right* to be angry?'

But Jonah refused to answer and by nightfall poor Jonah was feeling very unwell.

During the night God made a large tree come up suddenly and all next day Jonah sat in its shade and began to feel better. During the next night God caused the tree to wither and die, and the next day Jonah, as the sun burned down again on his head, again told God he wished only to die. He felt very miserable and mistreated and, what with the heat and dust and a very nasty east wind which had started up, he began to feel a bit odd in the head too.

'After doing all those things to me,' he muttered to himself, 'the shipwreck and the whale and the long walk and the waiting around in Nineveh for forty days, the least he could have done was to keep his word and wipe 'em all out. The *least*.'

The sun grew hotter and the dust worse. Poor Jonah slept for a while. When God asked him again if he still wanted only to die he said wearily, 'Yes, Lord, I really think I'd be better off dead. I've had enough. Oh, one more thing before I finish,' he said. 'I want you to know I appreciated the tree. It was a nice thought. But, as you can see, the poor thing's withered away. Shame. Beautiful tree. Oh well.'

There was a sound which might have been the wind but which sounded like a loving chuckle. Then God spoke. '*Poor* thing?' he said. 'You feel *sorry* for the tree, Jonah? You think it a *shame*?'

'Well, yes,' said Jonah.

'Well Jonah,' said God, 'if you feel sorry for the tree which cost you nothing, which you didn't plant or tend, which gave you no trouble, should I not feel sorry for Nineveh? Should I not spare a hundred and twenty thousand people – over whom I've taken a great *deal* of trouble? They may be foolish and slow to learn right from wrong, but should I not spare them?'

And Jonah, at last, got the point. Have you?

Poor Blind Tobit

And now another story of Nineveh. You may not find it in your Bible. Or you may find it tucked away in a sort of appendix of later books called 'The Apocrypha'. But it's a Jewish story and a good one. And it begins, as I said, in Nineveh in the days when Nineveh had been taken over by the Medes and Persians and when Jews were to be found in all the main cities of the east.

In a very poor part of Nineveh, in what was little more than a mud-hut, lived an elderly couple and their son, a youngish man, the child of their later years, the child they'd waited a long time for. Maybe because of this they'd over-protected him and maybe that was why he, Tobias, was rather timid. Pleasant, certainly, but a bit weak and with not much push in him. Very fond of his little dog called Toby – although I think we'd better rename the dog Sam. Otherwise it's going to be confusing for us all. I'll tell you why. Tobias's father's name was Tobit. Dad called Tobit, son called Tobias, dog called Tony. No; the dog henceforth shall be known as Sam. Tobias's dad, Tobit, was about sixty, maybe a little more. Marvellous old man. Truly humble, do anything for anybody; give away his last penny. Which his wife, old Anna, used to say he'd just about done.

And, mind you, she had a case. They hadn't always been poor, in fact they'd been pretty rich. Tobit had been a merchant, who supplied the court and sold to the people at the same prices and with the same fairness and honesty. His door was always open to travellers who were tired or brethren who were hungry. Anna never knew how many she was catering for. She used to get cross sometimes. Very practical sort of woman Anna was. 'Some of your so-called brethren,' she'd say, 'are just a lot of hangers-on and spongers!'

'Ah yes,' Tobit would say, 'but some are not, and all men *are* my brothers. God said so. Anna dear,' he would say, 'if we are well off, it is God's will; if we are able to help other people, it is God's will.' Mind you, Anna believed in God, too – but a good nag helps sometimes.

But one day – a dreadful day – Tobit went blind. He was marvellous about it, a bit puzzled, very patient. Kept on saying, 'It must be God's will.' No nagging from Anna during *that* time. Nor during the time which followed, when misfortune followed misfortune. They lost everything. People did not rush to help. They forgot their debts to blind Tobit who'd never asked for either thanks or receipts. New people at the court at first looked greedily and then confiscated the old Jew's business. Such things happen. And, let's face it, son and heir Tobias, was no *strong* man.

So, here we are. Blind Tobit, Anna and Tobias – oh and Sam the dog – in their mud-hut. Nothing in the place to eat. Suddenly, Sam's tail went between his legs and his hair stood on end and he seemed terrified. The light in the doorway was blocked by a tall broad man carrying a larve heavy-laden basket. The sunlight behind his head gave him a sort of halo, thought Anna for a second. Then she said, 'Halo indeed! What do you want, young man?'

The tall man lowered the basket. 'I want nothing. In the basket is food. Meat, bread, wine, fruit. A fair amount of each. Er – it is a gift. The message is, "peace to Tobit, Tobias and to you Anna". Goodbye.'

'Just a minute, just a minute,' said Anna. 'Gift, message, all our names ... who *from*, the gift – God knows we need it – who *sent* the message – and who are *you*?'

The tall stranger, who hadn't moved, said, 'Yes, God knew you needed it – er – who am I? Er – my name is Azarias – the son of Ananias of Nephtha.'

'Ananias of Nephtha!' said old Tobit. 'I knew your father very well. Anna,' he said – (and she knew what was coming) – 'our friend will stay to dinner!' And the tall man did.

Although it must have been obvious to him that, for Tobit and his family, this was the first decent meal they'd had for weeks, Azarias gave them no sign of it. He helped unpack the big basket and get the food ready and at the dining table he was polite and pleasant, ate little and spread a sort of calmness round him. Tobias's little dog, Sam, however, was not calm. There was something about this tall stranger that Sam couldn't fathom. And neither could Anna. Like many old ladies, she got 'funny feelings' about people and she had a funny feeling about Azarias. Tobit, enjoying the food and the company, noticed nothing, nor did Tobias. But Anna and Sam the dog were right. This *was* no ordinary traveller – and his name was not Azarias either. It was Raphael. And he was an angel. An archangel, in fact. Special one. On a special mission. And the badly needed gift of food was only a tiny part of the mission.

Azarias – or Raphael if you like – smiled at Anna gently and said, 'I've been admiring your seven-branched candlestick and that lovely brass and leather chest in the corner. Beautiful.'

Anna was pleased. 'Yes,' she said, 'our only two nice things. All that's left. We had a lovely home once. Servants and comfort and everything. A candlestick and a box full of rubbish! All that's left.'

Tobit reached out his hand. Blind people know quicker than others when someone's upset. 'Not rubbish, Anna dear. Your wedding veil and my prayer shawl and the little painting of Tobias as a child, and some other little things. Not rubbish, my dear. Show our guest the little painting.'

Anna went to the chest and rummaged around. After a moment she came back. Not with the painting but with a small parchment. 'This is odd,' she said, 'I don't remember seeing this before. It's a receipt for a loan of ten talents of silver you lent to Raguel. Who's Raguel?'

'Raguel?' said Tobit. 'Oh yes. Oh, a nice man. Yes, I remember. Wanted to move his business to Persia. He was in carpets. Thought he'd do better there. Nice man.'

'I've no doubt of that,' said Anna, 'but did he ever pay you back?'

'Well,' said Tobit, 'if we still have his IOU ...'

'Ten talents is a lot of money,' said Anna, 'and we need it. Where does he live in Persia?'

'I've no idea,' said Tobit.

'Ecbatana,' said Azarias.

'I *beg* your pardon,' said Anna.

'How do *you* know?' said Tobias.

Azarias said, 'Er – yes, well, it may not be the right one but there *is* a firm called Raguel Carpets in Ecbatana. I – er – travel a lot and I was in Ecbatana only recently. This Raguel, I am told, comes from those parts.'

'That's him,' said Tobit, 'unusual name, carpets – and it *was* to Ecbatana he went, it's just come back to me. We'll get in touch with him. Splendid!'

'How?' said Anna. 'Send a paid messenger? We haven't a bean!'

'Send Tobias perhaps?' said Azarias.

'Tobias!' said Anna. 'He's never been further than the city gates! He'd be lost in half a day!'

'What,' said the angel, 'if I went with him? I – er – have to go roughly in that direction tomorrow. Good experience for him. Company for me.' He turned to Tobias. 'What do you say, eh? Chance to help your parents. Chance to show your Mum you're a big boy now.'

Tobias, who quite honestly was not a very adventurous young man, suddenly felt full of strength and courage. 'I'll go,' he said. 'We'll leave first thing in the morning!'

Anna, who was not used to her only chick rushing off into the unknown, started to say a lot of things against the trip but Azarias stopped her. 'Don't worry, Mother,' he said, 'your son is in good hands.' And of course, he was.

Tobias Falls in Love

By midday next day Azarias and Tobias were well on their way. They'd been walking since before dawn. It was now very hot and poor Tobias was feeling it. He wasn't used to such an open air life. And his companion, who showed no sign of heat or fatigue, was keeping up a fast pace.

'Do you think,' said Tobias, 'we could stop for a breather? I'm puffed.'

'In about twenty minutes,' said the angel, 'we come to a river. We'll stop and you can have a swim. All right?'

Sure enough in twenty minutes they came to the river and sat down. 'Coming in?' said Tobias.

'Er – no,' said Azarias, 'I'll watch the things.'

'And me too, please,' said Tobias. 'I'm not a very good swimmer.' And in he went. He didn't go too far out but he splashed about and was having a great time. 'Come on, Azarias,' he yelled, 'it's marvellous in, what are you afraid of? I'm a rotten swimmer and I'm not – Help! A shark – a whale – it's *huge* – save me!' Azarias stood up. 'Take the fish by the gills,' he called, quite calm, 'and hold its head out of the water. Don't be a coward and we'll have *it* for *our* supper.'

Well, there was a great noise and yelling and splashing and then Tobias appeared dragging rather proudly a very big fish indeed. No shark; no whale; but very big.

'Well, Azarias,' said Tobias, 'what about timid Tobias now, eh? I fought him with my bare hands and beat him! And look at the size of him!'

Azarias smiled. '*He* is tremendous and *you* are brave beyond words. Get your knife. We'll have a splendid fish supper, but first, listen carefully, cut out his liver and his gall and put them carefully away in your bag.'

Tobias couldn't see the point of this but did as he was told. They slept well that night and the next day continued their journey.

At last they came to Ecbatana in Persia and to the house of Raguel who made Tobias and his servant (as he took Azarias to be) very welcome. 'How wonderful to hear again of my old friend Tobit,' he said. 'Sad to hear he's gone blind though. Very sad. Poor Tobit. Of course you shall have the money – *and* all the interest over these years, whether your father likes it or not. Eat first, then when you've rested and cleaned up you'll meet Sara my daughter who'll be home later.'

When Tobias and Azarias had eaten they went to their rooms. Tobias was so travel-weary he hardly remembered bathing or anything else. Later that evening he was awakened by Azarias who was sitting on his bed.

When Tobias was sitting up, Azarias said, 'Listen carefully, this is about Sara, Raguel's daughter. She's very beautiful and quite young. Are you listening?'

'Yes,' said Tobias still rather sleepy.

'Well,' said Azarias, 'some time ago a demon fell in love with her –'

'A what?' said Tobias.

'A demon,' said the angel, 'and as demons can't marry young ladies (and what young lady would want to anyway?) the demon said, "Well, if I can't no one else will." Mind you, one or two young men have tried. Seven in fact. Poor Sara has been married seven times, and seven times on her wedding night her new husband has been strangled by the demon.'

Tobias was now fully awake. 'What a fantastic story,' he said, 'seven husbands!'

'And,' said the angel, '*and*, unless I am very much mistaken, you, Tobias, are going to be her eighth.'

Tobias sat up in bed and looked in absolute astonishment at Azarias. 'Do you calmly sit there,' said Tobias, 'and tell me that I'm to be the eighth husband of a lady I've not yet met, whose previous seven husbands were all strangled to death on their wedding nights by a demon who's in love with the lady? A *demon*?'

'Yes,' said Azarias, 'his name is Asmodeus; very ugly; tail like a dragon and very nasty breath.'

Tobias jumped out of bed. 'You're crazy,' he said. 'I thought so when you made me keep the liver and gall of that great fish and now I'm certain of it!' He crossed to the window, very angry. 'Anyway, I didn't come here to get married. I came here to collect the money Raguel owes my Dad. I didn't come here to marry Raguel's daughter Sara.' He looked down into the garden. 'Sara's seven husbands and her demon are *her* business and – oh, Azarias, that is the most lovely girl I've ever seen.' He was transfixed. 'Azarias,' said Tobias, 'do you believe in love at first sight?'

Azarias crossed to the window. 'Tobias,' he said gently, 'that is Sara.'

Raguel, Sara's father, tried to put Tobias off. 'Your father, my old friend Tobit, was good to me when I needed help. I can't put you, his son, in danger. It's not fair. Also I'm tired of digging graves for Sara's bridegrooms. Makes me ache for days. Don't do it, son.'

But Tobias, who now was sure that Sara loved him as dearly as he loved her, had made up his mind. 'It may be,' he said to Sara, 'that to marry you means to die but not to marry you won't be really living either.' So Raguel gave his consent and the eighth wedding feast was prepared.

On the day of the wedding Azarias took Tobias to one side. 'Now listen,' he said, 'and do what I say without question. When you and Sara go to your room tonight, light a small brazier outside your door and on it put the fish-liver I told you to keep. Not the gall; that's for something else; the liver. It will make a bad smell, but you'll be on the other side of the door. No, not a word. I promised your fine old Dad I'd look after you and this is my way. Trust me. All will be well.'

And of course it was. It wasn't Azarias making a bad smell. It was the archangel Raphael dealing with a demon and bringing a lot of previous experience to the job. Between you and me, he rather enjoyed it. When the demon arrived at the door of the bridal chamber, there was a bit of burning liver and it stopped him dead in his tracks. He got very mad and was going to try something even nastier – when Raphael stepped out of the shadows. And the fight was on.

They were evenly matched. Wing-tip to wing-tip there was nothing in it. The demon, of course, had his great tail but the angel was in better condition through cleaner living. They fought it out high in the sky and it took most of the night. As Raphael flew down to earth again, tired but happy, all the birds, who had been silenced long before by the demon, burst into song. Poor Raguel who'd spent most of the night digging the eighth grave was helped next morning by a very-much-alive Tobias to fill it in. Sara was radiant. Happiness was everywhere.

Raguel, when his back stopped aching, got busy. It was to be the richest, largest, longest wedding party ever known. Nothing was too good for his lovely daughter and his fine son-in-law. 'In addition to the money I owe your father,' he told Tobias, 'there's Sara's dowry plus half of all I possess – and I'm the biggest carpet man in Persia. It'll take a little time to work out and gather together, so go and enjoy the party.'

Happy Ever After

Well, the wedding party went on for about *three weeks*! People came from far and wide – for the story of the demon and the seven husbands was well known in Persia. Tobias and Sara lived in a cloud of tenderness and love. But one day Tobias said to Azarias, 'Look, I think I'm being a bit selfish. My Mum and Dad must be worried sick about me and I've been far too long at this shindig. Sara agrees. We go home tomorrow.'

Azarias smiled down at this new rather decisive Tobias. 'Right,' he said. 'Don't forget to pack the gall of that fish I told you to keep.'

Tobias was right. His parents were worried sick about him. So let us go back to where this story began, to Nineveh. Outside their mud-hut sit Tobias' parents, blind Tobit and Anna his wife. They'd seen a lot of trouble but this was the worst of all. 'He should never have gone,' said Anna for the thousandth time, 'our only child. I must have been mad. My poor Tobias! Never been further than the city gates and I send him all the way to Persia just to collect a debt – and with a complete stranger too.' Then, as people in distress sometimes do, she looked for someone to blame. 'If *you* hadn't lent or given money to everybody who asked you in the old days, he wouldn't have needed to have gone! Three months!' she wept, 'Not a word. Not a sign. That man Azarias has robbed him or killed him or sold him or something. As soon as I saw that man I wasn't happy. Something odd about him.'

Tobit lifted his tired old head. He said, 'I *never* saw him, I'm blind, but I knew that Tobias would be safe with him. There *was* something different about Azarias, but it was a good something.' Suddenly Tobit stopped. 'Listen!' he said, 'camel bells.'

'There are *always* camel bells,' said Anna crossly.

'No,' said Tobit, 'these are silver bells – and there is gay music; weddingy sort of music. Far off!'

Anna got to her feet. She was trembling. At first in the glare of the sun she saw nothing; and then it was a sight to see! Raguel had kept his word. A huge procession of camels, asses, servants, the bride and groom, and gifts and riches beyond description. And the joy and the kissings and the happiness and the wonder and the overflowing love can't be described either. You can guess what went on.

Azarias, tall, handsome, stood quietly by and watched old Tobit wiping tears of joy from his blind eyes. As Tobias passed he grabbed him. 'Tobias,' he said, 'listen carefully. Go and get the gall of the great fish which you caught. Rub it on a new silk handkerchief and give it to your Dad. He's old and very happy so he's crying a lot. Be quick.'

Old Tobit took the clean hankie. 'Thank you, Tobias,' he said, 'very thoughtful, a long time since I had a silk handkerchief.' He wiped his eyes. 'So silly to cry so much – but only for joy. Wonderful sort of handkerchief, and such a pretty design too ... Tobias, I can see!' And he could.

Well, the next half hour I won't describe either. Tobias, later, said suddenly, 'Where's Azarias?'

And Tobit said, 'Yes, I want to thank him – and see him too with my new eyes – and, Tobias, we must give him a most generous gift.'

Then, oddly, there was a sort of hush, and, oddly, there was Azarias, a little way off.

'He's changed his clothes,' said Tobias softly, 'looks *bigger*.'

Azarias looked at them one by one with great affection. 'I can't accept gifts,' he said to Tobit. 'Tipping's not allowed in my job. *Doing* the job is enough.' A sort of glow came from him. 'Tobit,' he said, 'my name is not Azarias. It is Raphael and I am an archangel.' He smiled. 'Always sounds so silly to say it out loud. Tobit,' he said, 'all your life you have *given* – which, where I come from, is regarded very highly. Because of this,' he said rather formally but with a twinkle, 'I am instructed to tell you that you and yours will live happily ever after.' And they did.

The Beauty Queen – Esther

We come next to the Book of Esther, ten short chapters, in my Bible only seven pages. Esther who won a beauty contest and got a King of Persia for a prize! The one with a funny name, you remember, Ahasuerus. But in this story we'll just call him the King.

The story begins in the royal palace at Susa, where the King is giving an enormous party for all his chiefs-of-staff and nobles and governors of provinces. Gorgeous marquees in the garden. All the royal cutlery and crockery on show. Most of it solid gold. Every kind of food and drink served. First class cabaret. And all this to go on for a week. In another part of the Palace, the Queen was giving a party too. For all the women. Rather quieter affair. She was beautiful, the Queen, and that, I suppose, was the start of all the trouble.

By the seventh day of these parties the King was rather drunk. Not surprising. 'Bring my seven chamberlains,' he said. And when they were all before him he said, 'Go to the Queen and tell her to put on her best crown and so on and to come to my party because I want to show her off.' But the Queen didn't want to be shown off and said no and that was it.

The King felt pretty stupid and was very cross and sent for his wise men. They listened and then the wisest one spoke. 'Very serious,' he said. 'The palace is buzzing with talk and gossip. Tomorrow all the guests go home and the word will spread and soon *all* the wives will start disobeying.'

'What shall I do?' said the King.

'An announcement,' they said. 'Right away. That the Queen is fired and all her goods and so on will go to the new Queen who will be chosen soon. Thus,' said the wise men, 'wives will know their place and in every home the man will be king.'

'Let it be done,' said the King. 'Good sense. That'll show 'em. When do I get the new Queen?'

Well, the chamberlains got busy and the great competition was announced. All entrants had to be young and beautiful. There would be heats and the finalists would live in the Palace for grooming for one year. Applications poured in.

Now, in one of the back streets of Susa lived an elderly Jew. (The Jews, you remember, had been carried off to Babylon some seventy or eighty years before, and colonies of them were now to be found in most of the cities of the east.) His name was Mordecai, of the tribe of Benjamin, and with him lived a young cousin whom he'd brought up after she'd been orphaned. A quiet, wise old man was Mordecai, and this girl Esther was his pupil, his daughter, his life. And she was beautiful. 'You are a special sort of daughter to me,' he told her, 'and you would be a special sort of Queen too. You must enter the competition.'

'Do you think I've any chance?' she said.

The old man looked at his lovely, graceful daughter with the quiet eyes and gentle wit. 'How can you lose?' he said. 'Do as they tell you but say nothing of me or of your religion. I have a feeling that God, our God, the God of the Jews, is guiding me and he will tell us when to reveal that you are a Jewess.'

So Esther entered her name and things seemed to go well for her right from the start. She just walked through the first heats and when the finalists moved into the Palace for the beautifying and grooming year, she quickly became popular. People just liked her. Especially the two men in charge of the whole thing. Hegai and Shashgaz, the King's eunuchs. They gave her good advice, extra lessons, taught her how to give orders quietly, to remember that all people have dignity, to show respect, to be a Queen. When Esther was declared the winner, Hegai and Shashgaz wept with joy. There was a great crowning ceremony and a national holiday and certain tax reliefs were announced and the King was very happy and very generous. He loved his new Queen at first sight and she was worth it. Old Mordecai was right, she *was* special.

The King's Vizier

Not long after Esther became Queen, Mordecai told her he had heard two of the King's chamberlains plotting to kill the King. She told the King and the two men were arrested, tried and hanged. 'Write all this down,' said the King, 'and don't forget to put down the name of Esther's loyal friend, who gave us the warning.' After this the 'counsel of chamberlains' method was looked at and the King decided that he would appoint a Grand Vizier over all the chamberlains and princes and nobles of the court and he did. But he wasn't much of a judge of character, the King, and he gave the job to a chap called Haman, who not only had great ambition but also great cunning and cruelty.

Well, the new Vizier lost no time in making his presence felt. He had a throne made and sat always by the King's right hand. He treated people like dirt and made laws regarding his own importance. 'Everyone will show the Vizier great respect,' he had posted up. 'Everyone will kneel or bow as he walks by.' And everyone did. Except one. Old Mordecai, who was not young, and saw Haman for what he was, and was quite unafraid anyway. 'Also,' he would say calmly, maddeningly, 'I am a Jew, and we save our kneeling and bowing for God.'

Well, all this made Haman very angry indeed and he decided to destroy not only Esther's father but every single Jew in all the provinces ruled over by the King. He took his time and made plans and spoke often to the King of a 'strange people' scattered throughout the vast lands with 'their own laws and practices.' He hinted at disloyalty, rebellion, disturbance, sabotage, all the age-old reasons for mass murder. Having got the King thoroughly flustered and worried, he then put forward a brilliant plan for the final solution, the extermination of every single one. 'All on one day,' he said. 'Every one of 'em. At my expense.' He went on and on and the King, dizzy with it all, signed the orders and the notices went out. You can imagine.

Well, Mordecai heard about these arrangements for mass murder. When he told Esther, she was shocked. 'I don't know what to do,' she said. 'When the King fired the last Queen for disobedience, new rules were made. To go to him without being asked is absolutely forbidden. If anyone approaches the King without being summoned it means death unless the King points his sceptre.'

'Points his sceptre?' said Mordecai.

'Yes,' said Esther. 'If he does you live. If not, you die. Even me. I haven't seen the King for a month,' she said sadly. 'He's locked up with Haman from morning till night.'

Mordecai looked at his beautiful daughter. 'With God's help,' he said, 'you became a Queen. It may be that if you do nothing you will escape death. You will not die. Except,' said Mordecai, 'of shame.'

Esther stood up. 'Beloved father,' she said, 'gather your friends and let them fast and pray for me. I and my women will do the same and in three days' time I will go, unbidden, to the King. And if I perish, I perish.'

On the third day, Esther got up early. She'd hardly slept and felt rather weak from lack of food. She dressed carefully and wore no jewellery. She did her hair simply. Only a very little make-up. Her ladies-in-waiting, normally a talkative happy crowd, were silent. This could be the last time they would ever see their beloved mistress. One by one they came forward and kissed Esther on the cheek. Then they walked with her to the flower garden that separated the King's apartments from the Queen's. They stopped and Esther walked on alone.

It was quiet. The murmur of a fountain. A little birdsong, not much. The soft steady sound of her own feet. She came to the first door and, as she went into the cool corridor, she felt cold.

She walked on. Four more doors to the innermost private sanctum where the King sat with Haman.

One, two, three, four. Esther stood in the doorway. She was pale, quiet, still.

Then the King looked up. 'Hello darling,' he said. 'How nice to see you.' Then he pointed his sceptre. 'That's a nice dress,' he said. 'I like it.'

Esther let out a long fluttery breath and walked forward.

'You look a bit upset,' said the King. 'We can't have that, can we? Let me give you a nice present. Something *very* nice. You can have anything you want. Anything at all. Just ask.'

Esther looked into the King's smiling face, then at Haman, who seemed just lately to be more powerful than the King. She closed her eyes and asked God if this was the moment and God said not yet.

The King leaned forward and kissed her. 'Had a think?' he said. 'Well, what would you like?' She smiled. 'What I should *really* like,' she said, 'is for you to come home for dinner tonight.' She looked at Haman. 'You come too,' she said. And they did.

It was a splendid dinner and at the liqueur stage the King again told Esther she could have anything she desired and again she asked only that he should take an evening off. 'Tomorrow,' she said.

'Come to dinner again?' said the King.

'Yes,' said Esther.

'Me too?' said Haman.

'Yes,' said Esther.

Well, Haman went home that night and told his wife everything. 'Dinner with the Queen tomorrow *too*!' he crowed. 'Two days *running*! Just her, the King and *me*. Equal to the King I am! *Great* honour. I'm a great expert on honouring.' He went on and on and then stopped. 'And *still* that old man won't bow or kneel to me,' he said.

'I know what,' said his wife. 'Don't wait till your special kill-'em-all day, attend to the old man right away. Get some carpenters and have a gallows built, a nice one, near the Palace, and tomorrow tell the King you're going to hang the old man as a sort of before-dinner entertainment.'

Haman looked at his wife with great affection. 'You're a very clever girl,' he said, and he gave the orders right away. Then he went to bed and slept like a baby. Very happy.

The Tables Turned

But at the Palace the King couldn't sleep. So he asked to be read to. 'Bring the Book of Memorable Deeds,' he said. 'Read to me from that.' So the King's Night Reader was sent for and the King lay and listened. The Reader began with the most recent deeds and soon was telling how Mordecai had saved the King's life by discovering the plot by the two chamberlains.

'How was he rewarded?' asked the King, who had not even bothered to enquire the name at the time. Simply had it written in the book.

'In no way,' he was told. 'Nothing was ever done.'

'Disgraceful oversight,' said the King. 'Send for Haman.' So they went and woke him up and he came over.

Haman didn't mind. It would be a good opportunity to talk to the King about hanging Mordecai.

But the King was the first to speak. 'You're an expert on honouring,' he said. 'Tell me a really big honour for someone I'll be delighted to honour.'

Haman smiled to himself. 'He means me,' he thought. 'For my kill-'em-all plan.'

'For such a man,' he said to the King, 'only the best. Let him be dressed in a robe of the King's; let him ride on the King's horse. Let the horse be led through the city by one of the King's most noble princes who shall call out, "This is the man the King delights to honour".'

'Marvellous,' said the King. 'You be the noble prince and go and do all this for an old man who saved my life.' He picked up the book. 'Here's his name and address.'

Well, what could Haman do? It was the worst day of his life and made much worse by the modesty and lack of malice in old Mordecai who seemed to be looking up to heaven and smiling all the time.

When they arrived back at the Palace, it was time for Esther's second dinner party. Even better than the first and the King said so. Also he said again, 'Esther dear, I think you want to ask me something. What is it? Anything. I would give you half my kingdom.'

Esther stood up. She was a bit white but very beautiful and composed. 'I am to be killed,' she said. 'I and the people to whom I belong. Orders have been given and it is to be done quite soon. I ask the King,' she said formally, 'to spare my people and thus spare my life also.'

The King could hardly speak. 'Orders!' he roared. 'Orders? What orders? Whose orders?'

Esther pointed at Haman. '*His* orders,' she said. 'Haman's orders. Sealed with your ring,' she added gently.

The King got up. He was trembling with rage and shame. Haman was just trembling. The King went out into the garden and walked around to cool down a bit. He saw what he had nearly done. When he came back into the Palace, Haman, now terrified, was pawing and clawing at Esther as she sat, imploring that she save his life.

That was the last straw. 'Take your filthy hands off my wife!' roared the King. 'You're not fit to be in the same room with her!'

And that was the end of Haman. The gallows he'd had built was ready. He'd paid for it, it was his, it seemed a waste not to use it, so they hanged him on it. Then because the time now seemed right, Esther had Mordecai brought in and told the King that he was her father. The King was delighted to be related to such a wise and good man and offered his father-in-law Haman's job which the old man accepted. He called a meeting right away, borrowed the King's seal-ring and cancelled all Haman's orders. And so a lot of Jewish lives were saved. As I said when I mentioned this story before, we could have done with an Esther in Hitler's Germany.

Daniel and his Friends

After the Book of Esther in the Bible come the Wisdom books – the Psalms of David, the Proverbs of Solomon, the Song of Solomon, and the sayings of other wise men – not forgetting Job, who suffered so terribly – the loss of his property, his children, his health; unhelpful advice from his wife and his friends; and finally something of a telling-off from God himself, who afterwards made it all up to him. But these are not stories; we must pass them over. As also the books of the prophets – Isaiah, Jeremiah, Ezekiel. We've already seen the place of these great prophets in Jewish history. But the next book, the Book of Daniel, is different. Full of stories. He was a prophet, yes. But in Jewish Bibles his book is placed not among the prophets but among the histories. Straight after Esther in fact, though the stories it tells must have happened some forty years earlier, not in Persia but in Babylon, where the Jews had been taken into captivity by King Nebuchadnezzar.

Well, Nebuchadnezzar, King of Babylon, was no fool. He had use in his large empire for many skills and knew all about finding the right young people and training them. And now he had in his kingdom thousands of these highly civilized people from Judah. Valuable people who could enrich his nation.

So one day he sent for the head of his household, an old friend called Ashpenaz. 'These Jews,' he said, 'they are now of Babylon and their noble and royal families are as old or older than ours. Among them are many youngsters of a very good type. Go through them carefully. Select the best. Not too many. They will live in the Palace, learn our language and customs and at the end of three years I'll hold exams and they'll join the staff.'

Ashpenaz was careful. He knew the King had high standards. Eventually he sifted down his selections to the final group. He lined them up. Roll call. Given new names, by the King's order. The last four to be renamed stood together. Obviously close friends. They answered with their old names and Ashpenaz gave them their new ones. 'Shadrach,' he said to the first; 'Meshach' to the second; 'Abednego' to the third. Then he turned to the fourth. Handsome boy. Steady clear eyes. A gentle smile. Ashpenaz had marked him from the first. He returned the boy's smile. 'And what's your name?' he asked, although he knew. 'Daniel,' came the reply. And Daniel we shall call him in this story. His new name doesn't matter.

Then Ashpenaz issued all the other orders. Subjects to be studied, homework, lesson times, recreations, games, mealtimes. And food. 'The best food,' he said, 'from the King's own kitchens, and wine from the Royal Cellars. As much as you want. You are to be kept in perfect condition, and the King believes in good food.'

The boys looked pleased and Ashpenaz dismissed them. But Daniel and his three friends hung back. 'May I speak to you a moment sir?' he said. 'It is important.'

Ashpenaz nodded; this was not a boy to waste his time.

'It's the food and wine,' said Daniel. 'All four of us come from orthodox families and have never eaten certain foods because our religion forbids them. Neither do we drink wine. Do you think,' said Daniel, 'we might have fruit and vegetables and plain water instead?'

Ashpenaz was stunned. This was right outside his experience. He knew about eccentrics and cranks, the court was full of them, but these were quiet, well-behaved youths with a sort of dignity. He was flustered. 'It's very difficult,' he said. 'You see, it's not me, I don't make the orders. The King does. I only carry them out. To the letter. Good food means good condition. The King said so. If I do differently, if I go against him, I could lose my *head*. I'm not joking!'

'We don't mean to be difficult,' said Daniel, 'or to get you into trouble. Will you let us eat what we ask for ten days? Then compare our condition with the others. Then, whatever you say, we shall do.'

Ashpenaz was about to speak when Daniel added, 'We don't make the laws. God does. We only carry them out.'

And the old servant knew that the boy was not being funny. 'All right,' he said. 'Ten days. Keep it to yourselves. I'm not sure whether all that rich food and wine is good for the King either.'

And of course at the end of ten days Daniel and his friends were in great shape. Even heavier. Ashpenaz was convinced, and made all arrangements. He was very fond of 'the quartet' as he called them and they showed him great respect. As the months turned into years he saw his quartet sweep the board at every prize-giving. They worked hard and were always cheerful. They were much liked and bred no jealously among the other young men. As the end of the third year approached, the schooling changed its character rather. These were to be young men of the court, of the government, of the ministries, a certain polishing began. Particular talents began to emerge. Diplomacy, directness, leadership, oratory. Daniel possessed all of these and something else too. He discovered in himself the ability to interpret dreams, to understand visions. An extra sense. Special. God-given.

So. End of term. End of school. Passing-out parade. Diploma day. Ashpenaz sad but rather proud. 'I shall miss you four,' he said. 'You've passed out top. But now you're on your own.' So Daniel and his three friends entered the royal service.

They soon saw that the King's power was absolute, his every wish was a command. 'They are young,' said the King, 'but already men and wise. And that will be their job. Wise men. I want them near me at all times.'

But Nebuchadnezzar was no tyrant. Quite a human sort of person really. Bit of a worrier, often had bad dreams and would look pale and tense for a day or two until the soothsayers had soothed and the magicians and enchanters had cooked up for him a lot of rather flattering interpretations of his nasty dreams.

Daniel would listen and say nothing. Like his distant ancestor Joseph he had a true gift for reading the meanings of dreams and visions and he knew it. But he was a new boy and kept quiet.

One day, though, it was different. Daniel wasn't there, and neither was Shadrach, Meshach or Abednego. The King had got up in a shocking state and had demanded a full muster of all the magicians and sorcerers and dream-readers. They filled the Great Hall. Trumpets sounded, gongs banged and the King was helped to his throne. He looked awful. Pale and trembly.

They waited. Then the Chief Wise Man stepped forward. 'Tell us the dream, O Lord,' he said, 'and we will tell the meaning.'

The King looked up. 'I can't remember the dream,' he said, 'that's just it. I only know how it's left me feeling. Worse than ever before. It must be important. Tell me what it was. And be quick.'

The wise men blinked. 'We can tell you what it *meant* –' began one of them.

'I know you can,' said the King. 'This time that's not enough. First tell me what the dream *was* – and *then* tell me what it meant!' The King looked very bothered indeed and a bit mad.

The great crowd of magic-doers were thunderstruck. They began to play for time, to make speeches, to try to calm the King. The flattery began.

He stood it for a while, then got to his feet, white with fury. 'Send for Arioch the Captain of the Guard,' he said. 'A special job. The killing of every so-called wise man on the payroll.' Then he left.

Absolute pandemonium. Arioch posted up the notices, sent the message, drew up lists. Efficient man. He went himself to Daniel, whom he liked. Told him regretfully that as he, Daniel, now had the honour to be one of the King's wise men he was to be killed too.

'Arioch,' said Daniel, 'make an appointment for me to see the King. Don't kill anyone. I think I can help the King.' Then he and his friends prayed and God, who had arranged the whole thing, gave him the answers and Daniel told the King first the dream and then its meaning. Not flattery, not nonsense, but a logical-sounding prophecy.

The King, deeply impressed and comforted, then heaped honours upon Daniel and his three friends and forgave the rest of the wise men. Who however did not forgive Daniel *or* his friends who were soon made by the King rulers over whole provinces. Daniel himself the King kept by his side. Second-in-command, no less.

Nebuchadnezzar Humbled

Now, although the King had said some nice things about this God of Daniel's who'd helped with the dream business, it didn't stop him making a great golden idol over ninety feet tall and arranging a huge ceremony of dedication. Officials and delegates from every part of the Empire were invited. Special music was written for huge orchestras and this music was played at certain times and strict orders were given that when the music played all the people had to do a sort of all-fall-down and worship the great idol. If you didn't you would be thrown into a pit of fire, a fiery furnace. The idol was the *real* god, because it was the *biggest* – and of *gold*, so no praying to any *other* gods. If you did, the furnace.

The sorcerers and magicians and soothsayers kept watch and in no time were telling tales on Shadrach, Meshach and Abednego. 'Rulers of provinces,' they told the King, 'whom *you* honoured, who ignore the orders and pray only to their own Jewish God.'

The King who should have known better, especially after the dream business, lost his temper, and when Daniel's three friends flatly refused to all fall down he was even more foolish. 'Make the furnace seven times hotter,' he bellowed. 'Tie 'em up and let strong men carry them right to the flames and throw 'em in.'

All was done and the strong men were burnt to a cinder. The flames roared: white hot. In the middle, Shadrach, Meshach and Abednego, having a quite stroll in conversation with a visiting angel whom God had sent to keep them company! You can imagine the state the King was in. He'd thrown in three and he could see *four*. And when the angel disappeared and the three Jews came out there was not even a smell of burning on their clothes. Not a hair was singed. Only the ropes and chains which had bound them had gone. Completely. They walked free.

The King then made a lot of speeches and issued statements saying that the God who could do what they'd all just witnessed must be a special God. *Very* special, and that anyone who said anything different would get into serious trouble.

The King was too proud to say that he himself believed in the Jewish God and God noticed his pride. So God prepared another lesson. Rather harder one, but maybe God was remembering that the King had destroyed the beautiful Temple in Jerusalem. Anyway it took the form of another dream. Not forgotten this time, recalled in every worrying detail by the King. Who sent for his friend and right-hand man, Daniel.

Daniel listened carefully and then looked very worried for he liked the King.

'Is it bad?' asked the King. 'Never mind, I must know.'

Daniel said that he wished that what he had to say was about the King's enemies, for it *was* bad. Then he went on to give the meaning of the dream, which was that the King, the great and powerful King, would one day live away from men – in the open like an animal. He would eat grass and have long matted hair and claws. He would live wet and cold and naked. But the kingdom would be safe for his change-back, which would depend on how truly he believed.

All this took a long time to tell and the King was silent. What could he say?

'The dream doesn't say when,' said Daniel. 'Maybe if you change your ways a bit it might not happen. Be righteous, show more mercy, be less proud and so on.'

But it did happen. A year later, right in the middle of a rather boastful speech in which the King was telling of his great power and majesty. It happened exactly as foretold, to the last detail. A great king was changed into a strange creature, neither man nor beast. Set apart. Dumb, with no place. But time passed – twelve whole years – and a day came and the King changed back and there were other changes in him too. He was more humble and thus a better king. More simple in his way of life. Had no more doubts as to who the true God was. (No more bad dreams either.) And his new faith made him happy till he died.

Belshazzar's Feast

Now five years after Nebuchadnezzar died his son was deposed by one of his most ambitious subjects. So ambitious that he moved on into Arabia to do a bit more empire-building, leaving his son Belshazzar on the throne of Babylon. Meanwhile Cyrus of Persia was the coming man and Belshazzar had to pay tribute to him. That no doubt made Belshazzar all the more particular to assert his royal dignity in Babylon. Even made a point of speaking of Nebuchadnezzar as his father. But he had no use for

Nebuchadnezzar's new-found faith in the God of the Jews. Daniel soon faded into the background. Until the day when King Belshazzar threw his biggest dinner-party – and his parties were famous.

Belshazzar always tried to have a moment at each of these great gatherings when he would give his guests something to remember. A very special exotic dish, a unique cabaret, a costly gift for everyone, a moment. Well, he certainly gave them a moment on this occasion. Unforgettable indeed. The party was already at its height. Then a great clash of gongs and a silence. Up got Belshazzar. 'A special wine!' he shouted. 'Superb. And you shall all drink it out of very special cups. The vessels and goblets that my father, King Nebuchadnezzar, took from the Temple of Jerusalem. Let's see whether the wine tastes different in *holy* glasses! We'll toast all *our* gods!' he roared. 'Every one of 'em – from the god of wood to the god of stone!'

Out came the beautiful cups and goblets and bowls, all in gold and silver, and the wine was poured. As the King took the first sip there was an odd change in the light. The wall at the end of the great hall began to glow and shimmer. The laughter and shouting died away. Then, before everyone's eyes, a man's hand, just the hand, grew out of the air and with one finger wrote words on the wall and then faded away. The hand faded; the words remained.

The King was white and scared. The magicians and sorcerers and astrologers were sent for. Huge rewards were offered. Prime ministerships were promised. Nothing. Nobody could either read the strange writing *or* tell its meaning. No one.

But the Queen Mother, Nebuchadnezzar's widow, remembered something. 'Stop trembling,' she said to the King. 'There *is* someone. Daniel. In my husband's time he was the top man over all this lot. He interpreted dreams, explained riddles and read signs time and time again. Never wrong.'

So Daniel was sent for and the vast rewards and gifts were offered to him. The King made the offer himself. He was impressed by Daniel.

It wasn't mutual. 'Keep your gifts,' said Daniel. 'The meaning won't please you. Your father, as you call him, was taught by God, my God, the only God, that pride is a sin. When he was at the height of his power everything was taken from him and he was changed for a while into a creature neither man nor beast, with no place. The lesson he learned then – that *God* decides the fate of men and must be honoured – you seem to have ignored. You have used God's holy vessels to toast and praise idols that are nothing. As you are nothing; other than what God allows you to be.' Daniel paused. 'God has decided to end your kingdom,' he said. 'He has considered it carefully but you are not worthy. Babylon will fall to the Medes and Persians. And that,' said Daniel, 'is the meaning of the writing on the wall.'

All came to pass. That very night the King was killed. We don't know how. And Babylon was occupied by the Persians.

The Lion's Den

The King of Persia, Darius the Great, put in now governors of his provinces, a hundred and twenty of them, all answerable to three Presidents. He had heard of Daniel and made him one of those three top men of his kingdom. It mattered little to Darius that Daniel was not of Babylon but was really an exile from Judah, a Jew. It mattered a lot to the other top men though, *and* to all the governors and councillors who had to answer to Daniel. They hated him. And the more Darius trusted Daniel the more jealous they became. So they did a little plotting. Daniel was an incorruptible man, an absolutely honest man, a loyal man. Difficult to discredit or destroy such a man. So the plotters, knowing that Daniel was deeply religious and that he prayed every day to his God, three times a day, and had no time at all for their idols and images, decided to get at him *that* way. They prepared an order, a law dealing with a short period, called an *interdict*, which said that anyone making petition or request to any power but the King's within the next thirty days would be cast into the palace den of lions. They presented it to King Darius with so many heretofores and howsoevers and suitable legal language that he, poor chap, didn't know what he was signing.

Within the week they were back with lots of witnesses to say how President Daniel just ignored the new law and petitioned and requested and prayed to his God. Three times a *day*. 'And the law is of the Medes and Persians,' they shouted, 'and cannot be revoked.'

Poor Darius! He knew what he'd done and tried every way allowable to undo it, but it was impossible. He had established a law and it could not be set aside, not even for a friend. Daniel also knew how he had been betryaed but said nothing, just prayed as usual, three times a day.

Well, the plotters brought the order for Daniel's death and the King signed it and he and Daniel went down to the palace zoo together. 'You have served me with the same devotion you serve your God,' said the King, 'and I have killed you. May your God treat you better than I have.'

They shook hands and Darius could not see for his own tears. The cave of lions was sealed with a great stone and then with the seals of the King and court. Darius went to his Palace and mourned for his friend. He would eat no food and could not sleep a wink.

As dawn broke the King went back to the cave. He didn't know why, a wild hope, maybe Daniel's God could do even this thing? Daniel was quite unharmed. The lions had shown no interest in him at all though they had been starved by the plotters for days. When Daniel had lain down among them for warmth, they'd made room!

Darius was overjoyed. And when not one word of reproach came from Daniel, the King saw clearly who served him best and gave a few orders regarding the plotters and the lions didn't go hungry after all!

Then Darius made a great proclamation in all the languages of his great Empire that Daniel's God, the God of the Jews, was the living God, everlasting. A God who creates signs and wondrous things – 'and who saved my friend Daniel,' wrote the King, 'from the lions.'

THE NEW JERUSALEM

'Abomination of Desolation'

The second half of the Book of Daniel is taken up with dreams and visions. Dreams and visions concerning the various empires that would rise and fall. And their various rulers, some good, some bad, until the reign of a really terrible man. A man who claimed to be a god. That's what the second of his two names implies. Antiochus Epiphanes. Set up his own statue in God's Temple at Jerusalem. 'The abomination of desolation,' Daniel called it, 'standing where it should not.' But not for long.

Well, we left Jerusalem, you remember, under a Jewish governor, Nehemiah, its Temple newly rebuilt and rededicated and its people happy and united, left at peace by their neighbours, a semi-independent territory within the vast empire of the Medes and Persians. But soon the changes dreamed of by Daniel began and they were to be huge. The mighty Persian Empire had spread and reached out even as far west as Greece. Athens was burned. But when the Persian Empire fell, it fell to a Greek. To Alexander the Great, warrior extraordinary, a regent at sixteen, educated by Aristotle. A king at twenty. A conqueror. Stopped only by his own death, at thirty-two, of a fever, in bed. A remarkable, rare man. Every land from Egypt to India he took and, having taken, ruled with justice and without blood. After he died, a group of his army commanders cut up the vast Empire between them. They fought among themselves for years, like dogs over a bone.

One of these commanders, a man much trusted by Alexander, was named Ptolemy, and he ruled Egypt and Libya and Cyrene. He was an educated man and made Alexandria, named after Alexander, a great seat of learning. Over the years many Jews have made their home there, soon speaking only Greek. Legend has it that Ptolemy arranged the translation of the Law and Holy Books of the Jews because *he* wanted to read them. Seventy scholars, so it is said, did the work in seventy days. On a small island near to Alexandria. This version, the Septuagint, was of great use to the Greek-speaking Jews.

This Ptolemy founded a dynasty of Egyptian kings. Not all as good or enlightened as he, but all called Ptolemy. Another of Alexander's generals, Antiochus, founded a similar dynasty in Syria. Jerusalem was now part of what was called, till a few years ago, Palestine. As Ptolemy succeeded Ptolemy in Egypt and Antiochus Antiochus in Syria, Palestine changed hands between them many times. But in the main the people, with their careful Judaism, their religious way of life, were left alone.

Until this man who called himself Antiochus Epiphanes. Put on the throne of Syria by the Romans, who were the new great Empire, he decided that *he* wanted, thoughout his domain, which included Palestine, a new order. No more Judaism, no more God of the Jews. Jupiter was to be worshipped and himself as an incarnation of Jupiter. The Jews protested but he was an absolute monarch, a Hitler, with storm-troopers and special police. They robbed the great Temple and in the inner sanctum, the Holy of Holies, they put up an idol of Jupiter. There was burning of all holy books. All Jewish festivals, including the Sabbath, were forbidden. So was the circumcision of boy babies. The full terrors of religious persecution descended like a black cloud on the whole of Palestine. A crushing taxation began. Confiscation of property, rape, murder, slavery, concentration camps. Nothing is new.

The people were dazed. It seemed the end. But there was more to come.

Two years after the first great pogrom there was another. Whole streets were pulled down, whole families wiped out. Mass executions. Jerusalem, the golden city, became a rubble-piled waste area where half-starved people scratched a living. To be a Jew, to observe in any way, was to die. It was the law. On every side there were idols and pagan chapels. Once a month, right through the weeping land, there was a sacrifice day, and these were days of terror. On those days were slaughtered all Jews who had dared to practise their religion. Young mothers who'd had their baby sons circumcised died with their dead babies hung round their necks. Old men, too old to change their ways, fell with the blood running into their beards. Once a month a murder day!

In Jerusalem itself, as month followed month, very few Jews remained. Heathen, lawless men lived there, put there by the King, to further desecrate and despoil the city of David and its Temple. The nightmare went on and on. In every town and city of Judaea the storm-troopers would see that only heathen sacrifices and profane services were observed. There were many spies and informers, many who had given up the fight, gone over to pagan ways, to stay alive. In every public place, town square, crossroads, altars and idols. Sacrifice and prayer were compulsory. It was the law. If you broke the law, merciless whipping and torture. Slow death. A terrible, terrible time.

A New Resistance Movement

Just north-west of sad Jerusalem, about fifteen miles away, was a town called Modin. Not a big place. The people of the town had heard of the dreadful happenings all over Judaea but had not themselves suffered a great deal. Not like some places. But there was rumour that there was to be a shake-up; that a huge idolatrous altar was to be built in the square and that the King's special officers were coming to hold the first big sacrifice-meetings. It was true. The hard-faced men arrived and notices were posted up and the ceremonial altar built. The officer-in-charge knew his job; he'd done it many times before. He knew that there was always a top man whom a town looked up to. A leader of opinion whom people would follow. He knew also that most people had a price.

In Modin one of the elders of the community was a man called Mattathias. He was a Jewish priest, a religion whose practice meant death. He was an elderly man, too old he would say, to learn new ways, and a great worry to his five sons. 'Not that I am so old,' he would say. 'But the old ways are better. They are God's ways.' Often, though, his sons would see him weep for the broken Temple and its profaned altars. 'What point,' Mattathias would say, 'is there in living?' His sons, who were muscular, handsome men, were not too much upset by their father's low moods. They had inherited not only strength from their father but bravery also, and knew him to be quite fearless and of great resilience of spirit.

When the day of the first sacrifice-meeting came, a messenger arrived from the officer-in-charge. Polite invitation; no threats. The five sons waited. Mattathias rose to his feet. Tall, powerful shoulders still, silver hair and beard. 'Come,' he said to his sons. 'This, I feel is to be a special day.'

When they arrived the square was packed with people. By the new altar, near the new idols, were the animals prepared for sacrifice. Mattathias and his five sons walked forward to where the officer-in-charge stood on a small platform. He looked down at them cynically. He wasn't impressed. He'd killed many priests in his time, many sons of priests. It was just a job; get it over with. He spoke only to Mattathias.

'You are a leader in this town,' he said, 'with sons, and of a large and distinguished family. I have dealt with many such, and many have obeyed the King's order without argument. The others are dead. Now come, you show your people the way, you be the first, and they will follow. Make the first sacrifice, and the King will be your friend. He will reward you.'

Mattathias looked straight into the officer's cynical eyes.

'You ask me to be the first,' said Mattathias, 'to make the first sacrifice to an idol. A graven image. Because I lead the community and am a priest of God,' he paused and raised his voice a little, 'the only true God.'

The officer and his men stiffened. The five sons moved a touch closer to their father.

'If the whole country – and every other country under the King's rule,' said Mattathias, 'obeys these terrible orders to give up our covenant with God, my sons and I will not. Not one step will we take from the path of our belief. Neither to the right nor to the left.'

The officer sighed. These old priests were a bore. As if it mattered which God. 'Please yourself,' he said. 'We'll deal with you later.'

He turned to the crowd. 'All right,' he said, 'who's first?' There was a pause, then a man stepped forward. It surprised few people that he was the first. He bowed to the officer and his bow had a scrape in it too.

Mattathias was a priest, bred on the commandments, a mild man. But he felt an anger begin in him like heat. And a strength and power that he knew was from God. He moved forward, every sinew taut, springy as a dancer. He and the man reached the altar together. They were much of a size but Mattathias picked him up and broke him like a stick. It took a second. One scream, and the man was dead.

Then everything happened at once. Mattathias left the troopers to his five sons, who were already upon them. He himself turned, without hurry, to meet the officer, now pale, with a short sword in his hand. Mattathias caught the wrist as the sword came down and turned it as though it were putty. He looked into the officer's eyes, standing close, the point of the sword under the man's chin, the handle still in the man's hand. Mattathias reached up his other hand and put it on the officer's head like a blessing. He bowed the head and helped the officer to kill himself.

He looked around. His sons had coped very well. 'Come,' he said to them, and to the crowd of townspeople he spoke louder. 'We go, my sons and I, to the mountains, to hide and to plan, for this is not the end, it is the beginning. We are Jews and will not break the covenant. Let all who think the same, do the same.' Some came forward right away, and in half a day, leaving everything, they were gone.

Indeed it was not the end of the matter. The news of the revolt soon reached Jerusalem, where the occupation forces had their headquarters. Together with news almost as unbelievable; that after Mattathias and his sons and friends had gone to the mountains, no less than a thousand men, women and children with their sheep and cattle had left the town and were hiding away in the desert scrub-land. Soon where they were was known (there are always informers) and a large heavily-armed force set out.

The troops found the people on a Saturday morning. The officer-in-charge knew his job. 'Make no resistance,' he told the people, 'give up your religion as the King says, and you will live.'

'We will not give up our religion,' said the people, 'nor will we offer resistance. It would profane the Sabbath. Which is today.' And they did not resist. The soldiers went in among them and slaughtered every living thing. Men, women, children, cattle and sheep.

When the news was brought to Mattathias in the mountains, he wept. Then he gathered his sons and his friends round him.

'For over two years,' said the silver-bearded Mattathias, 'our country has lived in terror, in blood. Thousands have been killed, thousands more imprisoned, robbed, maimed; our beloved Temple in Jerusalem has been stripped and defiled.' He paused. 'In the inner sanctum an idol now stands. And to it *pigs* are sacrificed. All this you know. And now, another thousand of our neighbours have been massacred. The soldiers found them yesterday and they would not fight back because it was the Sabbath. So they were massacred. Everyone. Men, women and children. Even their sheep and cattle.' He straightened. '*We* will fight on the Sabbath,' he said. 'We will fight every day, in every way. To keep alive the Law of God we have for a while to break it. He knows and is with us. We have many Jews to avenge. We are few, but I have sent word to many. Come,' he said, 'let us fortify this place, our new home in the mountains, let us plan, and harden ourselves.'

Before a week was out their numbers had doubled, trebled. Every kind of man from pale young priests to mighty warriors skilled in the use of arms. A hard discipline began. They were outlaws, wanted men, revolutionaries. Soon they made their first raids, a highly trained, highly mobile guerilla corps. They would descend upon a town without warning. They would pull down every idol and image and wreck every altar. Every profiteer and informer would be punished. They took an eye for an eye, a tooth for a tooth. Their numbers grew, they seemed in ten places at once. They were a clarion call to the people.

The Temple Lives Again

It was a hard life, and sadly one of the first great losses was Mattathias himself. After about a year. As he lay on his death-bed, he asked to be propped up a little the better to look into the faces of his five sons. They drew nearer.

'My sons,' said the old priest, 'we live now in a time of ruin and fury. I die for God and am happy to do so. Show zeal for his Law. Give your lives, if need be. Keep faith. You will be in good company. Father Abraham never wavered. Nor did Joseph, nor Joshua, nor David, nor Elijah, nor Daniel and his three friends. So many, so many.'

No one spoke.

Mattathias began again, his voice firmer. 'Now listen carefully,' he said, 'for upon you, my five sons, rests a huge responsibility. Of you all Simeon is wisest in counsel. He shall take my place. Judas has been a mighty warrior since a youth –' he turned his head, and Judas leaned forward. They were a bit alike. Lean, wide-shouldered men, deep-set eyes, wide resolute mouths. The old man smiled. 'Judas the Hammer,' he said, 'Judas Maccabaeus. You shall command the army, and your brothers will be your spear and your sword. Observe the Law, avenge wrong. Pay back in full both good and evil.'

Then he blessed them and died.

Soon all Israel knew, and mourned, and soon the army of Judas Maccabaeus grew in numbers again. The old priest's call to show 'zeal for God' made a new name for the army. 'Zealots' they were called.

Judas was a fearless man. A born leader and a master of tactics. He created a vast information system throughout the land. He was always forewarned. And he knew the value of surprise and the effect of shock upon the enemy. The enemy now was huge. The whole army of occupation, controlled from Rome, was against him. An order arrived for the attention of Apollonius, who controlled Samaria, north of Judaea. Destroy Judas Maccabaeus and his rabble, it said. Apollonius gathered a large force and went out to do so. Judas, as always, was aware and prepared. He met Apollonius halfway, tore his army to pieces and took everything except prisoners. Apollonius was no coward and, when he came face to face with Judas, fought fiercely. Well matched. Judas killed him and took his sword. And used that sword in battle for the rest of his life. Many battles.

Antiochus was beside himself with fury. 'Two of my armies *beaten*!' he roared. 'By a lot of blasted Jews. I'll do the job myself!' So he gathered all his own personal army, which was huge – including the latest heavy stuff, elephants – and gave every man a year's pay in advance. Then he found himself a bit short of money. Not surprising. So he called in his Prime Minister, a man called Lysias. 'Look,' he said, 'you do it. Take half the army and the elephants and go and wipe Jewry off the map. I'll take the other half of the army and go east and raise some money. The tribute to Rome is about due.'

The battle took place not far from where Judas and his brothers came from. They knew the orders given to Lysias; all Israel knew. And before the battle they and all Israel prayed. And God looked after the whole thing. Even allowing for the do-or-die part, and the first-class tactics, it was still impossible that the Jewish army should win. But they did. And they took vast plunder, elephants as well. And when, next year, Lysias tried again with even more troops, the Jews won again. Lysias had never seen people fight like that before. He was, the Bible says, perplexed and discouraged. I should think so.

Judas called his army together. 'Our enemies,' he told them, 'for the time being, are crushed. Now let us stop fighting for a while and give thanks to God in the best way I know. Let us go to Jerusalem and make it clean and holy again. We will clear out the thieves and wicked men put there by Antiochus and we will cleanse our beloved Temple from top to bottom.' And they did.

Jerusalem, city of David, broke their hearts when they saw it. And when they came to the Temple they wept. Neglected, desolate, dirty, the beautiful gates burned and smashed. Empty of all its lovely furnishings. All its gold and silver vessels and lamps looted and stolen. The gardens overgrown, the altars filthy with the remains of pig-sacrifice. Idols and images everywhere. The people wept. And then went to work. They smashed down the idols and the defiled altar and built a new altar of rough stone. They restored and renovated and rebuilt and scrubbed and swept and wove cloth and beat metal and made lamps and found oil and sweet herbs.

And the day came. It was the same day of the month on which, three years before, the Temple had been profaned. Three years to the day. The Temple was rededicated with songs and music and happy tears. It glowed with light and was fragrant and spotless. The celebration lasted eight days. And on the last day Judas told the people that the rededication would be celebrated every year from then on. And it is. To this day. It is called Hanukkah, when the branched candlestick is used. A happy festival. A festival of joy and light.